Tessie
and
Pearlie

A Granddaughter's Story

JOY HOROWITZ

SCRIBNER

SCRIBNER
1230 Avenue of the Americas
New York, NY 10020

SCRIBNER and design are trademarks of Simon & Schuster Inc.

Set in Adobe Fairfield Light
Designed by Jenny Dossin

Manufactured in the United States of America

1   3   5   7   9   10   8   6   4   2

Library of Congress Cataloging-in-Publication Data is available.
ISBN 0-684-81395-5

For my children,
Trevor, Gus, and Lucy
And their children
And theirs

Memory believes before knowing remembers. Believes longer than recollects, longer than knowing even wonders . . .

WILLIAM FAULKNER, *Light in August*

CONTENTS

Shmegegge: Nerd

COMPARED TO MY GRANDMOTHERS, I'M A *SHMEGEGGE*. THAT'S *shmeh-*GEH-*gee,* Yiddish for nerd or ineffectual slob. They, of course, would fiercely deny that their granddaughter is a nudnik. How could I be anything but brilliant and beautiful in their eyes? Perfect, even. But the truth is that next to them, I am a regular shmo.

Take gin rummy, for instance. The last time I played Tessie, my father's mother, she killed me, 98–0. She knew she would. When I asked her to play, she replied, without malice: "Why? You vant to see how you can lose?"

As for my mother's mother, Pearlie, her particular genius resides in a ball of yarn and a crochet needle. You need a toilet paper cover? A doll with braids? A place mat, an afghan, a beret? You name it, Pearl makes it. She shouldn't, because of her arthritis. But sometimes a yarn master can't help herself and sneaks in a baby sweater for her great-granddaughter, packaged inside a knotted plastic bag. ("She's so beautiful, *kineahora,*" Pearlie tells me, invoking one of her oft-chanted Yiddish expressions to ward away the evil eye while pressing another crocheted goody into my hands for my baby daughter, Lucy. I am pathetic and bring Pearlie nothing. She waves her thin, veiny hand, as if to bat away my guilt, and says, "It's nothing, dahlink.")

My grandmothers are the strongest women I know. True, their health is fading. But in my mind, they're pioneers and adventurers, brave and fearless. *Shtarkers,* to be precise, who live by themselves. Tessie Weinreb in Queens, New York, Pearlie Feldman in Santa Monica, California. They're also the first women I've watched grow old, outliving, between them, twelve siblings, three husbands, one son, and most of their friends. Pearlie is 94; Tessie turns 95 this year. "Maybe," Tessie says with a shrug, "God forgot my address."

Always with the jokes, they can get on my nerves. They can even drive me crazy, with their Old World superstitions and Neanderthal attitudes about a range of issues. And yet, they are my gurus. Just as striking as their longevity is the sense of utter constancy they offer in a world that seems to speed along faster and faster. Like it or not, they are my personal guides into old age and the existential dilemma.

"You shrink, this you should know," Tessie advises.

"You shrivel up, just like a potato," Pearlie agrees.

Two matriarchs, they are my *bubbes*—the Yiddish term for grandmother, pronounced with the vowel sound in bubbles, BUB-ees. They are not in the least pretentious, nothing fancy-shmancy about them. And they offer no sugarcoated prescriptions for life: It is hard, it is complicated, it is not forever. There is joy in sorrow and sorrow in joy. Always, there is family. And passion. Even now, the titles of their favorite TV shows speak volumes. Tessie's is *The Young and the Restless.* Pearlie's is *Mad About You.*

The last of a breed, they are still close to their immigrant past, hardened by wars and the Great Depression and shaped by discrimination against Jews that began to dissipate only in the 1950s. Now they have little patience for basic questions. What is, is. Ask Tessie, for instance, why being an Orthodox Jew is so important to her, and she answers rhetorically: "Why does an Arab wear the *shmatte* on his head?" Ask Pearl why she continues wearing her wedding band, eighteen years after her husband's death, and she quips: "I'm married forever to him. All my life. I'm a Jewish nun."

I should say, at this point, that I am utterly baffled at how middle age has turned me into a sentimental sop. Pathologically so. I cry over stuff that is embarrassing—my 12-year-old's Little League game, my 8-year-old's musical-comedy debut, my baby's weaning. I am a boomer sandwich, eyeing my children's growth, my parents' aging, and my grandmothers' frailty as signs of my own mortality. So I unearth the past to make future connections, keeping the continuum alive. I go back to the source.

To Pearlie and Tessie. My grandmas. My heroes. My *bubelehs*.

I FIRST DECIDED TO INTERVIEW MY GRANDMOTHERS WHEN I realized that they were having a difficult time recuperating from falls they suffered in the summer of 1993. Both had slipped and broken their arms. Pearlie's stumble was especially traumatic, since it occurred when she was two-stepping with her folk-dance troupe, the Dancing Dolls, during the rousing finale of "Achy Breaky Heart."

I phoned them both to say that I wanted to write an article about them.

"*Oy vaysmere,*" Tessie complained right away. "Can't you get a better subject? I can't see. I can't hear. I can't talk. What else?" Translation: She couldn't wait to see me.

Pearlie was equally happy to comply. "Joyala, my life is an open book. You just tell me when."

In the eighteen months following those initial calls, I visited them with tape recorder in hand and on occasion, telephoned. When I stayed with Tessie, we were roommates, and her snoring drove me wild; Pearlie and I stole time together over tea and homemade Toll House cookies she served up from a coffee can. I found myself frantically jotting down notes about the details of their lives, as if the act of remembering would allow me to hold on to them longer. Then I resisted writing their stories with every journalistic bone in my body: How could I truthfully distill the very lives I most wanted to extol?

At first glance, Tessie and Pearlie seem as different as two women could be. Tessie can be secretive and has few close friends, though she is acidly funny; Pearlie, who tosses her head back and lets go a piercing cackle when she laughs, is vocal and has a range of acquaintances and relationships. Pearlie is ribald. Tessie is circumspect. Tessie boycotted my wedding eighteen years ago when I married my husband, Brock, who is not Jewish; Pearlie not only came to our wedding, just a month after her husband died, but she also joyously danced there, à la Isadora Duncan, in pink chiffon. Tessie strictly observes Jewish ritual, keeping kosher and attending shul as often as possible; Pearlie, who prays by writing letters to her deceased son and husband, believes that religion resides in the heart.

On closer inspection, though, it quickly becomes clear that my grandmothers face the same predicament: Both women, in a sense, have become invisible. As with the matriarchs of the Old Testament, you have to read between the lines to understand them—or just to find them. To be an old woman in American culture is to be cast off, dismissed as daft or ugly or worse. Jewish mothers, in particular, have become cultural icons and the butt of countless jokes. Yet, these public portrayals mask a deeper truth that is no secret: Women outlive men. Thus, their undisputed power resides in their longevity, as keepers of the family legacy. Tessie and Pearlie stand as symbols: Sometimes there are men around and sometimes not, but life goes on either way.

They tell stories about their past with the narrative panache of Isaac Bashevis Singer. Are their stories true? Some go back so far, to the middle of the nineteenth century, that they surely improve in the retelling. But accuracy isn't the point, really. What matters to me, anyway, is that I find the girl in the woman before me, still alive with possibility.

What follows is my ode to *bubbe*hood, a patchwork of interviews, recipes, and kitchen-table advice: Pearlie's wisdom and Tessie's *tsuris* (worries).

"You know what's *tsuris*?" Tessie asks, casting one of her deadpan looks. "Two Jews were sitting on the train and they were talking *tsuris*. And the Irishman was holding on to the strap in the train. And he hears them talking *tsuris, tsuris, tsuris*. He says, 'For God's sake, if you have a sore ass, why don't you get up and give me a seat?' "

May 1996

GRANDMA TESSIE'S

Amazing Matzo Ball Soup

First of all, the chicken should be fresh. A good chicken. Usually, the nonkosher chicken is not so fresh, because nonkosher can stay in the freezer who knows how long? But if it's a nice, fresh-killed chicken, I clean it up. Take out all the feathers and all. Clean. And then, let's say for a chicken, you need four pounds. It's a good chicken already.

You put in some water in the pot to cover the chicken. Slowly, you bring it to a boil and take off the stuff. It gets foam, like. The fat. Nowadays an hour and a half is a lot. You cook it slowly. You put in vegetables, like carrot and celery. I don't like onions. I don't use no pepper, just salt. Very plain. Other people put in other stuff, yet. It's not like liquid when it gets cold. It's so like Jell-O.

I take out the carrot with a spoon or when I pour off the soup. I like the carrot. I don't like the celery to eat. I remember my sister Leah, she used to put in all kinds of vegetables. And he, Harry, her husband, he ate it all, the vegetables. I couldn't stand it, to see him eat it.

The matzo balls, you cook it separate, not in the soup. Let's say I make two eggs, is more than enough. For one person it's even enough one egg. And I put in a little matzo meal, about a half a cup. I beat it up good with a little salt. You can even put in a drop of pepper, which is okay. A drop of seltzer makes the balls fluffier, maybe a tablespoon of seltzer. I don't know the measurements. That's why I can never give anybody any recipes. Because I just mix it and I see, when it starts getting thicker or so. It's important you should let it stay a few hours, so it hardens up by itself. Then I boil up a pot of water. Throw in the balls. But don't make them bigger than a walnut, or it'll come out like a big peach. Let it boil for forty minutes. And that's all. So what?

CHAPTER 1

Shmitchek: Whatchamacallit

Pearlie Rosenwasser, winsome at 16.

MOTHER'S DAY, MAY 8, 1994. 6:30 A.M. INSIDE TESSIE'S APARTMENT.
"Come, *mamashayna,*" she says as soon as she's hugged me
hello. "Come eat breakfast."

Bleary-eyed, I've just arrived on the red-eye from Los Angeles to
her one-bedroom apartment in Queens. She lives in a six-story
brick building, the Winston, in a tree-lined working-class neighborhood of Briarwood, not far from Forest Hills. In anticipation of my
arrival, she's already beaten the eggs for my matzo brei—scrambled
eggs with moistened matzo. Wrapped in a plastic bag and covered
with a paper towel is her homemade marble cake, my favorite.

At 93, Tessie stands just under five feet, though she once was a
couple of inches taller. She wears thick, pink-framed glasses, red
lipstick, a flowered housedress, and sneakers. Her right hand
shakes, her fingers are gnarled from arthritis, her sciatica is a
source of constant pain. Still, she manages to have her fingernails
painted fire-engine red.

"It's good to live long, but it's not good to get old," she tells me.
"You can't do what you want."

She sets a cup of coffee on the place mat. "Do you use sugar or
do you use your disposition?"

Her apartment, decorated with family photographs from decades ago, is furnished in neo–*I Love Lucy*: most of the lamps, tables, and chairs are from the 1950s. But they've held up for a reason. "This is what I learned from my husband, Izzy," she says of the grandfather I never met and for whom I was given my Hebrew name. "If you buy, buy good." In the living room, above an overstuffed couch, there hangs a pastoral oil painting of Stevensville in the Catskills. On a side wall, there are two ceramic dancers mounted in frames. Over her bed, too, there are framed prints of Degas dancers.

It's drizzling out. I ask about her arthritis.

"They wouldn't let me alone."

"Who wouldn't let you alone?"

"The arthritis. They stick to me. They like me." A jokenik, she deflects most questions with her highly idiosyncratic brand of humor. I offer her a Mother's Day gift—a box of soaps.

"Why spend money on me?" she asks.

"Why not?" I ask.

" 'Cause I hope I use it up." Meaning she doesn't think she'll live so long. "I hope not," she says.

"You hope not?"

"Because me no like it," she says, invoking the upside-down syntax to a favorite old Yiddish song, "*Oy, I Like She.*"

To listen to someone you love tell you that she'd prefer to be dead is dreadful. In my grandmother's case, though, it's predictable. She's been talking this way, without remorse or rancor, for the last several years, at least. But her depression is also understandable. Once stubbornly independent, she now must rely on her two daughters—my aunts, Cynthia and Bobbie—who structure their workweek around shopping for her and transporting her to the doctor or to the beauty shop. She has an attendant five days a week to help out. And she has an emergency button and the phone, her lifeline.

"I lost confidence in myself," she explains about her fall last year. "I don't trust myself anywhere. I don't go down for the mail myself. I do sometimes, but the cane—I hate people should see me. So I don't go some places I want to go." She ventures out twice a week now, to her Golden Age Club on Mondays and to Danny's Beauty Salon on Saturdays to have her white hair fluffed and sprayed into a bubblelike crown.

"Now, anything that I want to do, I can't do it myself," she says.

It takes her half an hour to fasten her bra, longer to clean a chicken. "So what is it? I don't want to aggravate the Man Upstairs, but it's no use. Why do they celebrate the 'golden age'?"

She reconsiders. "Maybe I'm too critical on myself, too," she adds. "The kids say that I'm too critical. Do you find me that way?"

Not at the moment. She's just served me a giant slice of cake for breakfast. Who am I to complain?

Minutes later, though, I'm fair game. For this trip, I've lugged along a breast pump so that I can continue to nurse my 10-month-old daughter when I return home. Tessie disapproves of the setup. "If she could do the four days without you, you don't need it," she says of the pump.

I disagree. "All right," she shrugs. "Nurse until her wedding day."

☞☜

THE BLUE DOOR TO PEARLIE'S APARTMENT HAS A LITTLE PLASTIC sign hanging from the doorknob, like the ones you leave out for room service in a hotel. But Pearlie's sign is a daily reminder of what it's like to live in the shadow of death: Good morning, I'm OK!

Kathie Lee and Regis are blaring from the TV set. Pearlie tells me she doesn't much care for Kathie Lee's new haircut. We guffaw over Regis's beady eyes. Pearl has high cheekbones, bright eyes, and a pixie haircut, like Peter Pan. I practically tower over her now, she's such a sliver of her former self. Though she moved to California ten years ago, her voice is still coated in Brooklynese.

"You want orange juice or what?" she asks. She lives five minutes away from me in the Silvercrest, a concrete apartment complex for seniors. Her building is sandwiched between a muffler shop and the Phoenix Bookstore, a hangout for hipsters. During the week, she usually eats her meals downstairs in the dining hall; otherwise, she cooks for herself in her tiny kitchen, unable to duplicate the lavish spreads she is famous for in the family. But on the kitchen table, there is an entire plate of chocolate chip cupcakes she baked fresh for my visit.

She speaks in code sometimes, expecting me to fill in the blanks of her sentences. She forgets words. Names slip her mind. She calls this "the 92-year-old thing." I tell her that I've got the same problem, but I'm fifty-one years younger than she. She cackles. So do I.

"They're no-cholesterol cupcakes," she explains, sitting at the table, which is covered by one of her crocheted tablecloths.

"Did you make them from scratch?"

"Yeah."

"Really?"

"And there's no cholesterol."

"Where's the recipe from?"

"From the box." A cake mix, in other words?

"Yeah. And they come out perfect, they're so easy. Yeah. Ya take 'em right out of the thing." The thing. She means the paper cupcake wrapper.

Her usual sartorial splendor is much in evidence. She wears a peach-and-white sweater with matching polyester pants and white Reeboks. She made the sweater not long ago, and it has gold-thread embellishments. Around her neck, she wears a gold charm that says Happy Birthday, a gift from her grandchildren for her ninetieth.

"You gotta enjoy your life," she tells me, worried that I'm over-extended. "Don't rush, rush, rush. Learn to enjoy while you have your health." Though she's slowed down recently, having stopped her volunteer work at the local hospital and cut out her weekly dancing with "the Dolls" for fear of another fall, Pearlie's great enthusiasm for life is undeterred by age. "I think if you keep your-self involved in lots of things and don't concentrate on yourself, it helps a lot," she says. "It's good to have outside interests, to keep the mind busy. It's like a sore in your heart to not be involved.

"Life is great, if we could only have it without pain," she says. "What's bad with life? There can be lots of fun in this world, lots of enjoyment—air to breathe, food to eat, places to go. What do we know what we have in the other world? Nothing."

Her mind is razor sharp, especially when I ask about her past. She conjures up vivid memories of having her tonsils extracted ("just yanked out with, like, pliers, but then I got to get ice cream with my father on the trolley"); of asking advice from the local health department on how to take care of her first baby, Jerry, because she wasn't sure if feeding him spinach at three months was advisable; of going through menopause ("The doctor said to me, 'Just lie down, put a cold compress to your head and chest, and relax.' And I didn't have any problems: It didn't last too long, about two years"). I survey her tiny apartment, decorated with recycled furniture from my parents' house, including the vanity table from my bedroom when I was a girl. Over the peephole to her door, she's hung a macramé object and little purple pompoms.

"That's a *shmitchek, shmitchkie*—a thing," she says, explaining this all-purpose Yiddishism (pronounced SHMITCH-*eck* and SHMITCH-*key*) of my grandfather's making. "If you want a hand, you say, 'Give me that *smitchkie*.'" She smiles mischievously. "Grandpa used to call this a *shmitchkala*," she says, pointing to her crotch.

I ask her to please not turn this into an X-rated interview. "*Shmitchek* can be any part of your body," she says. "A whatchamacallit."

Clearly, she was mad about Moe, my lusty grandfather who'd give me rides on his feet and make his biceps dance to the strains of Russian folk songs. She invokes his memory, his *joie de vivre*, whenever possible. When my younger sister, Peggy, recently reported how wonderful, kind, and supportive her new husband is, Pearlie asked only one question, à la Moe: "Is he a good luvah?"

A Bubbe Questionnaire

Do you have any famous relatives or ancestors?

TESSIE: None of them were in jail. To be famous? I can't recall.

PEARLIE: No, except on Grandpa's side. His sister's daughter's son was married to a gentleman who was a state senator. I forget his name. That's the only outstanding one.

What is your favorite health, beauty, or fitness tip?

TESSIE: Beautiful I was never. I'd rather go for health than beauty. But I can't control my health anymore. I like to be clean, neat. Fancy? No. Of course, I have my hair done and nails done every Saturday at Danny's. I'd rather look decent. So people wouldn't say, "That old lady, she looks such a *shlump!*" As for health, I just ate some potatoes.

PEARLIE: When I look in the mirror, I'm not happy to see the wrinkles. The skin changes so much in your nineties. The whole face changes. I don't know how to stop it. I just don't want to get to look any worse than I am now. [*She laughs.*] Because I don't want to look scary to my great-grandchildren—and it's bound to happen. Your face becomes crepe-y. Your eyes become smaller. Your nose becomes longer. I put on sunscreen when I go out. Just a little powder and lipstick. I can't pluck my eyebrows because the skin gets red and sore. I do the best I can. I brush my hair and wash it. Otherwise, no secrets. I never was one to stay in the beauty parlor. As long as I take a shower twice a day, keep myself clean. Not be a *shtunk*, smelly.

The word that best describes you is:

TESSIE: Not a blabbermouth. My children say critical. It's easier to criticize than be correct.

PEARLIE: Love.

Tell me the most unusual things about yourself or unusual things you have done.

TESSIE: I got married again. Maybe I shouldn't have. I don't know.

PEARLIE: I like to tell dirty jokes, a simple joke. It's nice to make people laugh.

How do you like to celebrate your birthday?

TESSIE: No wishes, no shmishes. That's all. I don't tell anybody it's my birthday. What's the difference? Those years that come, I don't appreciate it. I can't do what I want. I don't enjoy with the old age. To me, I'm not that thrilled about it. I'm living the longest of anybody in my family. So? Pish-posh.

PEARLIE: To be with the family. Oh yeah.

Can you love your children too much?

TESSIE: There is no such thing to love children too much. No. It's not possible. Or is it?

PEARLIE: When you give love, you give it with your whole being. I don't think I could love my children less, no matter what. Even my son-in-laws. My family is my life.

━━🖚🖛━━

IT IS A BEAUTIFUL, CRISP MORNING IN NEW YORK. BY TEN o'clock, Tessie and I are still wearing our flannel pj's, with no

intention of getting dressed. We've already broken into a box of choco-
lates I've brought with me from L.A. She likes the chocolate-covered
honeycomb. "We're not eating, just noshing," she explains.

A lifelong Democrat, she loves to talk politics and is presently cas-
tigating Paula Jones. "Maybe she really instigated him," she says, referring to President Bill Clinton. "This she wouldn't tell you."

We break out the cards, and I "wash," or shuffle, them. The
cards fly, ten to her, ten to me. She turns over a king of spades, double the points. Her joints ache, her cough won't quit, her ankles
swell—but over a game of cards, the physical ailments subside
and her mind is as agile as ever.

My grandmother always uses a deck of red Bicycle cards, the
ones with two cherubs atop bicycles in opposing circles. The drawing makes me think of Tessie as an angel, playing cards. The circle
of life. It's a nice reverie, a confection that has nothing to do with
reality.

"What kind of *meshuggeneh* (crazy) cards you gave me?" she
asks, surveying her hand.

If American Indians listen to their elders around a campfire, I
listen to my grandmother with cards fanned in my hands, a discard pile between us. It's our little ritual, practically sacred. For as
long as I can remember, we've related this way. First it was the
game of war, then go fish. Then, when my hands were big enough,
gin. She used to let me win while I'd stay with her while I was still
in college, the two of us smoking cigarettes into the night. Now
she's ruthless. I throw another card on the discard pile.

"See?" she chides me. "You don't know how to play. You gave me
the jack and the queen!"

I tell her it's because I'm kind. She throws another card that I
pick up.

"You take cards for *tromba*," she chides me again. "You know
what's *tromba?*" I shake my head. "For speculation."

My knowledge of Yiddish is extremely limited, but Tessie uses
these card-playing sessions to offer lessons. Amazingly, she has no
age spots on the back of her hands. This, she tells me, is because
her family had an oil business in Europe and her hands were constantly immersed in cottonseed oil. Her job as a teenager was to
teach the workers how to extract the oil. "I was never young," she
says of her childhood. "I was never a child."

Her father ran a brick and oil factory in what was then Austria, formerly Poland. Her mother never paid her a compliment. Raised "to be nice," she was born Toby Teitel in the shtetl of Kozowa in Galicia, not far from the Russian border. Her education was cut short when she was 13 because of World War I, though she could speak six languages. A refugee for two years, she crossed the Carpathian Mountains by horse and wagon to Czechoslovakia with her family and returned home around 1917, only to find that her Polish neighbors had taken her family's home apart, brick by brick.

After contracting typhoid fever and losing her hair, she supported her family by working the black market, trading oil and kerosene for flour and tobacco. Anti-Semitism was endemic. Since her father had a long beard and was easily identifiable as a Jew, he risked his life every time he walked outdoors. She, on the other hand, could pass as a *shiksa* in bare feet and peasant skirts.

Was she angry with her father for not protecting her? "The cannons were shooting over our heads," she remembers, "and if anything had to be done, I could do it. For me it was an adventure. An adventure to go, to do more than my father does. My father once said, we were having an argument, he says, 'I like to argue with Toby.' He knew I'd answer him right. And he liked it. He'd ask me my advice. He and I were really pals. Why should I be angry? I protected him, so he shouldn't have to go outside."

On August 15, 1920, she and her parents arrived in America by steerage. At Ellis Island, she had her first taste of white bread and corn flakes for breakfast and reluctantly agreed to change her name to Tessie at the urging of her sisters. Within a year, she met a dapper egg candler, Izzy Horowitz, whose job entailed inspecting eggs by candlelight to discard those that were bloodshot. He was a gentle man who didn't have much of a flair for business but adored the violin. Together they opened a mom-and-pop grocery store in Brooklyn, called Clover Farms, and had three children. My father was the only boy. Tessie lived up to the meaning of her married name, Horowitz: "works hard."

Was she in love with Izzy? "Yes, but I knew that I can do better than he. We were in business. . . ." Her voice drifts off, as if to

Coming to America: Grandma Tessie's passport.

suggest theirs was a marriage of convenience. What followed were the depression years, when they lost the store. While her husband worked as a grocery clerk, earning $20 a week in her brother's store, she raised money for the local hospital, the kosher one with two kitchens. During World War II, she sent her son off to war; he returned from Japan, wanting to become a clinical psychologist. Her daughter Cynthia became a bookkeeper, and Bobbie a schoolteacher. Not long after Izzy died in 1951, she married a milkman, Sam Weinreb.

For Tessie, it is a virtue to never reveal one's true feelings, especially sadness. When asked how she's dealt with her grief, she says, "I never made any sour face to anybody. Nobody knew what's inside of me. They still don't." She catches herself, as if she's said too much. "I'm talking now," she adds. "But I shouldn't."

"Why not?"

"Pheh," she replies, waving her hand.

It's twelve-thirty. She snaps on the TV. "Shut up!" she's yelling at the TV set. Her soap opera, *The Young and the Restless,* is on, and she's bored by one of the plot lines. She likes to watch this show for the blind character who she claims has never blinked, a sign to Tessie of fine acting ability. But more, she's interested in the trial of a woman who's been charged with killing her husband.

If she'd had the opportunity, my grandmother tells me, she would have been a lawyer. Or better still, a writer. She's never admitted this girlhood fantasy to me before. With my pen and notebook in hand, I search her milky gray eyes and feel my shoulders lighten. The flash of connection, a flesh-and-blood link of desire, spanning three generations. Not that she says any more. She doesn't need to.

She sits in her recliner chair with the blue embroidered cloth draped over the headrest. "Oh, here's the caca-mercial again," she complains.

⊲⊦☞

THE PHONE RINGS. BAD NEWS. MY MOTHER HAS JUST LEARNED she has breast cancer. Now, she's calling to tell me that she's opted for a mastectomy, deciding that the radiation treatments that accompany lumpectomy are too risky.

The phone rings again. It's Pearlie, her voice shaky, bordering on hysterical. She asks for my permission to call my mother, even though she's just spoken to her. She's made the same call to my older sister, Shari.

"I don't want to be a bother," she tells me, saying she doesn't want my mother to worry that she's worrying. "I hesitate ten times before I call. I don't want to be a nudge.

"See, when your children are babies and you learn to protect them, no matter how old they are, they're always your children. They're still your babies. And that feeling never leaves.

"I know I'm a pain in the ass," she adds, her voice cracking. "Please forgive me, Joyala. But she's my baby. My baby. Why can't it be me, not her?"

When I hear my grandmother, fragile, frightened, nervous, wanting to help but knowing she can do nothing, I hear myself—and I cannot bear to listen.

In the weeks that follow, while my mother is recuperating from surgery, I speak to Pearlie more often than usual. Normally, we talk on the phone weekly and see each other about twice a month—for family gatherings, brunches, birthday parties—and invariably she ushers me home with another batch of french toast for my kids. But now, we've become allies in the worry department. My mother's cancer brings me closer to my grandmother, who tells me that her greatest wish in life is that her daughter be well.

For the time being, anyway, her wish has come true.

In June, Pearlie, my mother, my daughter Lucy, and I watch my middle child, Gus, perform in a little show at the Odyssey Theater—a four-generation cheering section. Afterward, Pearlie hands me an envelope to deliver to him. In it, she's enclosed $15 in cash and a note telling Gus how much she loves him. Then, in the quiet of her living room, she writes a letter to her son Jerry.

June 19, 1994

Dear Jerela,

It is with a lighter heart I am writing you today. Thank God Shirley is feeling better. I know your prayers for her recovery helped.

Jerela, today is Father's Day and I know how your family misses you. They are all such good children, and I know how

much you will be missed as they know how much you are
missed double.
   Thanks again for your prayers.

                                    Always xxxxxxxxxx
                                       Your Mom

The following week, she bequeaths her old typewriter to my kids, too. Always giving, always bearing hugs and kisses, even in print with her xxxx's and ooooo's. And I wonder, how is it that someone who grew up with so little can give so much?

Born on the Lower East Side in 1902, Pauline Rosenwasser hated her given name, so she changed it to Pearl. Her parents emigrated from Austria in 1894. Her father pressed women's coats. Her mother opened a series of candy and dry goods stores in Brooklyn, often leaving her children unattended. While playing on a fire escape one day, Pearlie watched as a cousin fell three stories, suffering a minor concussion. She remembers her mother saying, guiltily, "It should only have been one of my children," and later wondering if she had cursed her own family. Of seven children, three died young—two baby boys and a 13-year-old girl, from a weak heart.

By the time Pearl was 13, she had to leave school to help support the family. Before she learned shorthand and began working as a stenographer, she sewed labels into coats for $5 a week. When she needed a winter coat, a family friend suggested she could get one wholesale from Morris Feldman, who worked on Second Avenue and specialized in tucking and tailoring coats for heavyset women.

"When I first met him and he invited me up to his shop, he took my measurements—and he never tried anything," she remembers, dreamily. "He was a total gentleman! I always respected him so much for that!" She fell in love instantly; he was so handsome—blue eyes and thick, wavy hair—and he taught her how to tango. Her mother disapproved, since he was Russian-born, not American. Pearlie couldn't help herself; they had a son and two daughters—a stockbroker, a schoolteacher, and an artist.

Not that everything was idyllic. She endured her husband's love for schnapps, cigars, and horse races and the shock of her son's death, at age 53, from a heart attack on a subway. At the funeral, Moe had no idea their son had died, since he had suffered a series of strokes. Ten years later, after nursing him through a terminal illness, Pearlie moved west to be closer to her older daughter, my mother.

Just how Pearlie managed to live this long is a question she's often asked, since she's outlived nearly everyone at the Silvercrest. "You got to listen to your body," she says simply, "like even if you get a corn, you soak your feet." There are some dietary concessions, including the no-cholesterol cupcakes. But truth be told, she's a big proponent of butter, of an occasional glass of wine, and of gargling with Cepacol at the first sign of a sore throat. And exercise is important: She walks to the Third Street promenade daily, jogs in place in her apartment, and takes an exercise class for her arthritis twice a week.

"I really think as long as you can move, you should keep on moving," she says. "Because when you sit, everything sits with you. When you hit 92, especially, the body sort of lets you know, 'Ah, you're getting old, take it easy. We're tired of taking care of you, the bones.'" Most recently, she's realized her taste buds have stopped working.

But back to the longevity question. "Oh, I think it's the family that makes me live this long," she says of her nine grandchildren and thirteen great-grandchildren. "There's so much enjoyment in this. I couldn't ask for anything more. No money. No jewelry. No anything could compete with the wonderful family I have." I assure her she doesn't have to say this for my benefit.

"I say thank-you to God for letting me live this long. And anything He gives me over that, I thank him again twice. But I want to tell you something," she adds. "If you're a good person [she pronounces it "poyson"] when you're young, you're a good person when you're old. And if you're a nasty person when you're young, you're a nasty person when you're old. Character doesn't change. Age don't change character."

What does Tessie think of Pearlie and Pearlie think of Tessie?

TESSIE: I like her very much. I admire her very much. She is a different type than I am. I grew up in Europe. She grew up in America. I don't know which way is better or worse.

PEARLIE: Tessie? She is a good person, a very interesting woman. She has a different attitude about life. She is looking toward death. She thinks it would be a relief. I don't figure that. I want to last as long as I can. I want to be on this earth. She says it would be great if she died in her sleep. But life is so interesting, you know? So much change. You find it interesting enough to want to stay.

❧ ❧

THE STATUS OF WOMEN IN JUDAISM HAS ALWAYS BEEN PROB-lematic to me. Things are changing, of course, but not by much. It takes a lot to undo five thousand years of put-downs. Just take a look at the Book of Leviticus and the childbirth purification ritual: A woman who bears a son is unclean for forty days thereafter, whereas a woman who bears a daughter is unclean for eighty days. Exactly how this hideous little forty-day difference can possibly be accounted for is unclear to me. Can anyone in his right mind really believe that girl babies are somehow dirtier than boy babies?

Here's my grandmothers' feeling about it: Gender shmender.

Still, to explain the exalted-cum-pampered status of males in my own family, Tessie offers a story. "My grandmother Toby, the one that I'm named after, she had a daughter. Then she had a boy. The boy died young. She had another baby, a girl. Another baby, a boy, passed away. The boys couldn't live and the girls lived. She already had three daughters and not even one son. And it bothered her.

"She became pregnant again. She had a dream that an old man with a long gray beard came to her, and he said, 'You know you're pregnant and you're going to have a boy. But name him after me. My name is Chaim. And he's going to live.' They had nobody in the family with that name, Chaim. You know, there was a Yousla, a Moishe, but no name Chaim. And the baby was born a boy, and she named him Chaim, which means 'Life,' and he was the only son. That was my father. He was a spoiled brat. He took advantage of his four sisters." Yet she idolized him completely. The story underscores how the value of a boy supersedes the long-standing tradition of naming a child after a deceased relative.

Hoping that Tessie and Pearlie would give voice to my own beliefs, I asked them the same leading question:

Are you a feminist?

TESSIE: Say it in plain English.

PEARLIE: What do you mean, a feminist?

Do you believe in equal rights for women?

PEARLIE: Definitely. Women need to work and be equal. But also, not to hurt yourself. It's hard to have a career and family. I love to see women get ahead in the medical field and all over. When we were younger, we didn't have that. We were treated like a pot on the stove. Really! We had to do the dishes and clean the house, and the men got so much more respect because they were supposed to be smarter than us. They had more education than us. Now, when I see these women doing things that men never even dreamed of doing, I think the coming world is great. We can expect much better and bigger things now.

TESSIE: Yes, that I would like. I wouldn't mind that at all. Politics interest me very much. If I'd be much younger, I'd run for senator, and I'd make the law even better for the women than the men. My mother and her mother were brought up to just get married and keep house and raise the children. When I grew up, they had to educate the boys. The girls don't need anything because they can wash diapers without education and things like this. A woman should have the same rights as a man. I wouldn't let my husband go above me. If he drives, I drive, too.

☞☜

JUST NOW, PEARLIE IS REMEMBERING HER HAPPIEST MOMENTS as a child and confides they were stolen and secretive—reading. "My biggest pleasure was going to the library, taking home seven or eight books—they'd give you as much books as you wanted— putting it under my cover in the bed, and after Mama would go to bed, I'd turn on the light and read for hours. I got more out of reading even than going to the movies."

Today, like the last few times I've seen her, Pearlie's eyes are red-rimmed. At first, she says the pinkness is caused by her allergies, but later she admits it's more often from crying.

"Living here," she says, "most of the people that die—and they die in their sleep—everybody else says, 'Oh boy, if I could only die in my sleep, it would be wonderful.' To be honest, everybody fears it. And they won't talk about it, either."

This is not the first time that Pearlie has spoken to me about her fear of dying. On more days than she cares to recall, another apartment in her building stands empty because of the death of a friend or neighbor. More than once, she has told me that she feels "desolated." Just a week ago, her 95-year-old brother, Marty, died.

Pearlie sits in her recliner from Sears, the one my mother and aunt bought for her last year. It almost looks thronelike, since she's covered it with one of her purple and orange afghans plus one of those fluffy sheepskin covers. She drifts off for a moment as the car mechanic next door checks another muffler.

"It makes you feel sad," she continues, shutting her sliding glass door to mute the noise. "Your family leaves you. It's like a tree grows, and the branches come down, and the tree looks so lonesome and lonely. But I don't feel abandoned. I still feel attached."

❦

I CALL TESSIE, WORRIED ABOUT THE HEADACHES SHE HAS begun to mention to my father. She recently was scared by a dream, of her parents calling out to her. Is her time near?

"How's your head, Grandma?" I ask.

"What head?" she rifles back, deflecting my concern. She asks about my children, starting with my older son, Trevor, one of her fifteen great-grandchildren. I report his latest accomplishment, placing second in a citywide math meet. As if to make up for lost moments (with my father, I wonder?), she instructs me to tell him how wonderful he is.

"You should!" she insists. "You should give him a compliment. When he deserves it. Don't be stingy! I'll teach you psychology. Really. No, this is a fact."

Then she adds, "Tell Brock hello." She has almost forgiven him for not being Jewish. When she was last in California, he teased her about flying off with him to the Caribbean. It's a joke she can't resist. "Tell him he's still my lover boy."

She says her health won't allow her to make her annual pilgrimage to California. She jokes that maybe she'll be "out of town," as in no longer alive. "If I don't come next year," she quips, "I'll come two years later."

I'VE PUT MYSELF IN AN IMPOSSIBLE POSITION. CONTRARY TO professional standards of journalism, I promised my grandmothers they could have prior approval of what I've written so far. Family over business, as they'd say.

What did they think?

"Praise the children more," Pearlie says of her daughters, Shirley and DeeDee. My mother, Shirley, now 68, is the older of the two; DeeDee (known as Dorothy Schwartz to the rest of the world) is the director of the Maine Humanities Council. "They're the best. They don't come better. And you make Grandpa sound like a finagler and a gambler. You should portray him as a family man. Family always came first for him. He was such a good man."

There is one other little thing, Pearlie says, laughing. "The Salvation Army runs this building. Do you have to put in the part about my, you know, crotch?"

And Tessie? "It's okay," she told me, obviously holding back. "It's all right. I still don't like that you're talking about me. I don't want to be popular."

Did I get anything wrong?

"If I didn't want you to write it, I wouldn't have told you," she adds, shrewdly reflecting the advice most press agents offer their celebrity clients. "It's my simple life. But it is so."

Yummy Marble Cake

I'll tell you the truth: I use the recipe from the box. But I doctor it up. I make it a little more rich. I don't make it from—whatchama-callit—scratch. Okay. So, you take a Duncan Hines marble cake mix. I put in a half a pint of sour cream. It does not call for it. It calls for three eggs. All right, so I put in four. I also add small chocolate chips, about six ounces. And that's what makes it so good. I also put in a package of My*T*Fine vanilla pudding. This, you must have. It's got the vanilla smell. It's very nice. I use half of what the box says for the water and oil, since I add the sour cream. Otherwise, it'll be too loose.

So you mix the eggs, sour cream, and water and mix at not a very big speed. A nice speed. I mix it for twenty minutes for sure. It comes out very smooth. Oh yes. In order to cook and bake, you don't have to be a college graduate. You just need patience and good ingredients.

How do you make it marble? When you have all the ingredients mixed, you put it in the baking pan. I use a nine-inch tube pan. You know, so the cake comes out with a hole in the middle? But in order to make it marble, you leave a little dough in the mixing bowl. Duncan Hines gives you a little envelope with chocolate and you make it with a knife—like marble. Back and forth. Into this here, you add the choco-late chips.

If anyone doesn't like it, let 'em sue me. What's his name? Duncan Hines? He's gonna have it on me. Oy.

CHAPTER 2

Shleps: Drags

*In Cleveland, ca. 1957, Tessie holds baby Peggy,
with Shari (right) and me.*

GROWING UP JEWISH IN CLEVELAND, I REMEMBER HAVING TWO
role models: Anne Frank and Totie Fields. Anne, the schoolgirl-
diarist, was dignified and scholarly and yearning for romance, but
forced to hide in fear; Totie, the yenta comedian, was hilarious in
a buffoonish way that made her famous enough to guest on *The
Ed Sullivan Show,* spitting out self-deprecating fat jokes. One died
because she was Jewish; the other, with her catch-phrase cry of
"Am I right? Am I right?," exploited her Jewishness by creating a
distortion so gross as to seem like caricature. The choice between
being brilliant but hunted down by Nazis or funny but fat seemed
less than appealing. Either way, I didn't see being a Jew as something to parade around publicly.

My parents sent me to Sunday school, where I dressed up for
Purim as Queen Esther from the Bible. All I remember about that,
besides getting to wear my mother's tiara (why did she have a tiara,
anyway?), was wearing my mom's sheer slip, thinking I looked
almost as beautiful as she, and having Robbie Baskin from Palmer-
ston Road notice something else. "Look, I can see your titties!" he
railed. Several years later, when my family had moved to Beverly Hills

and it was my mother's turn to drive carpool to the Sholom Sunday School, a progressive reform program on Olympic Boulevard, Mom informed me she didn't believe in God. I was stunned at the timing of the admission but not altogether surprised.

In our house, Sigmund Freud was God. And public education was a co-god, which would help explain why we moved to Shaker Heights and to Beverly Hills—the school systems were top-notch. My parents, who considered themselves humanists, eschewed prayer and ritual for cultural identity and happily settled in a predominantly Jewish neighborhood, like Beverly Hills, because it reminded Mom of "Flatbush with palm trees." We lit the Chanukah menorah and, occasionally, lit the candles on Friday night in observance of the Sabbath. But rarely. What was sacred was family, though we'd drive one another bonkers.

We were never assimilated to the point of having a Christmas tree in our home, like my best friend, Amy, across the street, but my father did see fit to dress up as Santa Claus one year for my brother's Boy Scout pack dinner. I had no idea Santa was Dad until he yanked his beard down to his chest and said, "Hey, there, Joy Joy." Not even Santa Claus would dare claim my father's nickname for me as his own. Or wear his Hush Puppies.

Against this muddle of religious ambivalence stood Tessie and Pearlie—Jewish stalwarts, albeit long-distance ones, my *Yiddishkeit* barometers. Did I love them so much because I knew them only from afar?

As children do, I believed that they would always be a part of my life. Not until later, much later, did I understand that even they could not stand as a buffer to my parents' mortality. Or my own.

Each summer, my mother would ply us with enough Dramamine to survive the car trip from Cleveland to New York—Mom and Dad smoking Kents in the front seat, the kids eating bologna sandwiches in the back—to visit my grandmothers. First, Pearlie and Moe on Dover Street in Manhattan Beach, Brooklyn. Friday nights at the Esplanade, there were fireworks, the first I had ever seen. I slept on Pearlie's sunporch, beneath her heavy crocheted blankets. Before going to sleep, though, I'd watch Gorgeous George wrestling on TV as my grandfather, in his white undershirt and boxer shorts, chomped on his cigar and laughed at the phony spectacle. Under Grandpa Moe's tutelage, I first learned not to believe everything I saw on television. We'd get up in the morning and race downstairs, the smell of butter frying for Pearlie's French toast mixed with Moe's cigar smoke. At the kitchen table—it was pink marble with wrought iron legs—he taught us how to crush Oysterette crackers into our soft-boiled eggs and squirt seltzer water from a blue bottle with a nozzle on top. Beyond the trips to Nathan's for hot dogs and Coney Island nearby, I was fascinated by Grandma's sewing machine upstairs and the chrome toilet paper dispenser that popped out of the wall at the push of a button. In the basement, I was in heaven, because I could play with a tantalizing collection of buttons, trimming, sequins, and lace—leftovers from Grandpa's car coat and apparel business.

When we crossed over the metal gratings that covered the road of the Marine Park Bridge—the buzzing sound beneath the wheels of our silver 1957 Chevy station wagon signaling our get-away—I knew we were closer to Grandma Tessie's, which was diagonally across from Macy's in Jamaica, Queens. At the time, she was the only person I knew (other than Lucy Ricardo on TV) who lived in an apartment, which struck me as enormously cosmopolitan, being a kid from the suburbs. Besides the Sealtest ice cream sandwiches that Grandpa Sam would pick up from the nearby grocery, there was always a candy stash—chocolate bars the size of a house. Playing the squirrel game with Grandma, where she'd fold up a hanky and make kissing sounds, as if it were talking to us. Playing gin rummy. Having our growth measured on her bedroom wall, notches marked in pen with our initials and the date. Grandma wearing an apron, her blue metallic glasses dipping down her nose.

But to be honest, much as I loved seeing them, I think the primary feeling I had upon arriving in either of their homes was wanting to get out of there. With Pearlie, her hugs were a little too squeezy. And, never the diplomat, Moe would constantly ask us, "So, when are you going home?" With Tessie, punch lines were invariably in Yiddish, which she knew we kids didn't understand. The feeling of being excluded, even though I was part of the family, was palpable. If she didn't want me to understand, I wouldn't bother to learn her language, either.

In truth, my grandmothers bored me. Their stories made me fidgety. In one ear and out the other is pretty much the way I heard them. I was still busy navigating my own childhood, believing that Cubby on the *Mickey Mouse Club* was cool and Swanson's frozen Salisbury steak dinners were a gourmet delight. I equated my grandmothers' endless recollections of my mother and father with torture. It took more than thirty years before I was really ready to listen.

Lucky for me, my *bubbes* were still around to tell their tales.

"Remembering makes the memories come alive," says Pearl.

"Thank God I still got my marbles," says Tessie.

AFTER HAVING A MAGAZINE ARTICLE PUBLISHED ABOUT TESSIE and Pearl, I call my grandmothers for permission to write a book about them.

"You have more to write?" Tessie asks, suspiciously. "You're looking for trouble?"

Pearlie, whose health has been flagging for the past few months, tells me something else. "Your book, Joyala, gives me a reason to live." The next day, though, she expresses her fears about my undertaking such a project. "I'm worried," she tells me, "that maybe you shouldn't make this investment with the book."

"Why not?" I ask.

"I wonder whether I'll have time on this here earth," she says.

I do, too, but I don't say so. "I'll just write against time," I say, trying to sound reassuring. "That's why God made deadlines." In this context, the word "deadline" takes on an entirely new meaning for me.

Then, I call Tessie back. In truth, she's peeved that I've revealed her age in public—a big-time no-no, tantamount to committing a sin (a kind of subset of Honor Thy Father and Mother). Vanity, even for nonagenarians, never dies. Over the years, she's figured out how to shut people up on the subject. When someone asks how old she is, she usually replies: "Can you keep a secret?" The questioner, made to feel like a confidante, usually says, "Yes," to which Tessie adds: "So can I."

But I've sent her a thick sheaf of letters I've received in response to the article, mostly all singing her praise. "*Shayna maydala,*" she tells me over the phone, "it took me three hours to read those letters. It makes me feel a little something, like I got a diamond. But even better."

She clears her throat. "Now," she continues, "I see you're really popular. This here, I respect you and admire you. That's a different kind of love. I mean, I've always loved you like a child. Now, I love you like a genius."

Just in case my head should swell, though, she brings me back to earth as I later overhear her talking about me as "the author of the whole mish-mash. Don't ask."

In the following months, Tessie and Pearlie load me up with stories, photographs, and documents from their lives. Pearlie, especially, is eager to pass on her prose and poetry. With each trip to her apartment, I find myself returning home with more and more plastic bags filled with her writings and papers, including:

A poem she's just written, entitled "Grandpa Moala."

When my Moala was feeling good
Out came that big cigar and he would puff away
When he would go to the races
And his horse came in
Or when his horse didn't come in
But to me it was his cigar that burned
And when my anger was aroused
He would say Babeala, Pearlala
I love you so but I also love my cigarala too.
So how could I compete with a love like that?
How I wish he were here today
Grandpa Moala to puff puff away.

A recipe, written on the back of Salvation Army stationery, for mandel broit.

A plastic bag filled with seven crocheted hats—pink, fuchsia, kelly green, dark green, yellow, orange, and purple—for my daughter Lucy, whose head is now bigger than Pearlie's.

A folder of letters she's written to her son Jerry, who died in 1975, and to her husband Moe, who died in 1977, since their deaths.

A scrapbook from her eighty-fifth birthday of pictures and letters written by family and friends, including this testimonial from her brother Maxie's son, Stuart, and his wife, Toni, and their children: "Aunt Pearlie's laughter is contagious and her love of life is inspiring. Aunt Pearlie is loved and missed very very much. New York hasn't been the same without her—it's a lot quieter! Love,

Toni, Stu, Chris and Matthew." And the lyrics to a song my husband, the songwriter, wrote in her honor and serenaded her with, entitled "Eat, Eat, Eat."

> *Come and gather round people*
> *I will tell you a tale*
> *Of exploits culinary to which all others pale*
> *I'll attempt to recount*
> *The events that unfurled*
> *When I pulled up a chair to dine with the Pearl*
> *There was bread piled high*
> *Food of every ilk*
> *There was beverage plenty I had tea, beer and milk*
> *I had seconds and thirds*
> *I can still hear the voice and those now famous words:*
> *Eat, Eat Eat, whaddya talking about full?*
> *Eat, Eat, Eat, Brockala you eat like a bird . . .*

The scrapbook, covered with a pastel floral print, also contains Pearlie's thoughts, like, "I know I can't live forever but I love my family so much I will wait till God will say, Pearlie, enough is enough. . . . Please God protect my family. Keep them well."

An envelope, labeled "birth certificate for Joy," containing a photostat of Pauline Rosenwasser's official record of birth from the City of New York Department of Health, which duly noted that she was born at 104 Avenue D to a 28-year-old father and a 30-year-old mother of Austrian descent, though they seemed to take their time filing the birth certificate since she was born February 8, 1902, and the document from the Bureau of Records—officially, No. 9975—is dated March 4, 1902.

A torn and faded marriage certificate, taped together on the back with a crazy patchwork of orange and white tape, of Pearlie and Moe's wedding at 1507 Eastern Parkway in Brooklyn on May 7, 1921, corresponding with the thirtieth of Nisan in the year 5681 of the Hebrew calendar, and written in Hebrew with a drawing of flower girls and top-hatted men with beards surrounding a bride and groom under a tented canopy.

A photocopy of my grandmother's life insurance policy, stamped Paid in Full, that covers her funeral expenses and is attached to a diagram of plots I and J, No. 7, at Section AA, Block 6, of Beth David Cemetery on Elmont Road, where she will eventually rest forever—between her father and her husband.

A nine-page, single-spaced autobiography she wrote a few years ago, beginning with these words: "Get to know oneself." Clearly, she is one to heed her own advice. Why else would she begin psychotherapy, at 92?

⊰⊱

A Bubbe Survey on Motherhood

How do you let go of your children?

PEARLIE: Oh, it's very hard. It's one of the hardest things in the whole world. It's so hard, I can't even tell you, Joy. I remember when your mother went on her honeymoon, and your grandfather, Izzy, called me up and said, "Is Mike there? Are the children there? I wanted to wish them well." I said no, and I started to cry. I just can't tell you how I cried. But it's very hard to let go of your children. Even when you took them to school the first day, didn't you feel sad about that? I mean, any time that you have to part from your children is very hard, very hard. And it doesn't get any easier. Instead of getting easy, it gets harder. Isn't that strange?

TESSIE: How do you let go? You'll be happy to get rid of them! But I mean in a good way. You feel that they're on their own, you've done your job. You miss them, of course, but that's all. You get so used to it. In some part of you, you get used to it. It hurts and it hurts and you get used to the pain.

⊰⊱

MY GRANDMOTHERS MIGHT AS WELL HAVE STEPPED OUT OF A time machine. When they were born, Alexander Graham Bell had yet to invent the telephone. Marie Curie had yet to win the Nobel Prize for discovering radioactivity. Thomas Edison was in his prime. In fact, Pearlie's sister, Stella, was married to Edison's personal secretary, Frank Strauss, a man who felt he needed to change his first name from Abraham to Frank because he suspected Edison of being an anti-Semite. ("I don't know why," Pearlie muses now about Frank changing his name. "We have Abe Lincoln and he wasn't Jewish.") The automobile, the airplane, electric power all lay in the future.

"Let me tell you, the good old days weren't so great," Pearlie says.

"*Ach,* what I've lived through," Tessie adds.

At the turn of the century, when they were babies, life expectancy was 49 years. Today, it's 76. At the rate they're going, Tessie and Pearlie may soon be part of the fastest-growing segment of the American population—its centenarians. At last count, the Census Bureau tracked fifty thousand of them, up from fifteen thousand in 1980. "I'm gonna outsmart everyone," Pearlie told me on her last birthday. "I'll be here to 100. There's too much fun to have yet."

She lets go of one of her cackles. "I'm lookin' for a guy. I don't know if I could get one at this stage. Maybe I have to change my face."

Tessie's view is quite different. "I started the twentieth century," she says. "I hope I don't finish it."

Originally, they were Pauline and Toby—two girls leading parallel lives a continent apart. Both grew up one of seven children. Both lived in a world of anti-Semitic taunts and decrees. Both scraped through the poverty of their girlhood by working hard and relying on their street smarts. And both kept reinventing themselves, over and over. For Pearlie, the lessons learned came mostly from the dark reaches of the heart; for Tessie, from the wits to outsmart anyone she could.

"I ain't talking, I'm so happy," Tessie says to me as I stash my suitcase in the corner of her bedroom, arriving for another one of our historical review sessions. It is a Thursday evening in fall, cold and wet. From the crimson wall-to-wall carpeting to the Shalom sign over her kitchen door, Tessie extends me the red-carpet treatment like no one else. A three-course dinner awaits: half a grapefruit, split pea soup, and potted steak with kasha varnishkes—all served on her good china, the old Passover dishes, gold-rimmed with tiny flowers, that have been relegated to a top shelf in her cupboard.

As she serves me a bowl of soup, I retrieve it, seeing her hand shake. "Oh, Grandma, you're making such a fuss here," I say. Of course, I love it. And she knows I do.

"I make a fuss about you?" she asks, teasingly. "I wonder why. Maybe you know. I don't." She cracks a half-smile.

When I first arrived, she instructed me to not act like a guest—to help myself and feel at home. But she keeps treating me like royalty, serving me. "No," she says, correcting me, as she hands me a spoon. "I'm treating you that you're my granddaughter. You have to eat. *Es gezin der hate.* Eat in the best of health."

She sits beside me in one of the wooden chairs covered in blue Naugahyde. It takes her several minutes to get adjusted, grasping the table for support. "Any time I see someone from the family, especially you," she says, "that's an injection to live longer. Maybe I'll tell you all not to come."

"Because you want to die?" I ask.

"I don't want to die," she says. "But I don't want to wait until I'll be very very sick. I mean, I can live another one hundred years provided I could help myself. I don't mean I should go out dancing. But at least I should be able to wipe my own nose. Period."

For the moment, anyway, there are two key things at which she's still quite adept: reminiscing and eating. So we do both simultaneously, tracing Tessie's history to a province of Poland-Austria, called Galicia. It was, she recalls, a land of bad breath.

In the beginning, there was halitosis. Not to mention marital discord. "He liked garlic, and she couldn't stand it, his wife," Tessie explains of Aaron Simon Teitel and his wife Toby. They lived in the shtetl of Kozowa in 1850-something, though the exact date is unimportant. What is important, though, is that the husband adored his garlic. He loved it so much, in fact, that he'd rub it on the crust of his rye bread whenever he had the chance. And as much as he loved his wife, she couldn't compete with the garlic factor.

"So, she took him to rabbinical court, which at that time was three rabbis and then Torah," Tessie explains. "That means the law of the Torah. And he went. When they send for you, you have to go. Like a subpoena. He went. And the way he was talking and she was talking, they made a decision."

The rabbinical decree failed to adhere to the patriarchal laws of the day. "They said she was right," Tessie continues, handing me a napkin. "She won the case. He stopped eating garlic. You know why? The rabbis said if she can't stand it, he can do without. He smelled!

"That's why I can't stand it. Maybe I take after her." Eventually, Toby-the-garlic-hater died. But her granddaughter, also loath to taste garlic, was named after her. And they shared a certain feistiness, a certain I'm-right-and-you're-wrong air.

Nearly one hundred fifty years later, the granddaughter Toby—now called Tessie—is trying to get out of her recliner chair near a television set, and she is stuck. "Why don't you get a derrick and pick me up?" she asks her granddaughter, a garlic defender.

"But garlic is so healthy for you," I say.

"Healthy shmealthy," she says, dismissively. "I'm 93 and I didn't eat garlic." She shakes her head. "My sisters all liked it," she adds. "So look where they are and where I am." Her sisters, Gussie, Leah, Rosie, and Sylvia, are all dead. Maybe she has a point.

Onions, too, were a problem. "Raw onion is the worst thing. I couldn't stand the smell. My throat would lock up. My mother used to say I'm crazy, I didn't like red kidney beans. But I really hated onions. When my sister Sylvia and I were fighting, she'd eat an onion and come over to me and go 'hahhhhhh'—breathe in my face. I'd cry and Mama would punish her." Sylvia called Tessie "Fatso." Tesse called Sylvia "Squealer."

Her home, which didn't have running water and was surrounded by fields of wheat and corn and potatoes, was situated about twenty miles from the Carpathian Mountains. It was modest—two rooms in summer, or one in winter, with no flooring and a roof of straw. In the backyard, there was a vegetable garden and a cow, chickens, turkeys, and geese. To scour pots, her mother used sand and ash. They lived about a kilometer away from town, because her father's brick factory couldn't operate in the city. Once, her favorite kaiser, Franz Joseph, passed by her home. She especially liked him because he had a Jewish mistress.

"My father wasn't very wealthy," she says of Chaim Teitel, "but he was known in the city." Her mother she remembers as looking like her—stocky, about five feet two. Jet black hair. Wavy. Nice soft face, a chubby face. Brown eyes. But she identified more with her father. "My father had gray eyes, like a cat," she says, clearing her throat. "Like me."

Toby was a tomboy who loved to "run around." She had no toys, only a homemade doll fashioned out of *shmattes* (rags). She especially loved to play games, like the Gypsy Is Sleeping—a sort of Old World version of Red Rover, Red Rover. And she and her sisters acted out an imaginary sleigh-ride game with a fat, short guy named Sam Weinreb, who pretended to be a horse.

At her all-girls school, which was a mile away, she excelled but was often bored by course offerings, such as how to do cross-stitching correctly. She knew, though, she'd have to learn it, because if her father ever caught her sitting around, he'd say, "So take a broom and sweep the floor or pick up a needle and sew. A Jewish girl should never be idle." But she was also a wiseacre who got into trouble, like the time she passed a note about the teacher, Rose, to her cousin, sitting nearby on a long, wooden school bench. The note read, "Rose is a monkey."

"The teacher got it," Tessie remembers, smiling. She munches on a piece of rye bread. "What did she do? She sent me out in the hall as a punishment. So what did I do? I left. I went home. She went to call me in, and I wasn't there. The next morning, I came to school, like nothing. So, she gave me a lecture at lunchtime. When the others went out to recess, she held me in class and told me she'd tell my father. Well, that was the worst thing she could do. I promised her that I wouldn't do it, and I never did again."

She was terrified of incurring her father's wrath, so afraid she couldn't bring herself to tell him her eyes were weak. Once, she defied him and secretly tried on his glasses. Realizing that they helped her eyes, she nonetheless was worried that God had punished her for disobeying her father's command to not play with his glasses. "I was afraid to tell my father, because he'll yell at me how come I don't see!"

In any case, Toby was in demand by classmates' parents. "The rich children, like the banker's daughter, were in my class. When I went to school, I had to pass by her house. She lived, like, in a garden. Like a forest. It was something beautiful, her house. Very rich. And her mother would always stop when I'd come from school. 'Why don't you play with Sally?' she'd ask. I didn't realize Sally was stupid." As she did for the other girls in her class, she'd help Sally with her homework.

Perhaps, above all, Tessie was a "nosy body." "When I saw two people talk, I was pushing in my face there." When Austrian soldiers practiced maneuvers before the war, she'd eavesdrop on them when they talked to one another via "telephone"—tin cans attached by string. Once, in the trenches not far from her home, she came upon the body of a Russian soldier who had apparently taken out an identification card just before he was killed. The card had Hebrew letters, which to Toby signaled his desire for a proper burial in a Jewish cemetery. She ran to tell her father, and the local burial society made special provisions for the young soldier. She considered this a *mitzvah*, a good deed.

The sixth of seven children, she shared a narrow bed with her older sister, Rose. Her sisters Leah and Sylvia shared another bed. Gussie, the oldest sister, left for America when Toby was only 2 years old. Her two brothers, Frank and Max, were the darlings of the household. Frank was a wild kid who convinced his father he should be tutored at home rather than attend school because he'd have to remove his hat in class—a sign of being a goy. Max was more quiet, less prone to roughhousing. Though he was older than she, it was Toby who would fearlessly lead her big brother to the outhouse at night.

No doubt, theirs was a close-knit family. But the Teitel household was, in truth, not what it appeared to be in young Toby's eyes. It wasn't until her brother Frank died of the Spanish flu in America in 1918 and her mother, Charna, wasn't sitting *shivah* (the seven-day mourning period in Jewish custom when the immediate family members rend their garments, cover mirrors, and sit on low stools to praise the dead) for him that she came to understand the truth: Her father had been widowed with four children when he married her mother. But since he insisted that the family consider itself "one for all and all for one," no one mentioned to Toby that Gussie, Leah, Rosie, and Frank had a mother who had died in childbirth.

"We weren't brought up, we were dragged up," she is fond of saying. "I was born to a poor family. Not poor—we had what to eat. We were six kids in a little house, all in one room. But we were happy. My oldest sister was already in America then." Her father, a tall man with strawberry blond hair and a full red beard, imparted a critical lesson early on: "He always told us, 'Don't look up—there's no end to up. Look down. There are those who haven't got what to eat.' That's how he kept us humble." It is, of course, one of the basic tenets of the story of Moses: humility.

Even now, she views her life in much the same way. When she washes her dishes, she must lean her elbows against the sink counter for support. When she coughs, her whole body shakes with the force of a gale wind. When she walks, her slipper-clad feet shuffle against the yellow-and-orange linoleum tile floor, unsteady and slow. Ask her how she feels, and she replies, "*Mashlep-se.*" It means, "I drag myself."

Then, she hastens to add: "I have a friend in Rockaway Beach and she says to me, 'Tesseleh, other people would like to *shlep* and they can't. Thank God you can do it. Thank God you can *shlep.*' And she's right."

Her mother, she says, was quiet. "She wouldn't hurt you because she wouldn't want to be hurt." But she was also capable of great scorn. "My mother, if I would be cold, she would say, 'Oh you're a *culta hevnick.*' I was a kid, and I would say, 'I don't want to do it, I was cold.' So she would insult me. She says, '*culta hevnick.*' That means that I'm a cold piece of shit. Because I didn't do what she wanted. My own kids don't even know that word. I never said it, 'cause I always hated it when my mother did. And she meant it." Ironically, her mother is remembered by my father and his sisters—her grandchildren—as a sweet, loving, and warm woman.

All this recollecting is exhausting. "Sometimes," she says, "you don't want to remember."

It's nine-thirty, past her normal bedtime. I turn on the tap to wash a pan. "If you pay me a million dollars, I wouldn't let you do it," she says of my doing the dishes. I know this game.

"Go to bed," I yell back at her.

"Not yet," she insists, downing two Tylenols. I find her determination and willpower inspiring and tell her so. "Willpower is a big deal," she explains. Usually, the way she says "big deal" drips with sarcasm. This time, though, she means it. "If you have no willpower, you're worth nothing."

Then, she offers me a huge compliment. "You have willpower," she says. "Who else would do it—leave their kids to come here? All right, you make a few pennies writing this book. But the willpower to work. Other people don't even have the willpower to live."

I ask: "When you remember your stories and you tell me about your life, do you know what an incredible gift you're giving to me and my kids?"

She replies: "Do you know what an incredible gift it is to me that I can remember?"

My first night of this visit, I sleep in the living room—on the old cot my father used to roll out in the kitchen. As I make up the bed, she instructs me how to double over the thermal blanket, the one she's covered with butterfly sheets stitched together by hand. She hands me a two-cell industrial flashlight before shutting off the light, "in case you need to go to the bathroom." She also brings me a pair of pink terry cloth slippers, "so your feet shouldn't be cold." Finally, I know she's really going to turn in when she issues the same singsongy pronouncement she's issued since I was a little girl, when I curled up on the two living room club chairs she'd pull together for me to sleep on.

"Good night. Sleep tight. Don't let the bedbugs bite. I love you very much." Her words have an ironic edge now, given the cockroaches in the kitchen she'd like to pretend aren't there. When I pointed one out earlier in the evening, she feigned ignorance, saying, "I don't know him, we haven't been introduced."

I tell her I love her, too. And I thank her for everything. "It's so good to have someone to talk to," she says. "Don't forget. I'm thirty years alone." She props a hand against the hallway wall for support, heading slowly to her bedroom, past the clown painting, the macramé wall hanging, the copper cowboy etching.

Then, she returns once again. "Before I forget, there are washcloths in the closet," she says. "And towels. You name it." She shuts off the hallway light.

Lying down now, I turn on my side and look at the puffy couch beside me, covered as it is with a swirling red and purple and green fabric, practically psychedelic in the dark. I can't help myself and sneak a peek beneath the slipcover. I'm thrilled to discover a trace of my childhood and of Grandma's past—the deep green, tufted velvet and smooth-fringed edging that originally covered this couch. I know, as I drift off, that my grandmother and I will be peeling back layers of time and memory together. Like the couch, what lies under the surface will be rich and evocative. But I can find it only if I lift up the covers to see, only if I bother to ask.

And I think of the message implicit in the joke she told me after we switched off *Seinfeld*. A mother complained to her son: He doesn't write to her. He doesn't call her. He doesn't ask about her anymore. The son says, "I'm sorry, Ma. You're right. I didn't call enough. So, how are you?" She says, "Don't ask!"

⌐◄╡ ╞►¬

A Bubbe Culture Vulture

Who is your favorite actress?

PEARLIE: The one that passed away that had tomatoes with that colored man? She and her husband acted a long time. She was so sincere about her acting. What's her name? Oh, yeah. Jessica Tandy.

TESSIE: She died a few years ago. Had gray hair. Not for acting I liked her but for the person. She was always calm. She had trouble with her family. I remember how she took it so nicely. *Oy,* I can see her in front of me and I can't say her name. Do I have to remember? Had a theater named after her, so she must have been a big shot. Yeah, Helen Hayes. How did you know?

Who is your favorite actor?

PEARLIE: No one I can think of.

TESSIE: Spencer Tracy for drama and Jason Alexander for comedy.

What is your favorite song?

PEARLIE: "If I Were a Rich Man" from *Fiddler on the Roof.*

TESSIE: "My Yiddishe Mama."

What is your favorite book?

PEARLIE: I like biographies. You know who I admired? Roosevelt's wife. There was a book out just recently about Franklin and Eleanor Roosevelt I liked very much [*No Ordinary Time* by Doris Kearns Goodwin]. But I felt sorry for her 'cause she had such a lonely life. She missed the best part of being married: She didn't have a man who was in love with her. It was just existing. There was not love there. And she was a good person.

TESSIE: The Bible.

Who is your favorite singer?

PEARLIE: I like that—what the hell's his name? The big fat guy who sings opera. Yeah, Pavarotti.

TESSIE: The Italian guy. What's his name? Pavarotti. Now
he's gettin' no good no more. He's losing his voice. I
mean it. I feel sorry for him. But a few years ago, mm-
mm.

☜ ☞

IN THE EMPTY CORRIDOR, DURING THE QUIET HOUR OF LATE
morning, she's like a shadow, small even for an old woman. The
hallway up on the fifth floor, with its pink wallpaper and brown
plastic handrail, seems to muffle the clacking sound of her black
cane each time she places it on the industrial carpeting. But it's
more than the hushed tones of the building, more than the time of
day, that renders my grandma Pearlie uncharacteristically mute.

"Oy, Joyala, I'm so *fedrayt*," she tells me, meaning crazy, as we
near the elevators around the corner. Her voice is actually quavering.
"I don't know why I'm so nervous." She pronounces it "noy-vuss."

Outwardly, she appears exactly the opposite—regal and poised,
it seems. Dressed in her typically baroque style, she's wearing a
fuchsia cape layered atop one of her crocheted ensembles: black
sweater trimmed with fuchsia and pink and a matching beret, with
black pants, black Reeboks, and pink socks. Plus a pink and black
scarf draped around her neck. She's fastened an old rhinestone pin
"from day one," she explains, onto her sweater, too. And unlike pre-
vious weeks, I notice she's decided to wear a bra.

"I can't stand them hanging down, like *shleps*," she says of her
breasts, as the elevator doors open.

Her nerves are on edge today, because we're on our way for

some medical tests—an ultrasound
and a CAT scan. For the first time,
Pearlie used her emergency button
the other night. She had shooting
pains up her side and back and worried she might be having a heart
attack. The doctor suspects problems
with her gallbladder and advanced
arthritis. The CAT scan is intended to
check for possible tumors.

Baby Pauline (Pearlie) with pacifier.

I park my Ford Windstar van. Pearlie carefully edges herself off the passenger seat. I congratulate her on taking her time.

"Yeah, I like my ass," she says, meaning that she likes life too much to not take care.

I offer her the crook of my left arm to lean on as we walk into the Santa Monica Imaging Center, a large, white building equipped with state-of-the-art machines for diagnosing illness. Grandma's appetite is virtually nil, and her weight has dropped to 112 with her sneakers on—down twenty pounds from just a few months before.

"I just keep *shtuping* [stuffing] it in," she says of food, once a main source of joy. She pads toward the reception desk and asks about my sons, Trevor and Gus, who she insists will one day attract throngs of adoring girlfriends. "There's no girl good enough for your son, that's definite," she warns me about the perils of mother-in-law-dom. "You wait. You'll see."

Then she asks after my daughter, Lucy. "Every time you kiss the baby, kiss the boys, too," she says, offering a bit of unsolicited advice, a Pearlie trademark. It is the hallmark of her love. "They shouldn't get jealous. Don't be afraid to give love."

At the reception window, she hands over her FHP card, wrapped in a white plastic holder, and pays $5 in cash. Since she is covered by FHP, a health maintenance organization, her payments for all medical visits are the same. Today the receptionist advises her that both procedures combined will cost $5.

"I'm gettin' a break!" she beams. She is at her happiest when she feels like she's working the system to her advantage, especially if she's getting something for free. She speaks in a loud enough voice that the other patients sitting nearby look amused. Her nervous energy is unstoppable.

"They have a hard time shutting me up," she says, laughing, to the strangers in the waiting room. She seems to be trying to work off an anxiety that doesn't subside. When she gets panicky like this, I can't figure out if she knows something we don't. Or if she's suffering, again, from the pressing feeling that she's too old to be of help. To herself or anyone else. For someone who's spent her whole life giving, the depth of her anxiety seems bottomless.

The technologist calls her name, and she walks steadily into the examining room, cane in her right hand and maroon cloth purse in her left.

"I need you to take off your shirt, but you can leave your pants and bra on," Brenda, the technologist, tells Pearlie.

"You mean to say you don't want to see my physique?" Pearlie jokes. But the crack is characteristic of her underlying pride in her body, even now, at 92; she's guileless about showing it off. A favorite photograph she keeps in her picture album is from a costume party, back when she was in her eighties, dressed as a slinky cat, in leotards and fishnet stockings. Varicose veins be damned. In my mind, it is no small irony that I wore a very similar cat costume the night I fell in love with Brock at a Halloween party in the Adams House Dining Hall at Harvard, back in the fall of 1973.

She slips off her sweater. "Ooh la la!" I tease her, because she's wearing a lacy black bra.

"I was feeling passionate today," she says, laughing. The top of her pants are held together by safety pins, because she can't stand the feeling of elastic around her waist. A hiatal hernia, which she either refers to as her "heyeenia hoineea" or "that stinkin' thing," has been upsetting her stomach for months now. In fact, it was only recently that she could wear a bra again. "I like it so each one stands in place, like a soldier," she says of her breasts. "One for each pocket."

A few weeks before, we had been sitting in the quiet of her living room, discussing how difficult it is to accept one's aging.

"All of a sudden, I don't recognize myself," she told me.

Why not?

"Well, they're a different shape now—flat," she said of her breasts. Still, she needs the biggest bra size ever, a 40. "I never took a 40," she said. "It's a 40C. I always took a 36C." A former sweater girl gets down.

She looked at me. "What happens is they get longer and thinner." Longer and thinner? "Like a cow," she said, nodding seriously.

Lovely, I thought to myself. Do I really need to know this?

"You go back to the animal stage," she added.

At that moment, she wanted to show me what she meant. And as she lifted her shirt for me to see, without shame or sorrow, I remember thinking, Please, God, spare me this. I couldn't handle seeing the gravitational pull of 92 years on my grandmother's bosoms, as she calls them. I needed to keep some of the aging process a mystery. But then, something rather remarkable happened.

With her shirt lifted, I saw two shapely breasts beneath a cotton tank top—voluptuous and soft, really. I thought she looked beautiful. "I only know one thing," she told me of her entering puberty. "When I started to develop and my breasts started to sprout, I thought it was so terrible. And my mother couldn't talk to me and tell me this is a natural thing, like a tree sprouts. My mother never gave me a brassiere or guided me that way. I used to take towels and safety pins and make it tight to hide it. You can imagine."

Presently, she seems impatient. "Look, darling, I didn't eat all day, so let's get on with this," she advises Brenda. She adjusts the paper gown—open in front—and ambles over to the ultrasound equipment, hoisting herself, *sans* cane, atop the examining table, covered by a fresh layer of paper.

As my grandmother has her gallbladder scanned, my mind wanders back to her stories about life at the beginning of the century. Her mother ran a candy store on Avenue C on the Lower East Side, selling lollipops and marshmallows on a stick, two for a penny. Pearlie watched as her mother, Annie—whose parents owned an inn in Austria and sold whiskey to travelers on the road there—cranked out homemade ice cream and seltzer at the soda fountain.

Pearlie turns over onto her left side on the examining table, looking fragile now and afraid. "Now when you press your hand there," she tells Brenda, who is pressing the ultrasound scanner against her abdomen, "it hoits."

When she was 6 years old, Pearl moved with her family to south Brooklyn, where the first subway line, the IRT, had just opened on June 8, 1908. Though poverty was endemic among the Italian, Jewish, and Irish immigrants who lived there, rents were cheap. Showers were a luxury item. To save on water and heat, her parents would have her bathe with her sisters, Stella and Edith, in the tub. She'd fight with Stella; Edith was the gentle one.

Annie opened her second store, Rosenwasser's Dry Goods Store, a long, narrow shop with many counters and three rooms in back. Since the local merchants were anxious to do business, they gave Annie merchandise on credit. Pearlie remembers that her mother would make them lunch, and since her cooking was so wonderful, they'd ask if she'd mind if they brought their wives, too. Annie never objected, seeing it as a way to extend her credit.

But business was never easy. Pearlie's father, Sam, was forever

accusing her mother of being too generous with customers, allow-
ing some to buy underwear with a small down payment, for example, when she knew very well they couldn't pay her back. And he'd
get after her for buying too much ruching, the colorful pleated
trim she loved to order in bulk but couldn't sell. Pearlie remembers her papa saying things like, "What I make on the job I have
to put in the store instead of our mouths." And no one was
allowed to speak Yiddish in the store, for fear of driving customers
away.

"There was a lot of—whaddya call it—racism," Pearlie remembers. "Hatred between the Gentiles and Jewish people. To me,
people were people. It didn't make any difference what they were.
But when my mother was running the dry goods store, people
came in and some of them would say, 'I wouldn't go in that store.
That's a Jew store,' meaning we were Jewish. And when I'd walk
home from school, I'd hear kids say, 'Sheeny, sheeny.'

"The Irish and the Jews, they'd fight with clubs. My brother
Marty came home many times with black eyes." Three generations
later, the Irish and Jewish kids in Pearlie's life are her great-grandchildren, my children, blended together.

Though Annie Rosenwasser was a daring woman—able to open
her own corner stores and eager to fly in a tiny prop plane, like the
one that Charles Lindbergh first flew across the Atlantic Ocean, at
Floyd Gibbons Airport near Rockaway—she was also a product of
her times. Before birth control, before Margaret Sanger defied
existing laws to open her first clinic in Brownsville, Pearlie's
mother was a woman who equated her husband's disrobing with
another pregnancy.

"Years ago, they didn't have closets," Pearlie remembers, smiling
at the memory. "So they'd hang the pants on the door. Mama
would say, 'Take down those pants! I never want to look at pants
again!' It was very hard for her to have those babies. She was very
small and round. She had to go through a lot to have the babies,
every two or three years. If she'd go into labor at night, she'd say,
'Take those pants down. I can't stand pants! Look at the trouble
they give me.'"

Pearlie, on the other hand, would later visit Sanger's clinic
sometime in the 1940s with her friend, Ethel. "I think we got Margaret Sanger's thing not to have babies—the little rubber cup, like

the plate you put in your *smitchek*," she says of the diaphragm. "Grandpa used to use the rubber things. Sometimes, we took a chance, and when we took a chance, we got stuck. But it was a sloppy thing. It got all messed up. Sloppy whichever way."

But no birth control for Annie meant more babies. And more babies in those days was a mixed blessing, since infant mortality was not uncommon. Pearlie remembers her mother having big brown eyes and dark silky hair and looking "very severe, but when she would look at you with her beautiful eyes and the sweet expression 'round her mouth, she was the most beautiful person to me."

"I put my mother and father on a pedestal," she explained, riding in the car earlier that morning. "What they said I followed. Any time there were poor people in the neighborhood without food or money, my mother would send me over with a package of rolls and coffee to hang on their doorknobs. I was the *shlepper*. All times of the day, never fearing something could happen to me. And I didn't think anything could happen to me, either.

"So maybe if you think good, good will come out of it."

Beep. Beep. Beep. The technologist takes another scan and the ultrasound machine squeaks again. "Are you breathing?" she asks Pearlie.

"Mmm-hmm," says Pearl, her eyes closed.

"Okay, good."

"It feels a little, like, sore." Within fifteen minutes, the procedure is done. Pearlie wipes the blue jelly that conducts sound waves off her stomach and thanks Brenda. "That wasn't so bad, dahling. Thank you very much."

On to the CAT scan down the hall. The room is 64 degrees. The machine, labeled Technicare Delta Scan 2060, seems to suck Grandma Pearlie right into it. Its whirring sound, the technologist cautions Pearlie, might sound like a toilet flushing.

"Just so long as it's not a toilet flushing," Grandma jokes. Amid the Hazardous Explosive Materials warnings, I watch Pearl rising into the giant circle of this medical tool, its cold efficiency a stark contrast to her fuchsia beret, still perched atop her head at a stylish angle, even when she's lying down.

When we pull back up to Grandma's apartment, I step around to the passenger door to help her out of the car.

"Watch your *tuchis*," she advises, concerned about the one-way traffic whooshing by. I extend my right arm as support when she steps up onto the curb. Then, as I roll down my window to say good-bye, she blows a kiss.

"Good-bye, puppy," she calls to me, not meaning that I'm a little dog but offering an affectionate form of Yiddish for belly button, *pupik*.

GRANDMA PEARLIE'S

Famous French Toast

I put in two eggs. I put in just a cup of milk. And I put in a little drop of vanilla. You can use almond flavor or vanilla. If you don't want to use it, you don't have to use it. And a little sugar. I start off with a teaspoon and I find if I feel I need more, then I just add a little more, but don't forget the children put syrup on it, see, so we don't need it that sweet.

You can use any kind of white bread, sliced, if they like white bread. If you like whole wheat, you use whole wheat.

Now, you can fry it in butter, you can fry it in the no-fat, no-salt margarine. If I haven't got margarine, I use butter. I prefer the taste.

Soaking the bread, that's the secret. You have to have your oil or butter or whatever you put in there melted, and you mustn't leave it in too much in the milk. If you leave it in too much in the milk and the eggs, then it gets sloppy and then you can't have it like one piece. So you just put it in, take it out. Put it in, take it out. Fast like. I don't use too much grease. While it's frying, I see if it needs it, and if it's starting to burn, then I just add a little more, because I try to use as little as possible.

And that's the whole big spiel.

CHAPTER 3

K'nocker: Big Shot

*Chaim Teitel, Tessie's father and
my great-grandfather, around 1918.*

ON A THURSDAY NIGHT IN EARLY NOVEMBER, THE TV NEWS IS
blasting at full volume. It is switched to the local CBS station.

"This guy," Grandma Tessie says of the newscaster, "has such
smart eyes. He'll go places." Intelligence is a recurring leitmotif,
her insecurity about her own education being a prime motivating
factor.

To understand my grandma Tessie, it is necessary to listen to
her running television commentary, more of a contretemps than a
soliloquy. Much as she gnaws on sugar cubes, hides her chocolate
in the linen closet, and chews chicken bones, she treats her television set as an idiosyncratic indulgence.

Actually, her TV taste is quite specific. There are only a few
shows she views regularly. Her favorite soap opera, *The Young and
the Restless*, is a must. So is the nightly game show, *Jeopardy!*, at 7
P.M., after dinner. More often than not, she tunes into the news
that precedes *Jeopardy!* And, occasionally, *60 Minutes* on Sunday.
She also makes a point of staying up Thursday nights till 9:30 so
she can catch *Seinfeld*, because the actor Jason Alexander, who
plays George Costanza on that show, is married to Daena Title, a

granddaughter of Tessie's brother Max, who called everyone "Toots" or "Little Monkey."

"He works himself up beautiful, Jason," she says, viewing an episode of *Seinfeld*. She means he's a fine actor. *"Ach,* if he had hair, he'd be a little taller." She's only too happy to show off a recent photo taken of Daena and Jason at the White House with the Clintons. Or to serve me tea in a white mug with the *Seinfeld* logo on it, a gift from Daena.

Earlier that day, we watched *The Young and the Restless* together, Tessie offering an insightful play-by-play of what she likes to call her "sob story." "I'm not happy he died," she says of one of the soap characters. "He's not the dying type." Meaning he wasn't a whiner.

One of the things that emerges from a television-watching session with Grandma Tessie is her ability to make snap judgments about just about anyone. To trust or not to trust. And, most of the time, her pronouncements allow as to how she is superior to those being judged—a reminder of how automatic her self-criticism is. To pray, in Hebrew, means to judge oneself. In this context, my grandma Tessie might best be understood as a nonstop praying machine.

"It's important not to say, 'I'm bigger than you or better than you,'" she tells me. "I can tell people are stupid, but I'm not smart, either."

It's not just that a Sizzler commercial, featuring a special on shrimp and steak, is greeted by her bellowing *"Trayf!"* (not kosher!) at the TV. Or that an unemployed voice-over actor who bets too little on *Jeopardy!* and loses his championship title is reduced to being drubbed "You stupid!" Rather, her worldview is almost invariably reduced to two main categories, like the subdivisions of her *Jeopardy!* show: One is stupid-smart; the other is Jew-goy.

For instance, at the moment there is a commercial on the small screen promoting a product called Belly Buster cream, at $30 per bottle. The commercial features a guy with a big, fat, hairy belly rubbing the cream onto his ample girth.

"Look at that!" Grandma groans. She can't take her eyes off the TV. "Isn't it disgusting!" Score one for the Stupids.

Then, a sports newscaster comes onto the screen and another Tessie edict is issued: "That's a Jew boy," she says. "You look at him and you can tell he's a real Jew boy." Score one for the Jews. Right after Double Jeopardy is played, she shuffles out of her recliner chair and into the kitchen to wash up a few dishes. And like clockwork, she's back for the final question, sitting beside a tiny electric heater set up on the floor on an extra scrap of red carpeting.

As she watches, I see there is a hunger to learn, to know more. Why does she keep wanting to learn? "Why not?" she asks. "If I want to know, I want to know. There's never a limit to know more. There is always something to find out. It's good to know." And it occurs to me that as much as this game show serves as a sort of continuing education forum for her, it also stands as a symbol of what might have been, what she could have attained had it not been for World War I and its lessons of sacrifice and self-sufficiency.

When she was 13, she was forced to quit school when the Russians invaded her village. The experience caused her to redefine basic ideas about happiness. "All you can think is how to survive," she says, during a commercial break. "Bullets are flying. The Russians and the Austrians were fighting each other right over our house. They'd make trenches on the road and catch people to help them dig the trenches—even my brother. The bullets were flying overhead. The first bombs that fell, I fell off the window seat to the ground. One Saturday night, my family was laying on the floor there all night. The Red Cross was coming back with the wounded soldiers in horse and wagons. The blood was coming from the cars. And, you saw that, and you thought, What was happy? You're not allowed to be happy. You don't know if you get a bullet in the head or what. No doctors. No police. It was a no-man's-land. You're happy to stay alive. That's all."

But her family had no idea what to do, where to turn. "We left everything," she remembers now, like it was yesterday. "The only thing I took was a bottle of ink. I liked the ink so much that between all the clothes I put in a bottle of ink. The bottle of ink broke, and *ach!* In the linens I put it. And it wasn't like a small bottle, either. An officer left it. He forgot it. I couldn't get such nice ink. Blue ink."

Gone for four weeks to the Carpathian Mountains, her father asked, "Where are we going? What's the use of running?" So, they returned. It was just before Rosh Hashanah, the Jewish New Year. "We came back with not even a stitch of anything—everything burned. *Oy.*" Her family moved in with her father's sister, whom she remembers being "as mean as they come." But she was rich and had room. Still, her younger sister, Sylvia, begged their father to let them move into an uncle's house, instead. "The soldiers were marching day and night there, to fight. But Sylvia said, 'It's better to die from the soldiers than to live with Tante Fraida.' My father said, 'Sometimes you have to listen to a child.' "

If there is one point in time that Tessie continually returns to in her mind, it is wartime in Europe. When she arrived in America, she vowed not to speak of her past; three-quarters of a century later, this is what she wants to discuss most.

"We lived in fear," she says simply. "And another thing, I never tried to pull away from my parents. I always tried to be close to my father and mother. No matter how, what, when. During the war, I supported them. I had to. I did everything. But we came out alive. People were getting killed for doing the same thing I did. Nothing happened to me." Her ability to size people up, in other words, is a product of her childhood being abruptly upended by war.

She was a smuggler, working the black market through the box-cars like nobody's business, but also coming back in time Thursday nights to bring her mother a chicken for *Shabbes*. One time, she was in Ternopol, a big city about five miles from where she lived. "I stayed overnight there," she says. "My sister-in-law—my brother Frank's wife that got killed by the Nazis—I would stay with her and my little nephew. I had lots of packages. Cigarettes. The regular ones. Without the filters. And at that time they wore the bell-styled coats. You know, loose. I had sewn the stuff into the lining. All illegal. And I was going for the train. Dressed nice. The coat was beauty-ful. What's inside the coat! So, I was fat.

"I see two policemen standing. And I had a little satchel. And I had plenty of stuff there. But elegant. And what shall I do? I must go by, but they'll check me. So, what I did maybe saved my life. Instead of avoiding them, I walked straight to them. And I said, in Polish, of course: 'Would you please tell me which way for the train? For the station?' Well, I knew with my eyes closed where the station was. But if they think I don't know, then I'm not one of those peddlers.

"And they told me. I thanked them. I got away with it. This I can never forget. All they had to do was just touch me, and I'd fall over, I was so full of contraband—tobacco, ready-made cigarettes, everything. I could have been arrested. They could have beat me up."

But Tessie's sense of trust, perhaps even more than by the

travails of war, was derailed by those closest to her. At 17, when she figured out that her three older sisters and brother had a different mother than she, she remembers feeling at once relieved and betrayed. Looking back on it, she says she had suspected as much when she figured out that her sister Gussie was just a few years younger than her mother. "But I didn't dare even to think it."

Alex Trebek, the emcee of *Jeopardy!*, is always good for a nightly thrashing, especially when he's not moving as quickly as Tessie would like.

"C'mon, hurry up!" she yells at him. "I have no time!" In fact, time is all she has just now. Commercial breaks are good for another story. I ask her to tell me the one about arriving in America penniless. It underscores her values of generosity and trust.

"The trip coming over here?" she asks. "All we had was sixty dollars. That's what we could sell of pots and pans, whatever. We had land, but it was worthless. The land you couldn't sell to nobody. And we had tickets. My sisters, who were in America already, sent the *schiffcartes*, they called them.

"We came to Rotterdam. The men and women were sleeping separate. We stayed at the depot there. My father heard a man crying. My father got up and went over there to where the voice was coming from. Mostly, it was Jews running away from Poland. He heard a man cry. Why did he cry? He said, 'We're going to America, and we're short of money.' He has an aunt in America. They're in Rotterdam, and they don't have money to stay there. My father says, 'How much do you need?' He says thirty dollars. My father said, 'Look, I'll give you the thirty dollars. I don't want to know where you're going. I don't want to know your name. This is my daughter's address in Brooklyn. If you want, you'll come to America and this is where you can get me.'

"So we only had thirty dollars to our name to come to America. So then we came to Ellis Island. We came on Friday. It was so busy that they couldn't process us. We had to stay overnight. They gave us corn flakes and milk. And white bread. We hadn't seen white bread in years. Friday night, my father had the thirty dollars and he sewed it in his vest pocket. He put it under his head. To make a story short, at Ellis Island, those *faygelehs* they know where to go. They stole the thirty dollars."

"'Those *faygelehs*?'" I interrupt. It is a derisive term for homosexuals, like "faggots."

"Today *faygelehs* you think different. By us, it's 'the little thieves.' So, he got up in the morning. No vest. And that was it. So we were without a penny."

On her first Christmas in America, two men showed up at her sister's apartment in Brooklyn. "They had no beards. They were dressed American-style, shaved. They brought us the money back. We were rich! We had thirty dollars!"

There is one significant element of the coming-to-America story she omits, though—the part about her father having murdered a man back in Europe. She looks annoyed with me for mentioning it. "Oh, Freddie's been spreading that story," she says of her nephew, Fred Scheffler, who is her sister Gussie's son.

"See, my father had little houses, little huts for the men who lived there, for the summer," she recalls of the brick factory. "If they want to stay for the winter there, they could stay, but they used to go look for better jobs. But anyhow, there was one man, he was a big drunk. And it came before Passover and it was, you know, my mother would make it. She had even the counter where you clean, but it was in the attic. So my father went over to the man. He said, 'Look, there is a little work table, and you bring it down because my wife needs it.' But he was drunk, and he went back to sleep.

"My father went to the bath, because you had to go to the bathhouse before the Seder. He comes back and my mother couldn't do anything. It's Passover evening, it's already the Seder. And my father got very angry. He goes into that hut where the man lived. He sees his boss come in, and he jumps up from his bed and says, 'Yes, sir?' And my father said to him, 'Why didn't you bring down what I told you from the attic?' And he slapped his face. Just gave him a slap.

"He fell down. And he died. And my father sees he's laying down. And my father, he got scared, of course. So, he called the funeral man and they buried him. But every businessman has enemies. You know, there's always competition. Somebody squealed that my father killed a man. That's all the police and the gendarmes had to hear. So, they finally decided to exhume the body.

"So they exhumed the body, and the doctor took a look at his liver. He said he didn't die from anything else. It was cirrhosis of the liver. He said, 'This liver is all burned up.' My father got free. But he thought that in case they're going to indict him, he was ready to run away to America. Maybe it would have been better. Because my father was born too soon. He was a very brilliant man."

The final answer on *Jeopardy!*, under the category Royalty—"*Collier's Encyclopedia* calls this man 'the most famous of Polynesians' "—leaves her stumped. And when she can't come up with the question ("Who was Kamehameha I?"—which I'm at a loss to figure out, as well), she must come out on top. So she makes another pronouncement.

"You know who will win?" she asks me. "The woman."

Since the woman contestant bet so little and correctly answered the question that the champion blew, Tessie is redeemed.

"Stupid! You stupid!" she berates him. "I was right! I was right! The woman wins."

✎

Bubbes on Expressing Anger

What did you do when you got angry with your children?

TESSIE: I don't say anything. They know if I keep quiet it's worse yet. The silent treatment, you'd be surprised, is very effective. I wouldn't yell at them. Oh, no. And give other people the satisfaction that I yell at my children? Then they would say, "See, she yells, too." I had more or less a better reputation. Quiet and more *balabatish*. That means come from a nice family.

Sometimes, I'd tell them *kishen tuchis*—kiss my ass. You know what *tuchis* means? There is a Hebrew word, *tachat*. *Tachat* means "underneath." And from this is *tuchis*. Like Sam used to say, "Why do they say *kishen tuchis* is such a terrible word? Every *tuchis* is clean! Some people have a cleaner *tuchis* than others have faces."

PEARLIE: I did what my father did. I'd bite my finger and go, "Arghhhhh!"

✎

"ONE, TWO, THREE, AND A KICK. ONE, TWO, THREE, AND A KICK."

"Right knee. Abdominals tight. Sit up straight."

Sitting on a white aluminum folding chair, Pearlie dances. She hasn't been to this arthritis exercise class since her hernia problems set in, but people are clearly glad to see her back.

"How are you?" asks a woman, sitting down in an elegant blue sweat suit.

"Coming through," says Pearl, smiling. "Coming through the rye." She turns to me. "Look at this man, Joy," she says of a fellow in his eighties who uses an aluminum walker to take his seat. "He can barely walk but he comes here."

Pearlie's teacher, Arlene, snaps on the cassette player, and Italian accordion music fills the room, reminiscent of a bad French film or maybe *The Lawrence Welk Show*. Every week, about twenty-five students attend this class. The room, which has already been decorated with fake Christmas wreaths and giant red balls weeks before Thanksgiving, is located in the second-floor community center of the Santa Monica Place, an indoor mall one block from Pearlie's apartment.

"One, two, three, and a kick," Arlene says, instructing them. She is wearing a salmon T-shirt and gray leggings.

"You look good," another student, Alice, says to Pearl. "You don't need to be home. You sit at home, you get more sick."

"Now right knee. Abdominals tight. Sit up straight."

Pearlie turns to me, smiling. "To get movement in your legs— it's so good. Especially for an old *kocher* like me." Back when she was in her eighties, she began attending this class.

"I've been telling my granddaughter how many years I've been coming," she explains to Arlene, who says she's been teaching for seventeen years.

"You're the best!" Pearlie says. "She is!"

Arlene looks pleased, if embarrassed.

"Gotta learn to take a compliment," Pearl advises, as Bobby McFerrin begins singing, "Don't Worry, Be Happy." The class stands, holding on to the backs of their chairs.

"Toes on the floor. Hold your backs straight. Lean a little at the hip, now bring the heels up. Hold on to your chair. Five, six, seven, and again."

I look at Pearl, raising her heels with style and verve, even adding a sassy little shake of her backside, and I'm in awe of her vitality.

Ever since she can remember, Pearlie has danced away the vagaries of life. It's not really stretching it, I think, to view her as a modern-day Miriam, the Old Testament prophetess who managed to pack her tambourine for the forty-year exodus in the desert, ready to sing and dance at the water's edge even when hope seemed a distant memory. Pearlie's faith in the saving grace of dance and music started back in her teens in Brooklyn, when her father was working as an errand boy and her mother was scrubbing stairs, the dry goods store just about to go belly up.

In the autobiography she began ten years ago , Pearlie wrote:

> Things were getting real hard for Mama and a band of Gypsies were traveling around, knocking on doors, asking if anyone wanted to have their fortunes told. Mama thought maybe they could advise her what to do about the store, so she let them in. There were about five of them. They were dressed so poorly and their hair looked as if it was never combed. I ran ahead of them and stood in the corner of the kitchen and watched. They asked Mama to boil up some tea to read her tea leaves, and they told Mama not to move the store: She would be losing a child if she did. Then they walked through the store, sprinkling some water over all the merchandise with one hand and picking up goods with the other hand and stuffing it in their pockets.
>
> Then my parents had to give up the store—they just couldn't pay their bills. And as much as Mama hated to move, remembering what they told her about losing the child, she did. It was right after that we lost Edith. And then our little brother, Philip. He died from brain fever. He was almost two. Then the baby who wasn't named died. Two baby boys in a row.
>
> Mama's heartaches were always about the children she lost. They took Edith to the hospital and she was there for a few weeks, and I remember Mama and Papa coming home from the hospital one night and hearing them both crying like babies in the kitchen, and Mama telling us that our sister passed away. I'll never forget the smell of her body in the living room, where the people from the Jewish funeral society washed her. My parents were so in debt they didn't even have enough money to give her a decent funeral. I think it was $10 for the horse and carriage. It took Mama a long time to get over her loss.

Mama said she never knew my little brother, Philip, was so sick. Mama never used a thermometer but tested Philip's fever by his forehead. He was running such a high fever, and when she ran to the doctor with him—I went, too—the doctor told my mother, "Mrs. Rosenwasser, this child is dying." There was nothing he could do for him. My other little brother that died, she said she didn't have enough money for a good confinement doctor and took a very young doctor with very little experience. If he was a good doctor, she would say, he could have saved the child, because the child was alive when he was born. She would tell me what a beautiful little boy he was. Mama's eyes would fill up with tears when she talked about them, but she would say, "Thank God for my other children."

Mama always said the Gypsies knew.

Looking back, Pearlie has come to associate her sorrow over her sister's death with her own burgeoning adolescence. "After my sister Edith died I was, like, out of this world," she told me one afternoon, sitting in her apartment. "Terribly, terribly upset. Mother was so busy. She had been like a mother to me, Edith. When I lost her, my whole world turned upside down. I loved school, especially Shakespeare, but I couldn't concentrate and never even got my diploma from eighth grade.

"After she passed away, about a year later, that was the time I started to get a bust. I wanted to hide it, and I didn't know how. I just couldn't stand myself, sprouting and thinking I was getting fat. And my mother—it's very strange—she was such a good mother, but she never figured that maybe it was embarrassing to me."

To her family, she had always been "Paulie." But after Edith died, she became Pearlie—the name change signaling her yearning to cut free, to begin anew. In 1915, after learning shorthand and touch typing on a Remington typewriter, Pearlie was earning $7 a week and quickly worked her way up to $15. Her mother promised she would put down a deposit on a player piano with the first $50 she brought home.

"With your feet you had to do it," she says of the piano. She had little time to take lessons, though.

Pearlie worked as a stenographer six days a week, from 8:30 to 5, with lunch but no coffee breaks. Her job, down on Warren

Street, was at Stanley and Patterson, an electrical concern, where she became "a very, very fast typist." On her way home from work some nights, if the weather was pleasant, she'd get off the elevated train to walk over the Brooklyn Bridge, looking up through its giant cables and webs of steel. The American poet Hart Crane had once called it "the most beautiful bridge in the world." She agreed with that assessment.

She lived on St. John's Place in the Brownsville section of Brooklyn at a time when unions were first emerging. Rent strikes, subway strikes, even kosher chicken strikes, were not unusual. When she thinks about this time, her memories come back to her in a rush of cinematic flashbacks.

"They raised the price of chicken, so people on the block decided to strike and not buy chicken," she says, now sitting in her blue bathrobe in her living room. As a storyteller, Pearlie waves her hands and narrows her eyes, wiping the saliva from the sides of her mouth. There is something quite beautiful about her, in the act of remembering. "They said nobody was allowed to buy any kosher chicken, because there was a strike against the butchers. But someone smelled chicken soup. They followed the smell. Went to an apartment. Rang the bell, walked in, took the chicken. I was outside talking to a friend, and I see this hot chicken soup they poured right in the gutter. And that poor woman, coming and running, yelling, 'My chicken! My chicken!' And all the people standing there, laughing. I'll never forget that. It stands out in memory."

One recollection begets another. "Did I tell you about the superintendent that lived in that house? His wife had an affair with a furrier who was quite wealthy. And the super found out they were doing monkey business. And I remember coming in the house, and seeing the superintendent with a hatchet, screaming, 'I'll kill that son of a bitch! I'll kill that son of a bitch!' And they ran upstairs. We didn't have no elevators then. Went upstairs and ran on the roof. And the furrier running up on the roof. Ya know, there were black rooftops, attached to the houses, one after the other.

"I ran upstairs to tell my mother, and my mother ran to the window, right away. Everything happened by the window. She could see that the furrier was being chased by the super. The houses were attached one to the other. Fortunately, the last one had a door where you could go downstairs. That's where the furrier ran, and the super couldn't get him."

Annie watched it all, standing at the window where she'd talk to the neighbors. Theirs was a crowded, four-room flat. In the dining room, decorated with Dutch shelves of green dishes Annie won from the movie theater, there was also a couch, usually occupied by another cousin from Europe whom Annie had agreed to take in and try to help find work. Pearlie's extended family was always around: Her mother's brothers both married her father's sisters—cousins looking like siblings.

To listen to Pearl's version of this is a little like listening to Abbott and Costello's Who's on First? routine: "Wait, I wrote it all down," she says, grabbing notes she's jotted down to refresh her memory. "Okay, so Anna Leffenfeld—that's my mother—had two brothers. Uncle Hymie, we called him Uncle Hymie, but his real name was Herman Leffenfeld. And she had another brother, David Leffenfeld. Now, what happened is that my father's name was Sam Rosenwasser. Blanche Rosenwasser and Sam were sister and brother, and Molly Rosenwasser and Sam Rosenwasser was another sister and brother. So they each married into the family. One brother and one sister, and two brothers and two sisters. That was the relationship. Can you figure that out?"

When she'd come home from work, she was responsible for washing clothes—boiling them in a big round tub on the stove, scrubbing them on a washboard, soaking and finally draining them out. Every Friday, her mother would bake seven challahs, loaves of braided egg bread. Since there wasn't enough room in her little stove, she'd send Pearlie to the local Italian bakery, and for a nickel the baker would brown the bread in his giant oven. "It used to go so fast I can't even start to tell you," she says. When she was married, Pearlie carried on the tradition of baking seven challahs every Friday, distributing them to her neighbors and family.

As a teenager, her pleasures were few and simple. Bread and butter and jelly. Riding the train to visit her brother in Harlem, where he was studying for his bar mitzvah. Putting on a white sailor cap and midi for the Fourth of July fireworks with her father. Riding the handlebars of Frank's bicycle as he pedaled. Getting into the movies for 5 cents and staying until they threw her out. And playing "Tipperary" and "Beautiful Ohio" on the player piano. She had boyfriends, but she usually wasn't interested in the boys her mother was, because "the nicer he was, the more I objected to him." And there was an occasional dance.

Annie Rosenwasser, Pearlie's mother and my great-grandmother, on her twenty-fifth wedding anniversary.

"There was a canteen during the First World War, and I went as a volunteer," she says. "And we danced there. My cousin Helen was with me, too. We danced and we played spin the bottle, and this very handsome guy—he wasn't Jewish—kissed me. And I really liked that fellow. That was the only fellow I ever kissed besides your grandpa." She met my grandfather when she was 16.

Back at the arthritis class, Pearlie stands in a giant circle for a conga line. She sways in time to the hokey music. The art of living, the spirit of survival—you can actually see it in the spring of her step. But then, she abruptly decides to leave. She says she doesn't want to press her luck.

Later, she tells me it made her nervous to see people's pitying looks. I never noticed.

"It hurts," she says. "You see you're no longer a *k'nocker*." No longer a big shot. A somebody.

"Do you think I expect too much of you, Grandma?" I ask, worried that I've maneuvered her into returning to this class before she was ready.

"You don't want to accept, Joyala, that I'm not as strong as you think I am."

❦

TO SET THE RECORD STRAIGHT: MY TEENAGE YEARS COULDN'T have been more different from my grandmothers'. They were forced to grow up faster than anyone should, to support their families, to act like big shots—*k'nockers*—in the face of fear. Both Pearlie and Tessie changed their names, symbolic of their desire to become something they weren't. I loved my name, Joy, and felt lucky to be living the cushy life in Beverly Hills, even if we did live south of the tracks. My parents offered me every lesson imaginable:

violin, tennis, dance, horseback riding, piano. The biggest trauma came in shopping for school clothes at Ohrbachs instead of Saks to stay on a budget. And when I left home to attend Radcliffe College, the leap back to Boston was cushioned by a single comforting thought: I'd be able to visit Pearlie and Tessie more often.

THE ONE THING, OTHER THAN A TABLECLOTH, THAT GRANDMA Tessie keeps on her dining room table is a portable speed-dial phone. This, even more than the remote control on her TV set, is her favorite invention of the twentieth century. "If not for the telephone, I'd go crazy altogether," she says. "That's the only thing, the telephone, that keeps my sanity a little bit in place."

On the phone, there is a little yellow Post-it note from my father, offering Grandma simple operating instructions: "To use phone memory no's: Pick up phone. Press TALK. Press MEM. Press number (from 01 to 16). Do not dial." Seeing the note inexplicably makes my throat constrict. It's not jolly tidings that move me, but precisely the opposite. There is, beneath the simple block letters of my father's handwriting, a more immediate message: Stay in touch.

"My son," Grandma says of my father, "a better son than he is I don't think there is."

FRIDAY, DECEMBER 9, 1994. I'M HIDING IN TESSIE'S BATHROOM, crying. Grandma is on the phone with Eva, her niece in Lakewood, New Jersey.

Somehow, observing the aging process up close has overwhelmed me. The night before, Grandma took out my father's report card from fifth grade. His perfect attendance records. The birthday cards she's received over the years. The yellowing notices of appreciation in her honor. All kept inside Izzy's tin ledger from the store. And I think, This is what life comes to?

Earlier in the afternoon, she chided herself for doing nothing, as her father might have. "Why am I sitting?" she asked no one in particular. She really wasn't sure if she had spoken these words aloud or to herself. Such distinctions seemed beside the point now. "I've got so much to do."

She measures her time by way of chores to prepare for *Shabbes*. "As soon as my *knaydlach* [dumplings] are ready, then I have to get dressed for the Sabbath," she told me, rolling her eyes heavenward. She made a face because "getting dressed" doesn't mean what it used to. Now, she removes her red-and-white flannel pajamas with the moon and stars and keeps on her red-and-turquoise floral housedress, her stockings rolled to her knees.

Getting ready for the Sabbath, she sets out a variety of objects. There is the aluminum tray that Jerry, my mother's brother, brought her some fifty years ago. On it, she places a silver candlestick holder with five prongs—one for each member of her family—that belonged to her mother seven decades ago. In each prong, she places the Rokeach candles that Cynthia made a special trip to pick up for her. Next to the candles, there is a braided challah beneath a satin cover from Israel.

And I think, She's so alone. So alone. Everything dies. Nothing lasts. Who knows how long before this apartment will be a memory? Tessie, too.

In the bathroom, the tiles—gray and white checks on the floor—and pink towels have lost their grandmotherly charm. Now, I think, they're just old. Decrepit. The ceiling, too, is caving in. The plaster hangs precariously overhead.

The elaborate setup in the tub—a railing to hold on to the side of the tub, a special plastic chair to perch herself on while showering— is also a reminder that Tessie can no longer take baths, because standing and sitting are too difficult. The shower curtain pole is filled with empty hangers. She's hung up a yellowing plastic sheet over the window. Atop the heater, there is a copy of the *Reader's Digest*. Turning to the humor section called "Laughter, The Best Medicine," I can't find a single funny joke. They're all lame.

I miss her already. And she's not yet gone. I dry my tears and take a deep breath. When I open the door, something odd happens. I feel as if I've stepped into a dimension without time, without place.

It is actually minutes before 4:11, the official time of sunset. But as I watch my grandmother light the *Shabbes* candles, I'm struck by how such a simple ritual can bring order and meaning into a world of chaos and decay.

She covers her head with a silky mesh scarf, long and rectangular. She calls it her *shmatte*. She lights five candles and, in a circular motion, waves her hands toward herself three times—as if to draw the warmth and glow of the candlelight into her life. As I watch her, it dawns on me that she might as well be a priestess, bringing the *Shechinah*, the Divine Presence, into her home. Then she covers her eyes with her fingertips and in a low, deep voice, prays:

"*Baruch ata Adonai Elohenu Melech Ha-Olam.*" Her pronunciation of the Hebrew words, which she learned by listening to her mother, is, as she puts it, "just plain, the old-fashioned way."

"*Ashair kidishanu. B'mitzvah tov vetsyvanu. L'chadlik ner shell, Shabbat.*"

She adds a personal prayer: "Dear God, I ask for *gezint* [health] for my *kinder* [children]. And also, don't forget me."

The phone rings. I can tell by the lilt in Grandma's voice that my father is on the other end. The timing of his call is uncanny, almost eerie.

"Hello, Son!" she says.

"Hello, Mother," he replies. I can hear his voice over the receiver in Tessie's hand. Their rapport is formal, stilted, yet deeply loving. Yiddishisms fly and Tessie's face looks bright and alive.

She hands the phone to me, and I try to keep the tone light, playful. But the weight of my father's words hangs over me like an anvil.

Just as I did in August, when I last visited Tessie, I sit in her kitchen, speaking to my dad by phone. It was then that I first heard him utter the word "mesothelioma." Cancer of the pleura, the lining of the lungs. I vaguely remember having heard the diagnosis associated with the actor Steve McQueen.

Now, my father fills me in on the latest. X-rays showed the tumor pressing on his lungs. He's growing limited. His ability to breathe has diminished. Shortness of breath is a new problem. I hear it in his voice, which sounds shallow and pained. A lung specialist, though, tells him to keep working and seeing patients. Keep swimming, if he can.

"What should we do?" he and Mom asked the doctor.

"Live," came the reply, as if to suggest he didn't have long to do so.

I dimly take it in. Lots of mmm-hmms. Ohs? And reallys? To mask my fear.

Mom gets on now, and we make arrangements for her to look after Lucy and Gussie while Brock coaches Trevor's soccer game tomorrow.

Tessie knows nothing. My father, ever the dutiful son, feels the knowledge of his illness will only cause her pain. So I remain a part of this conspiracy of silence. And I hate myself for it.

WHEN I RETURN TO LOS ANGELES, PEARLIE CALLS TO TELL ME she saw George Burns, a lifelong idol, on TV. "He looked awful," she says. "He had drool coming out of his mouth."

She calls back. "Joyala, I was thinking about the book," she says. I can tell from the tone of her voice that she's scheming, dreaming. She's gone from being an accommodating interview subject to a merchandising madwoman.

"I think it's a good idea to get out *bubbe* dolls. It could bring in a lot of extra money! If I could get two dolls, I could make a little outfit. Maybe sell it with the book. It gives me something to think about. Something to wanna live on."

Meshuggeneh Matzo Brei

You want to see how I make matzo brei? My hands are clean. My mother washed them when I was a baby. You don't need any secrets for it. I'm Julia—what's her name? Yeah. Julia Child.

Two eggs. Two matzos. That's enough. If you want more, you make three, you can make all you want. You see, what I do is I wet the matzo first, under the tap, and then I put in the egg with the matzo. You crack it up into thirds. Put in a little salt. So you mix the eggs, but don't add milk. It has the water already. When you soak it too much, it soaks in the water. I cook it in the unsalted butter. I like it dry. Some people like it light. I like it well done.

I serve it in the bowl I mix it in. Cynthia showed me that. You can soive it with jam, but I'll need you to open the jar. I haven't got the power in my hands to open.

CHAPTER 4

Sex Shmex: Sex Shmex

*Pearlie and Moe Feldman,
cavorting at Coney Island.*

NO MATTER WHAT SHOES I WEAR, I CAN PRETTY MUCH COUNT
on Grandma Tessie hating them. She eyes my Nike hiking boots
with undisguised contempt.

"*Oy vaysmere*—what are you, in the Army?" she asks.

On another day, I'm greeted by a similar refrain. "*Oy*, what kind
of crazy shoes are these?" Tessie asks me with a disapproving gaze.

"They're cowboy boots, Grandma," I explain of a favorite pair of
black pointed boots.

"*Oy*, how can you even wear them?"

She should talk. My grandma Tessie might best be thought of
as the Imelda Marcos of the Yiddish set. She is a complete shoe
freak. The door to her closet is ample proof—twenty-five pairs of
pumps, heels, flats, and Mary Janes of all colors and grades of
leather hanging in a shoe tree. And inside the toe of each shoe,
she has meticulously wadded up tissue paper to preserve each
shoe's shape. On the closet's top shelf, there is a matching handbag for each pair of shoes. Not that she wears any of them anymore. I'm not sure she would qualify as a fetishist, but there is no
question that her life story can be traced to her shoes.

There is, for instance, the matter of coming to America on an old Dutch boat, the *Rindam,* that had been sunk by the Germans during World War I. "It was *shlepping* fourteen days on the ocean," she says of the rickety little ship. Besides feeling horribly seasick down in steerage for two weeks, she remembers arriving in a pair of red shoes. Not red, really—more reddish brown. First, she tells me they were high heels, the slip-on kind. Then, she corrects herself, saying they were definitely lace-ups, above her calf.

"It was a very nice leather," she recalls, gnawing on a sugar cube over a cup of Sanka one morning. "It was good material, and they were high." But she worried they would be considered hopelessly out of style when she arrived, at age 19, in New York in August 1920, wearing a black-and-white gingham dress and matching velvet headband (the kind that was split in two with a sliver of hair peeking through), her cheeks flush with excitement.

"Charlie Scheffler used to say—he was about twelve years old when I came to this country—he said he never saw a girl with such red cheeks as he saw on me. He knew I had no paint on or so." She laughs softly at the memory of her nephew. But she also knew she was lucky to arrive—part of a crushing sweep of immigrants from Eastern Europe. In 1920, five thousand aliens arrived in New York every day for one hundred consecutive days. The immigration figures doubled the following year, leading to an emergency immigration restriction law, the Quota Act of 1921, which was basically intended to restrict people like Grandma Tessie from gaining entrance to the United States. In the Bronx, for instance, builders were tacking up signs on their swank new apartments: NO JEWS ALLOWED.

Her sisters, who had pawned their wedding bands to buy her family tickets for passage to the United States, greeted her at Ellis Island and promptly advised her to change her name, which she had officially listed as Toni. "My sister Gussie told me, 'Tony is the icemaker. Tony is the shoemaker. Tony is the dressmaker. You can't be Tony.' " She settled for Tessie, a name she wasn't really fond of since she thought it was short for Theresa. "We tried to fit the names to the American style," she says of her immediate attempt to Americanize.

On that Saturday in August when she first set foot in Brownsville, she felt like royalty. "Ah! People were looking at us as if we had robes on," she remembers. She is sitting beneath the

Wandering Jew plant that hangs in front of her kitchen window. "There was a crowd. We were almost the first ones to come from the war zones. We came very early. We were the first ones from Kozowa to come to this country. When we came, maybe for three, four weeks steady, was company in and out and out and in to come to see us—whether we still have our faces on."

Not to be a *greeneh*—this was of supreme importance. Since she spoke only Yiddish, she began attending night school four times a week at PS 150 with her brother Max. "I would be a *mensch*," she says now, "if I would have been an American."

Beyond language, there was the value of clothing, another means of becoming Americanized. "Without a hat you didn't go out. You always had to be dressed. If you come in like a slob, you get treated like a slob. But if you come in dressed nice and you talk nice, this is different." She says she could have been a half-size model since she was a perfect size 15½, short-waisted and top-heavy, no stomach and no behind. She thought she was built like a horse, but her skinny sister Sylvia used to insist: "Dammit, you have shapely legs."

Her first week in America, she went to pick out a pair of eyeglasses—her first. She went to the optometrist with Harry, her sister Leah's husband, so he could translate. She remembers with an immigrant's vulnerability: "The guy came over to me and said something in English. And Harry started talking Yiddish to me. He must have said that I don't understand. So I felt hurt. And I tried my best to understand. But he sold me the glasses, anyway." They were pince-nez style with a golden hairpin and chain, no earpiece.

Mostly, her life then was about work, about making a living to support her parents. In return, her mother gave her a nickel for carfare and a sandwich. "I didn't do what I wanted," she says simply. "I did what I had to do."

On Delancey Street, she found a job in a negligee factory. It was a disaster. She burned a hole in a nightgown with an iron and boxed it up, anyway; her boss discovered her blunder and she was promptly fired. She then worked with her brother Max, attaching linings into valises. She turned over her salary in an unopened envelope to her parents, who paid $19 a month for rent on a rat-infested apartment behind a vegetable store at 348 Christopher Avenue, near Livonia and Dumont.

There were, of course, the language gaffes. Ice cream was

"itchy cream." When the train for Jamaica arrived, she'd invariably call it "Yamika." Chauncey Street was pronounced "Hanshe Street." Or there were To Let signs she'd mistake for a toilet. But above all, she talks shoes.

Late on a Saturday morning, she is rummaging through a drawer to find a tiny Phillips screwdriver. The handle to her white Corning Ware coffeepot is wobbly. She tightens the screw, explaining, "I had very good luck: Both my husbands didn't know how to hold a tool. I was the handyman." When I ask her about first meeting Grandpa Izzy, she tells me about aching feet.

"His *landsleit* [fellow countrymen] made a banquet. Uncle Benny Gottfried is his cousin, a forty-second cousin, but a cousin. Benny's mother was related, I think, to his father. But they had a banquet. My sister Rosie was pregnant with Ruthie. She and Uncle Benny liked to dance. He said to me that he's taking Rosie to the party but he'll have nobody to dance with. He wanted to take me so he'll have someone to dance with.

"Then, he said, 'There's a nice fellow. He's my cousin or whatever, but he works Saturday night.' He worked in a grocery. The groceries at that time used to be open until ten, eleven o'clock. He worked for somebody else. He says, 'I don't know if he'll come or not.' So, I went with them. They picked me up."

She sips her coffee. "Anyway, to have small feet was very stylish. Not big feet. I had no money. I was a few months in this country. I came here in August. That must have been in January. So, I bought for four and a half dollars—I'll never forget the shoes—A. S. Beck, that was the cheapest store for ladies' shoes on Pitkin Avenue, which was the main drag, like Fifth Avenue, in Brooklyn. Anyhow, so I bought those shoes. At that time, four dollars was a lot. Pumps. I think they were brown. Just little pumps."

She smiles, looking out the window. "But they saw that the shoes was too small on me. And I wore them because I wanted to have a small foot—be up-to-date. The smaller the foot, the nicer it is. What an idiot. I needed, let's say, a six. So maybe I bought a four. To make a story short, since Rose was pregnant, I'd dance with Benny. So we took the train—the IRT—and we came to Washington Heights and we went to the dance. And the shoes were so tight, when I came back from the party I couldn't take them off. They were so swollen, the feet were so swollen from the shoes. That's how stupid!"

I crack up. Then I look at her puffy ankles. "Now you have swollen feet for another reason," I say.

"Maybe that's the reason!" she says.

She continues. "That was Saturday night. I didn't work on Saturday, because it was *Shabbes*. I worked Sunday for half a day. My brother Max and I worked at the same place. But I couldn't go to work. I couldn't put on the shoes! I didn't go home. We went to Benny's house. The plan was that Sunday morning Max and I would go there from work to Manhattan downtown to sew the linings in the valise factory. Usually, we went by train, the subway. But Benny had a car. Then, who had a car? One in a million had a car that time."

And what about the dance? Meeting Izzy? "There were more than one hundred people there. It was someplace downtown. One of those dancing places where society used to meet. Whaddya call? Not a dancing hall. It was very nice. I'll think of it. And there was a band. It cost a lot of money. I didn't pay. Benny must have paid. I sure didn't have the money to pay. But I had a nice dress. I don't remember, but it must have been brown to go with the shoes. I looked pretty good.

"About eleven o'clock or so, Benny introduced me to a fellow, Izzy. I think I danced the waltz with him. I think I danced once or twice with him. But not on my own feet. Those shoes! Don't ask!"

The fourth of eight children, Izzy had arrived in America eight years before Tessie with three of his siblings; the other four journeyed to Argentina. He was honest to a fault, so much so that if Izzy raised the pot in a poker game, everyone knew to fold because he wasn't a bluffer. But it wasn't his decency that drew Tessie to him. "You know, he was a good-looking fellow," she says, putting her coffee cup in the sink. "He had a very clean face. That meant an awful lot to me."

Nicknamed "Itchy" by his Austrian

Tessie and husband Izzy Horowitz at the Brooklyn Botanical Garden.

buddies from Husiatyn, my grandfather could speak the language Tessie was so eager to learn. She thought him a roué, his English seemed so marvelous at first. It wasn't until a year later that she came to see him as a greenhorn, too, his English peppered with the Yiddish inflections of Brownsville. In fact, Izzy was unable to read English.

She gave him her phone number at work. "We had no telephone at home," she explains. "So who could afford a telephone? So I gave him my shop, the telephone. He called there lunchtime. He called but I wasn't there. They told him I didn't come in. And then the swelling went off. I was only making twelve dollars a week. That was almost half of my earnings for that pair of shoes. Dumb."

Now, her ankles are so distended—"old lady feet," she calls them, the result of too much salt in her diet—that she can wear only sneakers. Usually black Reeboks or Rockports. But never with socks. "I couldn't," she says, horrified at such a thought. "Not respectable." Only hose and sneakers.

⊰⊱

A Bubbe Sex Survey

Did your mother tell you about sex?

PEARLIE: Oh no! She never discussed sex with me. She never discussed anything.

TESSIE: You must be joking.

Did you enjoy sex?

PEARLIE: I certainly did. But it was from love, you know? We would kiss and love and—you know, I attribute sex to the next thing after you kiss and you love, that's the next thing. It's like a sentence. You start a sentence, and then you think about it, you write a couple words, and then you finish it. Same thing with this here, with sex. Like you love somebody and then you finish your love by having sex with them.

TESSIE: Of course, yes. Why not? Who doesn't? I used to read a lot about it—Polish books, German books. Love stories. The first book, it was German, *Die Ashten Lieber*—"The First Love." I knew more or less what's going on. I mean, but I didn't practice it. Not before I was married. I'll tell you something. When I got married, I didn't know that you can do it without getting married. There was no such thing.

But what is love, really? It's not when you go to bed. It's when you care for someone, when you consider the next one a *mensch*.

When was the last time you had sex?

PEARLIE: The last time I had sex. Well, you know, even Grandpa, when he was sick and his mind wasn't working, we slept in one bed. And he wanted to have sex. And we had sex. And then when he was in the nursing home, the hospital, I remember coming to see him. And he asked me, so politely, like a gentleman, he said, "Oh, I want to have sex with you so badly." And I says, "Forget about it." He was a very passionate man. But he never pushed himself on me. It was always with love and kissing that we worked up to passion. It was never, never just going to sex. There was always a lot of loving. And then he always played the part that he wasn't interested, that he didn't want, like it was only me that wanted it. "Okay," he says, "you want it? I see you want it. Okay, Pearlele," he says. But it wasn't true. He really wanted it!

TESSIE: Oh, my God. Who knows? Let's say in the early fifties, maybe. Forty, fifty years. So what? You can live without it. To me, sex shmex, doesn't mean a thing. If I had it, I enjoyed it. I thought you had to do it. You must. It's in the marriage license. To please my husband, I did it. But I enjoyed it, too. Sure. Listen, I wouldn't have become pregnant three times.

Do you miss having sex?

PEARLIE: No. I mean, you forget about it. You know that it's not there anymore and it's a closed issue, you know? When you're with your family, you get kissing from your children, you know, and you get that affection, so it sort of makes up for it.

TESSIE: No, no, no. Definitely not. I have no illusions. I have no fantasies. I live just a practical, plain life. I read stories or so.

BOTH MY GRANDMOTHERS TELL ME THE SAME THING: THEY CAN literally feel the life force leaving their bodies. It is a slow, inexorable, but distinct feeling that comes in your nineties.

"It's not that you're faint, no. But a feeling. It's so terrible, that you're expiring," says Tessie. "I start feeling like hot and then I don't know anything. And I sit here and I hold on tight to the table. It takes only a few seconds. Not faint but out—nothing, nothing, nothing."

"It's just a weakened feeling, Joyala, it's very hard to describe," says Pearlie.

Of the two, Pearlie is most fearful of death. "You know your time is limited, but you don't want to know it," she says. "You don't want to think about it. It's so hard to come face-to-face with it. I think you have to have a really good strong character to be able to talk about it."

I tell her I think she does have a really strong character. "You do?" she asks, sounding unconvinced. "I dunno. The fear of what's gonna happen to you is so intense. And yet, you know there must be an end to the life you live. And you don't want to talk about it. It sort of depresses you. You want to think about lighter things." So, she has taken to calling Tessie for death pep talks.

"I told her to just leave it go," Tessie tells me. "Whatever will happen will happen. What can you do? Just let it go. That's all. If you really look at it and face the truth, you can't be good-looking and die. So what?"

THE PHONE RINGS. "HELLO, JOYALA?" IT'S PEARLIE AT EIGHT-thirty on a Wednesday morning, the last day of Chanukah. Having dropped off the kids at school, I'm wearing my workout clothes, ready to exercise. Pearlie has other ideas.

"I soaked the potatoes overnight and got them all peeled," she says. "You wanna come over to make latkes?"

Exercise or eat fat-soaked morsels of delight? Tough choice. "I can be there in ten minutes." On this morning, I'm to be her *sous-chef* and short-term memory bank.

When I arrive, she has the ingredients neatly set up on her yellow Formica countertop—the flour, eggs, baking powder, salt, and potatoes. It looks like she's ready for her own cooking show. "Aw, c'mon," she says, casting off a compliment. Then, with the seriousness of a surgeon who has just scrubbed up, she turns to me and says, "Now, we're going to do the procedure."

There may be nothing nutritionally worse for you or more delicious than potato latkes. Naturally, I'm biased, but Pearlie's are especially sinful—not too crunchy, not too greasy. Perfect for a serious case of gastroenteritis. Next to her cans of Ensure, there is also a Tupperware container she has ready for me to bring home— a veritable pigfest for my children.

To watch my grandmother fry up a batch of latkes in her aged frying pan is a wondrous thing, bordering on the sacred. "The secret is to have the oil good and hot," she says. She's wearing purple bed socks, the ones the building management gave her as a little Christmas gift, and a white silk blouse and flowing silk pants.

"Look, Shar-ah-Joy," she says, whirring her blender. I'm used to her calling me by my sister Shari's name or my mother's or my aunt's. Usually, it takes her a few tries before she hits mine.

She is perfecting the consistency of the batter, demonstrating the finer points of how much egg to throw in with the potatoes. "See? That's where I get my liquid from." The blender whirs again. "See how it is? I take some more. I loosen it up. Then you've got your juices, so you don't have to worry about it getting dry." Her right hand holds the top to the blender and her left hand clicks on the buttons that control the speed.

"Turn on the light under the frying pan, Joyala." Her aluminum frying pan, with its sides charred black from constant use over the years, looks prehistoric. She hasn't the vaguest idea where or when she got it. "You've gotta do this fast 'cause the potatoes turn dark." She courageously tastes the batter, the uncooked potatoes and onion and eggs and flour. Bleh.

"A little more salt," she tells me. I toss it in.

"Is that called *shitting*?" I ask, trying to show off the smarmy little bit of Yiddish I've picked up over the years.

"Yeah, I *shit* that. Right." She means, poured in. Her face is hot, flushed from the heat of the stove.

A worried look descends across her face as she eyes the giant glass flour jar from which I've just scooped out two tablespoons of flour. "Did you put in the flour already?" She's somehow forgotten that one, too.

Pearlie makes it clear that no matter how spectacular a cook you are, you can still act like a basket case in the kitchen. Insecurities abound. Suicide threats are not uncommon. "I'll kill myself if they don't turn out," she says, worried about the efficiency of her tiny electric range. "Jonathan, he's so crazy for my latkes," she says of my cousin, who's at Dartmouth Medical School. "But you never know. Sometimes you can make 'em, they come out wonderful. Sometimes they're not so good." The self-doubts never stop.

She checks the oil, which is Wesson's canola. "This is the way the oil should be. Bubbly. God knows how many calories."

She begins to spoon the mashed-up potatoes into the skillet. "Before we go any further, watch your eyes," she says. "It shouldn't spurt." This is pronounced "spoit."

I ask her about her courtship with Grandpa Moe. "We were such hot lovers," she says. "I remember Grandpa Moe stopping at every corner stair to hug and kiss and squeeze. Very passionate love. I'm sure he went home with wet pants." Translation: He had an orgasm.

She flips the potato pancakes. "He'd say to me, 'C'mere, Boojie. I wanna kiss ya.' And he'd start to kiss and *kvetch* [squeeze]. His *shmitchek* started to go up, ya know."

The description makes me laugh. "Yeah, and my father would wait. He couldn't fall asleep until I was back in the house. And I'd get, 'So late! Did you have to stay out so late!' And I thought to myself, Papa, if you knew what we were doing! 'Cause we were fooling around."

She grows silent, checking the latkes. "By the way," she says, "it's *yahrtzeit* today." She means that it's the anniversary of Moe's death, seventeen years ago. A little night-light

Pearlie and husband Moe on their wedding day. Her dress was handmade by her sister Stella.

with Hebrew letters is plugged into an outlet near the stove in his memory. It is the modern-day equivalent of a candle. She keeps it lit from sunset to sunset, a sort of connection to immortality.

"Ya know, Shari-Joy, give me a spoon," she says. I hand her a soup spoon. "I'll tell you a secret. It's good to have another spoon so you can turn it over." She flips over a potato pancake with unparalleled panache. "See? You can hold it a little better." She pours in a touch of oil. "I don't like to use more oil, but you have to. That's the secret of them. To have them good and hot."

She talks about the latkes, but I can see her mind is elsewhere. She looks at me, her dark eyes fathomless. "You know, Grandpa wasn't perfect, but neither was I. And I don't think in this world I could have ever loved anybody more than I loved your grandpa Moe. With his faults and with his everything."

Do you remember your first kiss with Grandpa?

TESSIE: No. I'm sure there was a first. But I don't remember. I really and truly don't remember. Maybe I was embarrassed? I know I didn't make the approach.

PEARLIE: Yeah, I remember very vividly that first kiss. I didn't want to stop. We were going up the stairs, and he stopped me and kissed me. My father put on the light. He was afraid he'd do something wrong to me. Oh, that's such a hard time for parents. You want to protect you child and you don't want to interfere. Both at the same time.

ON A SATURDAY AFTERNOON IN DECEMBER, I FIND MYSELF sitting beside Tessie inside Danny's Beauty Salon in Whitestone, Queens, as she has her hair styled and her fingernails manicured. Six pink plastic chairs sit in a row before mirrors with peach-painted frames, decorated with blinking Christmas lights and gold tinsel. The linoleum-tiled floor is covered with snippets of hair, and the shop reeks of chemicals and hairspray and nail polish.

By the sink, there is Annie, the manicurist, peering out over her glasses perched on the tip of her nose. By the chair closest to the pot of coffee, there is Anna, the hairstylist, with curlers in her hair, who has been beautifying my aunt Bobbie, my father's younger sister, for three decades. It is Bobbie, a New York public school teacher for forty years, who usually gives Tessie a lift to the hair salon. And my aunt Cynthia, even on days that she works a second bookkeeping job in Manhattan, drives Grandma back home. By the wall, Grandma sits in a chair by a dome hair dryer, waiting her turn for a wash and blow-dry.

As she does every week, she's brought a tiny bottle of her favorite shampoo, Johnson's Baby Shampoo. Her cane is propped between her knees as she appears to read her *New York Post*. But, actually, she's not reading. A longtime eavesdropper, she's slyly zoning in on conversation around her.

She turns to me. "When she starts talking to you," she says of one of the women gossiping nearby, "you can go to sleep and come back."

Paul Newman is on the cover of the *New York* magazine I'm reading, with the caption, "The Sexiest 70-Year-Old Man Alive." "That's Paul Newman?" she says, aghast. "No wonder I'm so old."

When she was 15, my grandmother had no hair at all. Typhoid fever. "Why I remained alive, I still don't know. No, I mean it. No, let's talk." She sounds vaguely like Joan Rivers, but the comparison would infuriate her because she finds Rivers so vulgar. "Hundreds of people were dying daily from that fever, and I happened to be the one that made it. And another thing. It's contagious. Even my doctor was once sick with typhoid fever. But my father, my mother, my sister, they were all in the house, and all my mother could do for me was take a basin of water, put it on the end of the bed, and then the *shmattes* to put on the head. It took two weeks, two or three weeks that I didn't know if I am or who I am, and then when I opened my eyes, my mother didn't believe that I will survive.

"And then, when she took a comb, all my hair came out. You know, like you take off a *sheitl*, a wig. And my father, he was so worried. A girl without hair? But it happened in the fall. I used to wear a kerchief, a wool kerchief on my head. All winter long. And it came in the springtime, it started to come out, like you see the flowers, the grass, that's coming up. That's how, it was beautiful. And you know, my face was young and the hair was just curls, all over curls. Natural curls. But one thing, I had lighter hair than yours, even, and it came in black."

Sitting in the beauty shop, it seems appropriate to ask her about her own sense of beauty. "You want to hear something?" she asks me. "When I came to this country, I was nineteen years old. I heard that girls would have to work in shops, that all their lives they're old maids and they sit and sew. And they don't get married. There weren't enough men to go around to girls. There were more women. Now, too, there are more women than men. And I said to myself, I'm not going to be an old maid. But who's going to marry me? I'm ugly.

"Then, as I stayed there on the sidewalk near a little park, I see a woman wheeling a baby carriage. And she's *really* ugly. And I said to myself, If she could get married, then maybe I'll get married, too. My sister Sylvia, she used to call me Fatso. Fatso. I wasn't fat, really. I was solid. I had a healthy complexion, like a peasant. Mama would kill her for calling me Fatso. There is a Polish proverb: Before the fat get skinny, the skinny's gonna die. If she'd call me fat, I'd say in Polish to her, 'Before the fat get skinny, the skinny's gonna die.' That was a joke."

She grows silent, thinking. "I'm never told that I'm ugly. I'm never told that I'm pretty. Just another girl. Another girl."

Perhaps the most revealing story she tells me, waiting her turn in the beauty shop, is of her mother's morning routine in the New World. In hushed tones, she says, her family lived upstairs from a Jewish grocery. Since there were no refrigerators at the time, her mother would go downstairs every morning to buy milk and butter. When she'd return home, she'd laugh and relate another story of the grocery lady downstairs, who would brag about her son, the doctor-to-be, and joke to the yentas that her son is so economical he even sends home socks to wash.

In recounting this memory, the light in Tessie's eyes grows dim. "One morning, I said to her, 'Ma, you don't have the worst children in the world. Would you ever tell to anybody how good your children are?' She says to me, 'If I have nice children let other people tell me.' " It is a guiding principle that Tessie would come to adopt as her own.

Now, she watches as Anna does her magic on a client's coiffure, using a hot curling iron and then blowing dry what hair an older woman has left.

"Did you see how she only had a few hairs on her head?" Grandma asks me, marveling at the process that she, too, will soon undergo. "Now, she's got beautiful, big hair. It's unbelievable what she does."

Thinking that this little Saturday afternoon diversion must be a source of pleasure, I ask Grandma if she enjoys coming here. "Do I have a choice?" she shoots back. Meaning that she is confined by the dictates of her two daughters. "I'd rather go somewhere in my neighborhood on Sunday, not on *Shabbes*. But Bobbie and Cynthia, they work during the week and this is their only day to come. So?" In truth, Tessie is no longer *shermer Shabbes*, someone who strictly observes the religious rituals of the Sabbath, such as not handling money, not riding in a car, and not even turning on a light. It is a point that pains her, because she equates the celebration of the *Shabbes*, including such prohibitions, with redemption.

"Okay, Mom, let's go," Annie says to Tessie as she takes off her glasses for her shampoo. Since my aunts refer to Tessie as "Mom," so does everyone else in this shop.

Bobbie, wearing a red sweatshirt and blue jeans, reminisces. "She was a great dancer," she says of Grandma, who has her head tipped back in the sink as it's rinsed and shampooed. "She and Uncle Benny—they were better than Arthur Murray."

Florette, another customer with very big hair and long red nails, says of my grandmother, "God bless her—I gotta knock wood." She knocks on the wall. "She's up to the minute with everything and she tells it like it is. I've confided in her. I have a daughter-in-law I don't like. Your grandma tells me, 'You can't be like that. You're wrong.' I love her. And she dresses beautifully. *Kineahora*. Knock, knock, knock."

As Tessie emerges with her hair wrapped in a brown towel, in a sort of relaxed turban, I mention that she bears a certain resemblance to Mother Teresa.

"A Jewish Mother Teresa, please!" Anna corrects me. An Italian enclave, this is not exactly your politically correct beauty shop. It is the sort of place where the Italian clients openly discuss their heartbreak over a son's falling in love with a Jewish woman or a Jewish mother can be heard bemoaning her daughter's plans to marry an Italian guy. The clannishness of life goes undisguised—is celebrated, in fact. I hear talk of "eye yaps"—short for "Italian American Princesses." And, somehow, I can think only of the Totie Fields routine, "It's hard to be sexy when your feet are swollen right over the shoes! You think it's easy pushing fat Jewish feet into thin Italian shoes?"

As Grandma has her white hair blown dry and then sprayed, her feet not touching the floor, a woman in a blue muumuu says to no one in particular, "Where does the time go, huh?"

"It goes fast," says Florette.

Now, with her hair washed and fluffed and sprayed, Grandma slowly ambles over to Annie's manicure cart and sits before it. She's chosen Pink Nude for today.

The night before, she told me how she set off to make sure Izzy was "legit," playing detective to make sure he wasn't already married: Why else would he not tell her where he lived? He told her that he had been engaged, but he broke off the engagement because he wanted to go into business and his girlfriend didn't want to join him in a mom-and-pop venture. "He lived by a 'misses,' they called them—she had an extra bedroom—in Manhattan. And she was the aunt of the girlfriend. Then I realized he never wanted to tell me where he lived. He was afraid that I'd go and find out something. I don't know what. Maybe that I'd meet the girlfriend."

Determined to find out where he lived, she set out for Manhattan herself. "My cousin who lived downtown, her father was a *landsman* to Izzy. That means they came from the same town—Husiatyn, in Austria. I told her to ask her father's cousin, he also lives downtown. It was right after Christmas, I think. They were taking inventory at my job so I didn't work. And I got all dressed up. All *farputz*, as we used to say. Borrowed my sister's fur coat. And I went to 250 Fourth Street, on the Lower East Side. But there was no such number. It was a vacant lot. So, I said to myself, She meant to say 'fifty-two,' because in Yiddish, you say it backwards from what it is in English. *Zwei fiftsik* means 'two hundred fifty.'

"Sure enough, there was a big building. There was a woman there, and I told her I just came from Europe. From his town and his mother sends regards. And I make believe I don't know that he's working. And I acted like a real *greeneh*. And that's how I found out where he lives. So I found out he wasn't a married man. No jokes! For that I was afraid."

By trade, Izzy was an egg candler, inspecting eggs by the light of a candle to make sure none were bloodshot. On their first date, he brought her a gift of three dozen eggs. Her mother gave him homemade cake and a cup of coffee. Soon after, she started sneaking out to meet him. "He worked half a day Saturday and I worked half a day Sunday. I never worked Saturday. While we were living in my father's house, we never worked on Saturday. So, he'd come on Saturday to Aunt Gussie's house. And I would meet him there, so my father wouldn't see him. 'Cause he rode on *Shabbes*, ya know, my father wouldn't even let him into the house if he knew that.

"On Saturday after, I'd get dressed and go out to Gussie's. It was only about two blocks away. He was outside there. He was waiting." It was summertime. "Every Saturday, he'd take me to the Jewish shows. The Parkway Theater in Brooklyn. Beautiful. And you buy a box of candy at intermission in the theater." He never really asked her to marry him. It was a Jewish holiday, Succoth, and he came with his brother, Dave, to Tessie's on a Saturday night and brought her a diamond engagement ring.

Together, they opened a corner grocery under the El. She gave up her job to work there. That Passover he bought her a beautiful navy suit and a beaded handbag to match. "And a blouse," she says, "I'll never forget. It was pink. Um, sheer. Whaddyacall? Not chiffon. Crepe. He always tried to impress me he had the money. He vos vorkin'. I made twenty-one dollars a week, and I gave it to the house, because only Max, Sylvia, and I were working."

It's inspiring to imagine my grandmother working side by side with her husband-to-be—so modern, so ahead of her time. But the conflicts between holding on to the values from the old country and trying to Americanize were excruciating. To hold on to your religion or make money. "I'd tell my parents that I'm going to my sister's on Saturday morning. But I was at the store, working. I didn't tell them because I didn't want to aggravate them. But when I tore off the first piece of butcher paper, I felt something tore inside of me. How my heart went, that I worked that Saturday. I'll never forget that feeling that I had that morning. And then, ya know, you get used to it. 'You're a goy,' Mama would say. 'It's only hard the first time to do it, but then it goes away.'

"It's easy to become a goy, but it's hard to be a Jew." Their first store was in Greenpoint, Brooklyn, in a predominantly Polish neighborhood. "I spoke Polish. Oh, they loved me when we were in business there. And the Polish customers would say, 'Give me a can of shmagetti.' They couldn't say 'spaghetti' if you killed them. It was shmagetti. I said to them, 'You want shmagetti, I'll give you shmagetti.' "

But one of her most vivid memories from this time was the hurt Izzy inflicted on her. A regular customer, who lived around the corner, had his eye on Izzy as a prospective son-in-law. Not wanting to alienate him, Izzy introduced Tessie as his sister rather than as his fiancée. Was he embarrassed she was his wife-to-be? Was he trying to hurt her? "He was just stupid," Tessie says, in retrospect. "This was his *chachma* [wisdom]. He was laughing that he fooled the guy."

It must have bothered her. "It bothered me that the man lost the respect of him," she says. "It wasn't right, that's all."

Did she have boyfriends before Izzy? "There was one guy that taught us dancing in Europe yet. He came to America, he wanted me, but I didn't want him. He had six brothers. Six butchers. Hirschorn. Myself, I wanted a nice, smooth, clean face. He had a little acne or what. His face wasn't so pretty."

She turns to me. "You want a manicure?" she asks. A nail-biter from way back, I'm very much my mother's daughter. Though I mostly grew up in Beverly Hills, Mom eschewed beauty shops for me in favor of trimming my hair herself. I've adopted my mother's sensible approach to beauty, fingernails never being high on the beauty agenda.

"No, thank you, Grandma."

"Okay, so you're not a JAP," she tells me. *Pas moi.*

"Thank you," I say. "I consider that a compliment."

Annie examines Grandma's fingers, filing them with an emery board. "Your nails are very good," she says.

"I play a lot of solitaire," Tessie explains. "It breaks the nails. That's why I must have them done."

Not ever having had a manicure, I ask Grandma if it feels good. "It's not pleasant," she says, "but I like when it's done."

Annie looks up over her glasses. "I hurt you? You tell me."

After a while, Tessie looks pleased. "See, to put on stockings, the nails are smooth. This is good."

Her hands are lifted skyward, so her fingernails will dry. She looks down at her feet—at her black Reeboks.

"Would you believe I wore those shoes last week to a fancy-shmancy bar mitzvah?" she asks. "So I said if no one would like it, I would not look." Ever the stoic, her sarcasm covers the shame. But then, she reconsiders.

"I put a little nail polish to attract you to this," she says of her hands, "and not look at that." She eyes her bulky ankles, then her feet. Her shoes.

⊰⊱

HOW PEARLIE AND TESSIE SUMMON THEIR ROMANTIC HISTORY is a study in contradiction: Pearlie is romantic; Tessie is pragmatic. Though both had parents who disapproved of their prospective husbands—Moe was Russian-born and Izzy's father managed a bathhouse in the old country, considered déclassé at the time— their recollections reflect their inner selves: Tessie on guard, Pearlie a sucker for sweet talk. Pearlie remembers feelings, kisses, the sensory world. Tessie recalls dates relative to holidays, places, and the cost of clothing. How could she be swept off her feet if they were so agonizingly squeezed into a pair of shoes?

"You know what got me?" Pearlie asks of falling in love with my grandfather. "His blue eyes."

Tessie, whose prodigious memory astounds, even now, likes to recall how Izzy would tease her about her memory. "He used to say I got such a good memory that I remember the grandmother I'm named after," she says. It is, of course, an impossibility since Ashkenazi Jews tend to be named in honor of a deceased relative. But when I ask her a basic question—what color were his eyes?— she grows melancholy. Not because she misses him so much but because she doesn't know the answer. Her inability to recollect such a basic fact causes her to slump over in her chair and develop a wicked headache.

"I feel," she says, "I'm falling apart."

The following day, she tells me they were blue.

⊰⊱

AS I START WASHING UP THE DISHES, PEARLIE SINGS IN A WARBLY voice reminiscent of Marge Simpson, the character on the TV show *The Simpsons*.

"What a beautiful day, for a wedding in May," she sings. It is "their" song, Pearlie and Moe's. "See the people all something, at the dada dada." The lyrics escape her for a moment. But then, they come back. "See the people all stare at the lovable pair. She's a vision of joy, he's the happiest boy . . ."

Suddenly, she looks worried. "You put the money away?" she asks me.

If truth be told, there is a certain quid pro quo about my latke connection with Pearl: She offers up her *secrets de cuisine* and I do her banking for her. Like Tessie, she lives on a fixed income, mostly from Social Security payments. Pearlie wants me to deposit the monthly interest from her modest savings account into a checking account and then bring back cash.

She sits on her brown plaid sofa—once my father's analysand couch—and stares off into the kitchen. Hanging on the wall beside the utility closet, there is a single Wedgwood plate patterned in a red-and-white floral design. The china plate, part of a set from England on which she used to serve up lavish spreads, stands as a last, scraggly reminder of her brilliant culinary past: Most of her kitchenware came crashing out of the cupboards during the massive earthquake that jolted her awake January 17, 1994. What amazes me is not the extent of her loss—we all had to sweep up shards of broken glass afterward and endure cracked walls and racing hearts during each aftershock—but that she chose to put the plate back up at all, a symbol of her capacity to start over when everything comes crashing down. Like a phoenix, she rises up.

And yet, the quake remains a demarcation point for Pearlie's inability to overcome her anxiety. It has become a kind of metaphorical fault line through which her feelings of shakiness can no longer be swept aside. In rapid succession, Pearlie lost her sister, then her brother. Her daughter was stricken with breast cancer, though that's in remission. And just months later, her son-in-law was diagnosed with a fatal form of cancer. It's as if the earthquake ripped apart the fabric of her love—the security of her family—by taking away the health they so long enjoyed.

Here in her living room, she is often in the business of keeping her husband alive. Or at least staying in touch. Seeking solace after the big quake, Pearlie took a pen in hand and, for the first time in more than a year, wrote a letter to Moe, dead now for seventeen years. Her letter writing has always been a form of therapy. When she jots down notes to her deceased husband, it is a way of reminding herself of what she values most in life.

February 1994

Dear Moishala,

Yesterday I was thinking so much of our life together. Where has it gone? Life, my darling, is like a dream. I can't tell you how much I miss you.

Recently, we had an earthquake and I thought this will be the end. But God is so good and let me live a little longer to enjoy our wonderful family. Moishala, it would be so wonderful if you could see what beautiful children, grandchildren and great-grandchildren. They are all so good to me. Here I am 92 and still don't want to give up the ship! Our daughters could not be nicer or better than they are today and that I am sure is because you always respected and loved me.

I love you my darling, Moishala.

Pearlala

But now, the letters to Moe have stopped. Pearlie worries that she can't keep enough of a distance from his death to her own.

"So what else do you want to know, Joyala?" she asks me.

I ask her to tell me again about her courtship with Moe. This is one of my diversionary tactics. "Your grandpa was very affectionate, but he wouldn't put his arms around me," she explains. "He was the one that liked to be kissed and hugged."

In Pearlie's mind, there is always one person in a couple who shows affection more easily than the other. At least, this was also true for her own parents. "My father was more huggable and lovable than my mother," she says. "My mother loved it, but didn't show it. Sometimes, he'd take her and kiss her and hug her, and she'd yell, 'Stop! Stop!' But she loved it, ya know."

Clearly, she loved the way Moe would boss her around. "He was the one that really taught me how to dance," she says, smiling. "When I met him, he taught me how to do the tango," she says. "At that time, they didn't dance so close, face-to-face. But the hand was always on the shoulder. And his hand was on my back, and if I made a misstep, he would take his finger and poke it into my back: 'Now do the way I show you! Do it the way I lead you! Don't you lead me, I'll lead you.'"

Each memory is like a little love pact, a means of transcending his absence. When she remembers, she sits quite still, moving only her hands as she speaks. "He was very charming," she says of their first meeting in a freight elevator on the way up to his shop. "Very charming. Really brushed it up high. Right away I was attracted. And he never let me pay for that coat. Never."

Her mother and father remained unimpressed, however. The son of a tailor, Moe Feldman was the youngest of six children raised on a farm in Minsk. Soon after arriving in New York from Russia, his father was run over by a trolley car in Harlem, not far from the tenement house where his family lived. He began working for the government as a carpenter, building barracks for soldiers during World War I. At 19, he became a "cloakie," a ladies' coat manufacturer who, like other young men of his era, didn't hesitate to relax after work by paying visits to the high-class call girls working on the west side of Manhattan, many of them recent arrivals from Russia.

Undeterred, Pearlie went out with him again. He was good to his mother, and he was trying to Americanize—going to night school, taking ballroom dancing lessons. "There was one date that I remember very vividly," she says. "He used to go to the barber shop to get all prettied up. He'd take a very good massage and he would do his fingernails and he'd smell from cologne a mile away. It was a sweet cologne. And his hair was shampooed. He had very wavy hair, so he tried to flatten it down.

"So one time he had to stay later and he came later to me and he comes in the dining room where my mother and father were. And there was a little white thing sticking out from the front of his pants. And I saw it but I didn't say anything. And my father saw it. So my father said to him, 'Mr. Feldman,' he says, 'come, I want to tell you something in the next room.' Took him in the next room, he said, 'Your pants—they're unzipped.'"

They were going out together for six months when Moe told Pearlie he wanted to marry her and gave her a diamond ring, which she wore to work. "I showed the girls at work my ring. And I brought in the picture of Grandpa. They said, 'Why are you marrying that kike?' I cried. I felt terrible. I thought they'd say, What a handsome guy! To me, people are people. It didn't make any difference what religion you came from as long as you was a good person, a fine person, and I respected you."

Still, her mother wished only that she'd marry a doctor. "Another guy was after me. When the subway strike broke out, I really used him. He took me to work. But I couldn't stand him.

Even though my mother wanted me to go out with him, see, the only one I went out with was Grandpa. This guy was older than Grandpa Moe, but he had a lot of money and he had a car. In those days, if you had a car, it was a great thing. Grandpa didn't have a car until we were married about a year. That was the Star car. That was the first car we had. He bought it for nine hundred dollars. Oh, that was such a big thing."

Not only did my grandfather not have much by way of finances, but he'd lose things. In fact, Pearlie remembers how her mother threw an engagement party, but Moe's family was so excited about coming that they left their gift of a set of silverware in the taxicab. "My mother-in-law was heartbroken," Pearlie says of Moe's mother, Dora. Pearlie especially liked to watch the way Dora would sip schnapps and hike up her skirt to dance. "They were exciting. They were Russian people, and they liked to drink and eat a lot of sharp things—lox and all these different kind of fishes. They were a good family, a loving family. But kind of on the wild side."

Mostly, she remembers being crazy about Moe. "We were terribly in love. We wanted to really be together. Physically, I mean. Well, rules were rules at that time. And you just didn't. That's all. And in fact, just before we were married, we decided that we'd like to take a honeymoon, but he wasn't in such good circumstances that we could afford a honeymoon. So we took a bungalow at Brighton Beach with my family. We were five people, so we each put in one hundred dollars, and we had the bungalow from April until the end of September. And these bungalows were divided into three bedrooms and a living room and a dining room–kitchen. There were no doors—just little curtains were hung up. And that's where I spent my honeymoon in May.

"Let me tell you. It was miserable, that honeymoon. All these bedbugs were driving us crazy! One day, just when Grandpa and I were having a good time, my brother knocked on the door. Well, we weren't going to stop for my brother. So what does he do? He comes in through the bedroom window. I coulda killed him.

"And I went there a week before my wedding. My sister said, 'Pearlie, come, we'll fix up the bungalow so that you'll be able to enjoy your honeymoon.' So Moe had a bedroom and I had one and Stella and Frank had one. So Moe said, 'You know what, I'd love to sleep with you, Pearlie.' I said no. I said, 'You can't. Not before we're married.' He says, 'Look, I'm sure Stella will let you. Ask her.'

So I asked Stella and she says, 'Oh no!' She said, 'Not until you're married.' Grandpa even offered to keep his feet on the floor. But I do remember him coming in and kissing me good night, and I hated to see him go.

"I remember Frank put a horseshoe over our bedroom. He put a horseshoe and a banana in there, and the banana started to mold and get brown by the time Grandpa and I got there." She laughs at the memory.

"And I remember we were eating supper together with Stella and Frank, and Grandpa again said he wanted to sleep with me the night before."

"He wanted to sleep with you the night before your wedding?"

"But Stella wouldn't let me do it. And I just let them argue about it, and I didn't say anything. But after I went on my honeymoon, I said, 'Well, if Stella would have let me sleep with him, I know I couldn't have been a whatchamacallit.' "

"A whatchamacallit?"

"What do you call it?" she asks, at a loss for words. "What do they call it again, when you're pure?"

"A virgin?"

"A virgin, yeah!" she says. "So anyway, I realized when you're loving and sex is there when you're both so young, who could stop it? Nobody can stop it."

The doorbell rings. Pearlie goes to the door, and screams, "All right, Dora!" Then she shuts the door, never even seeing her next-door neighbor. This is their signal that it's time to go down to lunch, to line up on the chairs in the recreation room to be first into the dining hall.

<hr>

When Tessie and I return to her apartment from the beauty shop, I try to extract the details of her romance with Izzy. Much as I want to romanticize her past, she'll have none of it.

"I'll tell you the truth," she says, circling a word she's found in the Wonderword puzzle of the *New York Post*. "I wanted to get married to get out of the house. There was so much poverty." Not to mention zero privacy—the bathtub was in the kitchen. "I felt he's doing me a favor, marrying me. I mean, that I'm getting a bargain."

She circles another word. "Look, when you love someone, you have to allow for faults," she says. "Because nobody's poyfect. There is no such person in this world that should be perfect. If you like your child, and you see the child did something wrong— either you tell him or you be quiet—but you love him just the same. This is how I look at things."

Did Izzy go to her father and ask for her hand in marriage? I wonder.

Tessie looks at me like I'm an alien creature. "What kind of nonsense is that?" she asks.

"That's what they used to do, I thought."

Tessie shakes her head. "They didn't do that. I never saw that."

"So, he came over and brought the ring and what—did he just sort of throw it in your lap or did he say, 'Will you marry me?' "

She's growing slightly agitated with the line of questioning. "No, no. We were sitting and talking. He did not propose. He brought the ring and he put it on and that's all."

"You're so unromantic," I say, frustrated.

"Who talks about romance?" she asks, turning on the gas burner to warm up a pot of Manischewitz kosher vegetable soup.

"I do," I say.

"You do," she says, peering into the fridge. "Well, you're the next generation. The third generation." Then, as if to placate me, she adds: "It was nice. I was happy. The next morning, I went to work, and I showed off to my boss that I got a ring. Everybody, I showed it off. So they knew that I was going out with a fellow and we got engaged. So, what was there to make a big to-do of it?

"Now I'll ask you questions. What are we going to have for dinner?"

❦

Tell me about your wedding.

TESSIE: I got married November 18, 1922. It was beauty-ful. It was the first wedding my father was able to attend of one of his children. There were three hundred people to the wedding. Izzy paid for it. My father didn't have any money. He didn't even work. We used to pay his rent, even after I was married I used to donate to the household. He was fifty-five when he came to America, and that was considered very old then. My father sent out invitations to Europe to his friends. In each invitation he put in two dollars. For carfare. [*Laughs.*]

I hired a white dress with a white cape. It was a beautiful wedding gown. With a veil yet. At that time, there were no couples suppers. You'd send out an invitation. They didn't have to answer. They came! And some didn't come. So they didn't come. Izzy had a lot of friends. He even invited his first girlfriend's uncle and aunt. It was a beauty-ful wedding.

It was about five or six blocks away from where my father lived in Brownsville. It was a big hall. Saturday night. We didn't have no pictures on account of Kayla, Izzy's sister. She was so—I didn't know what was the matter with her. She wanted her fourteen-year-old daughter to be my maid of honor. And I didn't want her. I had flower girls. I think Sylvia was my maid of honor. There were bridesmaids. Max, my brother, got engaged at my wedding. He gave Aunt Ida a ring there.

We had music, of course. People were dancing. One woman came with a hat with an ostrich feather. Cost a few hundred dollars. It was Izzy's friend's wife. Came all *farputzed* [dressed up]. It was a lot of people. But we had so much leftover food that my mother, father prepared. Cooked food like chickens and soups and fish. About fifteen blocks from where my father worked, there was a home, a Jewish home. Do you know how much food my father brought there, with the horse and wagon, for the people? 'Cause what are you going to do with it? Throw it out? There are no refrigerators. You had to use it. So we gave it to the poor.

But I'll be frank with you. The whole wedding I didn't enjoy. Honest to goodness. On account of those pictures—we never got pictures of the wedding because Kayla, Izzy's sister, she made such a stink. I was upset on account of that she was . . . an open prostitute. She lived with a man in the open, and she had a daughter fourteen years old. Her husband was a *shmegegge*. They had two beds in the bedroom. I don't know if she slept with him or with both of them. I didn't want to know.

PEARLIE: My wedding was in our house—a six-room railroad flat with front windows. We lived on the second floor. Mama would sit and watch the trolley cars from that window. Later on came the buses. People would stop on the corner. Our house was right on the corner. St. John's Place. I think it was 1711, but I'm not sure.

For the wedding, Mama moved all her furniture downstairs. And she hired benches and tables upstairs. And she hired two or three cooks. They did all the kosher cooking in the house. There must have been one hundred fifty people. My mother couldn't afford a wedding in the shul. She made all these *fludens* [fruit strudel]. All the chicken was kosher. And Mama didn't let anybody go out without eating. She'd watch!

My mother was so afraid that Moe would forget his ring, that she took his ring and put it in her stocking. Then, when the rabbi asked for the ring, my mother turned around and got the ring from her stocking. I was so embarrassed!

My sister Stella, she was really a genius. She made my wedding gown. I don't know how she made it— with these panels back and front. And she embroidered the whole thing in pearls. And I didn't really appreciate her efforts. I really didn't. I don't know why I took her for granted. Maybe because we used to fight a lot. I don't know what it was.

Grandpa made my suit for after. It was like a horseman's suit. He made me a gray suit, and my sister made me an orange sweater underneath it. Double-breasted and pleats in the back. And I had an orange hat with a feather. Gray stockings. Can you imagine?

❧ ❧

I ASK MY GRANDMOTHERS TO DEFINE THEIR HUSBANDS' SALIENT characteristics. Pearlie tells me Moe was a big tease, pretending not to be interested in her or acting like she was the aggressor so she'd smooch him more. "You never could stay angry at Grandpa. He'd always make you feel good. No matter how angry I'd be at him. Sometimes he'd come in, put his arms around me, and say,

'You know I didn't mean it.' And that's all I'd need. Then I would fall his victim. You could buy me off with love very easily. More than money. Money didn't mean anything to me. It never meant anything."

Tessie tells me Izzy was a softy, a man who cried easily. "Izzy would cry if you could see a worm get killed, he could have cried," she says. "Right away he was crying. I told him, 'You're like a woman. A man don't cry.' Crying is silly."

Maybe she doesn't cry enough, I offer.

"Maybe," she says. "Maybe. I take it."

Luscious Latkes

It's six medium potatoes, peeled and cut up. It's either a small onion or half an onion. A teaspoon of baking powder. Two eggs. Two tablespoons of flour. Salt and pepper.

What I use, I use the blender. I take them after they're peeled. But you can't put in all the potatoes at one time, because the blender won't hold it. So you take in some part of it, like as much as it can hold. And you take part of the egg and put it in, because you must have liquid there in order to blend. You know what I mean? And don't forget your salt and pepper.

And then dump it out and put it in again, some potatoes and some part of the egg. But you must have the liquid there, in order for the blender. When you're all through, you mash it all together. But leave in some shtickla, little pieces.

Put oil in your pan. You can use whatever you like for frying. I use corn oil or canola. It's very good. Then you mix it all together. Don't forget the flour. And two teaspoons of baking powder, I told you about that. You take some batter in the tablespoon, and when the oil starts to heat up—watch it, 'cause you can hurt your eyes since it spurts, ya know—you put some in the pan to fry. But watch it! You can blind yourself with it!

I used to wring out the moisture, but I found out it's too much work. The old-fashioned way is to let the moisture out, but they claim the starch that remains inside is good for you. Then after you fry 'em on one side and then the other, you take your paper towel and put 'em on the paper towel to get the grease off. That's the whole megillah.

There's no secrets about it. You can freeze 'em. You can do whatever you want after they're done, but usually they never last that long. Make it only when you got time and when you're at ease, because you can get into trouble.

CHAPTER 5

Farmagan: Treasure

Pearlie and baby Shirley,
my mother.

Izzy and Tessie with baby "Mechel,"
my father Mike.

IT'S NOT EASY SPENDING A LOT OF TIME WITH MY GRANDMOTHERS.
First of all, there's the heat factor. No sooner do I walk into
their little apartments than I'm ready to pass out. It can be 90
degrees outside and both of them will have their heaters cranked
up to, say, Hades levels. I'm not exactly sure if it's due to thinning
blood or because they have less flesh on their bones. It could be
psychological—memories of walking home from school, hip deep
in snow (Tessie), or of having no heat in her Brownsville railroad
flat except a coal stove (Pearlie) and her mother wrapping bricks
heated from the stove inside pieces of flannel to warm her feet in
bed. But whatever it is, I'm quite certain that when I spend
enough time with them, I'm in serious need of a nap.

Sound is another problem. Pearlie and Tessie listen to their
television sets at mind-numbing levels. My head throbs when I
watch TV with them. If I surreptitiously attempt to lower the volume, they notice right away—and we're back to the ear-crushing
torture trip.

Then there are the painful concessions I watch them make to
old age. There is a reason our culture is so youth-oriented, so

obsessive about looking wrinkle-free. Mick Jagger was right: Getting old *is* a drag. We can focus on how much there is to learn from old people and hope that old age brings wisdom, but let's face it: Old age also means loss. Loss of physical functioning, loss of personal stature, loss of one's former self, loss of your future, loss of loved ones. As hip as my grandmothers are, as much as they know how to fine-tune survival strategies, they're still not exempt from the misery and bad luck of the human condition.

"Every head has its own *mishegoss*," Tessie tells me.

"It's not easy sitting on half an ass," Pearlie says of the arthritis creeping up her right side.

So even though I look to Pearlie and Tessie for their inspirational disquisitions on how to get through life's more difficult moments, I'm also wary. Wary of their platitudes: "You have to have rain before the rainbow" (Tessie); "Health is everything" (Pearlie). And wary of their maxims: "To suffer is to live" (Tessie on her childhood); "You shouldn't hoit y'self" (Pearlie on my taking something out of the oven).

The problem is, I look at my grandmothers and I see myself—the web of wrinkles, the bowed posture, the sagging skin—in fifty years. If I'm lucky. This is not easy to take. Tessie's vertical lines, like quotation marks between her eyes, from furrowing her brow—they're mine, too. Pearlie's puffy eyes—they're mine when I wake up in the morning, only exaggerated by a half-century more of gravity. All their complaints about not recognizing themselves in the mirror are mine, too. The crinkles around my eyes, the chin going south, the flesh losing its elasticity.

But what really annoys me about Tessie and Pearlie is the very thing that makes me adore them most: their questioning. Their resolute not-knowingness. Even now, in their nineties, they're still trying to figure things out. Still asking questions about life's mysteries that can make you totally insane if you ask enough. Pearlie and Tessie, though, have the courage not to stop.

Why do people have to suffer before they die? Tessie wants to know. "If I had what to say in this matter, I would make a law that people should live and exist as long as they can help themselves. I can go where I want. I can say what I want. Must people get very sick to die?

"There must be a reason. But if I would be God, I would make it different. You live seventy years, eighty years. It's enough. What do I accomplish by living now? To bring someone else into sin?"

Pearlie, too, weighs in. "Oh, Joyala, why, why, why?" she asks of my father's being stricken with cancer a third time. "It's like a window. I can see right through it."

While most of us coast through life pretending we'll live forever, or maybe thinking we can wrap ourselves in a cocoon of love and remain only dimly aware of an end way far away, my grandmothers tell another story. They, at least, have the guts to face the truth: Death is a part of life. They are mavens of the epistemological.

What they show me, much as I don't want to comprehend it, is that the natural completion of one's life is just as messy as the beginning. There is no peaceful going-into-the-night stuff. Instead, there is confusion and anxiety and selfishness, like the rest of life. Maybe even more so.

"This test, boy, I had real golf balls," Pearlie tells me, offering yet another update on her bowels, a current obsession since she's had more medical tests requiring a special liquid diet. "I tell you, anybody could play golf with it: shit balls." The next day, after another test, she calls back: "I thought my stomach would boist from all that water. They put you through hell, I'm telling ya.

"So listen, kiddo, come over tomorrow."

A Bubbe Poll on Maternal Instincts

What makes a good mother?

TESSIE: Well, that's the sixty-four-thousand-dollar question. What can I tell you what's a good mother? What does it matter? She takes care of the children. Doesn't talk dirty to them. If you take care of them—feed them, give them good clothes, good food, and you take them from school and you show interest in school and put them to bed early—what else can you do for a child?

A mother can always tell when they don't tell the truth. When you look at the child, you can actually see it's written. No child can fool a mother. This is why I say when they catch a teenager robbing or stealing, the mothers should be punished.

PEARLIE: Put the children on a pedestal. That's important. So you give a feeling of security to a child, making a child feel that he's not just a small child—he's a person. He means a lot to the family. You've got to give the child a feeling of goodwill, responsibility, that he belongs in this family, he's something in this family, he's an attachment to it. And when you give that child an attachment when they're small like that, it stays with them forever. It stays with them forever.

By giving them affection. By listening to them. If they talk to you, don't cast them off and say, Oh, okay, okay, I'll see you later. Make it important, what they say. Make them important. And they'll always be important to you. They'll like that. They'll have that feeling of security.

Is there a difference between raising sons and daughters?

TESSIE: I had no time to observe those silly things. My son was more closer to me. He was always more considerate of me. Even though he was a boy. And the girls more of their father.

PEARLIE: You fuss more with a girl—how she looks, how she walks. You expect more from a daughter. A girl you want more perfection. If a boy will say a rough word, well, he's a boy. But you don't want your daughter to be that way. You want her to be fine, silky. Somehow, you feel a boy can take care of himself more than a girl. Of course, that's not so.

⊲∥⊳

PEARLIE IS AN INCORRIGIBLE FLIRT. YOU CAN TELL, JUST AS soon as you walk into her apartment, how big a flirt she is: Right there, under her kitchen table, is the evidence. It consists of extra bottles of water—twenty, at last count—from the Arrowhead water delivery man, Gary, who calls her by her first name.

At first, I thought the stockpile of bottled water was my grandmother's response to the earthquake: Pearlie wanting to be prepared, setting up a survivalist's outpost up on the fifth floor of the Salvation Army building. But then we got to talking one day in the beauty shop about how much she loves male attention, how good it is to have a man call her "Pearlie." This never occurred to me before, whether a man or a woman calls you by your first name. But maybe she has a point. Not to put too fine a spin on it, Pearlie craves male company.

This, I've come to believe, is why she keeps making doctor's appointments. There's nothing like a reassuring man to tell you that you're doing just fine. She demands attention. She insists on action. She refuses to be shunted aside. From the doctor's vantage point, I'm fairly certain my grandmother would be labeled a GOMER, as in Get Out of My Emergency Room. That, anyway, was the attitude of her last doctor, who laughed off her stomach complaints and told her to drink some schnapps, patting her knee as he condescendingly recommended liquor as a tonic.

"He treated me like an idiot," she says now, grateful that she had the good sense to switch doctors. Her current love, Michael Lutsky, talks slowly and deliberately, just like Mr. Rogers. She immediately changes the subject.

"How's my Lucy Anna?" she asks. She includes Lucy's middle name when she asks after her, because she was named after Pearl's mother, Anna. "I have more berets for her. Kelly green."

"Listen," she continues. "She has a larger head size than me. She's a wonderful child. God bless her. And your boys, *kineahora*. They're so beautiful. You're gonna have to fight to keep the girls away, they're so handsome. You've got a *farmagan* there. Do you know that word?"

"No, how do you spell it?"

"I don't know. But it means the whole world—a fortune." It's pronounced *far-*MAY*-gan*.

I thank her for teaching me such a wonderful word. For the moment, anyway, I've taken away her worry about her health. And I've convinced her that she's given me something, taught me three syllables that convey so much.

"Oh, Joyala," she says, sounding so grateful. Ecstatic to feel useful again. To be needed. "I love you."

The TV news is on. A commercial comes on for Taco Bell, one of its "run for the border" ads. Suddenly, she stands and begins dancing—a little shuffle step, then a two-step—in time to the beat. "I hear the music and I can't sit," she says, pressing her lips together as she swings her arms. "Gotta keep my feet going.

"It makes you feel alive!" she says, still bopping. "It makes you feel that you're living! I think when you sit you can forget." At home, we've trained our children to mute the sound to TV commercials. Pearl dances to them.

❦

AT SUPER CUTS ON WILSHIRE BOULEVARD IN SANTA MONICA, part of a chain of hair salons, Pearlie is staring at herself in the mirror as a beautician named Tahayra Manjra sprays moisturizer and conditioner onto Pearlie's fine hair. She's walked in off the street for a haircut without an appointment.

Normally, Grandma Pearlie clips coupons to have her hair cut for free by beauticians-in-training down at Sassoon's on the Third Street Promenade. "But it's a pain in the ass," she explains. "First the hairdresser comes in. Then comes in the teacher. So every time they cut a couple of hairs, they have to get it okayed. And you never know what you're going to look like. It's a three-hour deal."

Tahayra tells her this shouldn't take more than twenty minutes.

"When you get to my age, you're so glad to have some hair on your head," Pearlie says. She eyes her reflection and thinks aloud of having had long hair until Jerry was born, when she spent her days washing diapers by hand and boiling bottles, unable to nurse. "I wasn't a milker," she says. For excitement one evening, she and her sister snuck out to get their hair bobbed, over the objections of their husbands.

Tahayra mists Pearlie's gray locks. "We'll put on some conditioner," she explains.

"Whatever you say. You're the boss," Pearl says.

"We'll make you beautiful," Tahayra adds.

"Is that possible?" Pearl asks, joking.

Pearlie continues: "I have thirteen great-grandchildren. When you get old and decrepit, you still love them so. They're the best."

Tahayra says she has a child of her own, which allows Pearlie to launch into one of her child-rearing sermons, the kind that can make any working mother feel enormously guilty. "Children need a parent's guidance all the time, like when they come home from school," she advises. If there is some sort of mother gene that's coded Be Home When Your Kids Get Back from School, I've inherited it from Pearlie. Not to mention from Shirley, my mother, a stay-at-home mom of the 1950s who never felt compelled to leave.

Tahayra nods her head in agreement. "Unfortunately, I can't be there."

"Mothers and fathers don't give enough time to children," Pearlie says, sounding genuinely worried. "They don't. There's no time. But it's important for families to get together. And talk what's good for the children. We don't take enough time with the children. We take them out to the movies. We run run run run. But we don't give enough time to the children." I'm not sure if this is intended as a sideswipe at me. She reconsiders. "But even when you put so much into your children, you never know how it's going to come out."

Pearlie surveys Tahayra's work. She eyes me in the mirror. "She's doing such a beautiful job on me, I'll have to look for a guy now," she says, laughing. "I have a man who delivers me water. He goes out of his way to deliver water. I said to him, 'Don't try to please a lady so much. She'll fall for you.'"

Tahayra changes the subject. "My grandmother is eighty," she confides, sounding worried, "and she doesn't get out."

"Ya gotta keep walking," Pearlie advises.

"That's right!" Tahayra says, as if she's speaking to an ancient oracle. "But she won't listen to me."

Pearlie has an idea. "Tell her Pearlie says if you stand still, everything stands with ya." Satisfied to be dispensing advice, Pearlie stares contentedly at the mirror. "She knows I want to look young and beautiful. Even if I can't—I can dream!"

She's so lit up, she begins to belt out a song in a scratchy, nasal pitch, à la Ethel Merman. "I can dream," she sings, her silly-crazy melody improvised. In truth, she's worried about another diagnostic test for her liver later this afternoon. But for now, she sings. "I can dream."

☜ ☞

THE NIGHT MY FIRST CHILD, TREVOR, WAS BORN, I DREAMED I died. My-father-the-shrink analyzed the dream, saying it was about guilt. But I don't think so. I think it might have been prophetic. That's because my second child was born dead, the umbilical cord wrapped around his neck. My third baby, Gus, came out laughing. My fourth baby, with his perfect teeny hands and toes, was born fourteen weeks early and died. When my fifth baby, Lucy—our first girl—was born, my doctor looked skyward and took the words right out of my mouth. "Thank you, Lord," he said.

Maybe it's because I've had the misfortune of burying two infants that I see the connection between birth and death as inextricable. Every baby a miracle of nature, a sacred link to history. To genetics. To survival. But why are we born?

I ask the question of Tessie, and she replies, "To die."

Pearlie answers differently: "We don't know why we die, but we know why we're born: We're born out of love."

❧ ☞

TESSIE'S BEDROOM IS AN INTERESTING AMALGAM OF JUNCTURES in her life. The bookshelves offer an eclectic collection, ranging from a Thomas Wolfe reader to *The Last Angry Man* to a compendium of *Five Thousand Years of Great Jewish Quotes*. There is also a Passover Seder plate, a framed certificate of appreciation for her volunteer work from the Sisterhood of Beth El Hospital (1940), and a yellow flashlight. Her lace lampshades are covered with plastic, and her twin beds are framed by a large walnut headboard, scalloped at the ends. She bought the beds, now covered with orange floral bedspreads, before she married Sam in 1953, because she felt too guilty sleeping in the same bed she shared with Izzy. On the dresser top, there is a mirrored tray with eight bottles of perfume and photographs of her grandchildren from thirty years ago. I study my brother's bar mitzvah picture from 1962, our smiles frozen—Steve in *tallis* (prayer shawl), Shari in white gloves, Peggy in braids, and me in a dumb, Heidi-looking dress. On the wall is my father's framed pebble artwork from his bohemian days in Berkeley (1961), when he'd relax by doing mosaic art, a sort of paint-by-numbers set with colored stones. Plus a souvenir pennant from the Rose Bowl (1971), the year my brother kicked a field goal for Stanford and beat Ohio State. Not to mention the sepia-toned photographs from my father's college graduation (1943) and my aunts as little girls (1938), wearing Shirley Temple curls and pinafores. In the corner, on top of the control panel that hooks up Tessie to an emergency medical service, there is another photograph of Grandma on one of her Beverly Hills visits (1968), standing beside my siblings, my parents, and me.

"You getting dressed?" I yell out to her from the kitchen.

"I'm not putting on an evening gown," she yells back from the bedroom.

It is a freezing Monday in December. Tessie is getting ready for her Golden Age Club meeting that convenes at the Jewish Center of Kew Garden Hills. She wears lined woolen pants, a flowered silk blouse, and a maroon vest, the same one she wore to sleep the night before, over her flannel pajamas. She spritzes perfume, Obsession, on my neck, and motions to me to clasp the back of her gold-chain necklace, "just to give it a *kvetch* [a squeeze]," she says. She snaps on big pearl earrings, the clip-on kind.

I tell her she looks beauty-ful. She dismisses the compliment, rolling her eyes. "People say, 'You look so good.' I say, 'You need new glasses,'" she says. She slides open the top right-hand drawer to her dresser for lipstick. It's Elizabeth Arden, Tenderberry. She draws her lips over her teeth and, with the flourish of a makeup artist, runs the wand of lipstick over her top lip and then her bottom, inspecting her work with a plastic magnifying mirror.

She studies her reflection. "What am I?" she asks me. Her smile is uncharacteristically rueful, the irony all drained out. I've just shown her an old photograph in which she's dressed to the hilt in fancy pointed heels and smiling broadly beside Sam. My little trip down memory lane is upsetting her. "Am I that person, dressed so fine? Happy? What am I supposed to think? You tell me."

Some days, she grows so melancholy about being old that the weight of her sadness seems unbearable. "It's nothing for nothing, what's the use?" she asks, upset because, just before leaving her apartment, she's decided to sew a button onto her turquoise jacket. But her fingertips have lost their sense of touch.

She has me thread the needle. "This is why I'm not happy," she says, now pulling the needle through the buttonhole. "It's such a minor thing, and I can't accomplish it. So what good is it?"

But by the time she hooks her left arm into the crook of my right one—it is 34 degrees outside, with a wind chill of 12—she boards the shuttle van with an air of nonchalance.

"I'm so happy to come here, I need a rest already," she says, standing atop the stairs and out of breath, next to the bus driver. He smiles. "You think I'm joking?" she continues, a mischievous look creeping across her face.

She takes a seat. "Okay, I dood it," she says, invoking the words of Red Skelton, one of her favorite comedians.

The driver stops at a red light, and the bus idles. Tessie leans forward. "No sooner they see him come," she announces, "instead of putting out the red carpet, they put out the red light."

The driver laughs out loud. "Hey, that's a good one!"

"You know my jokes or so—maybe I wouldn't be here no more without it. That keeps me up." No doubt, my grandmother's humor is her ultimate weapon.

"I live alone for the last thirty years," she says.

"Wow," says the driver.

"Somehow, I'm never lonely. I'm never bored. I can always find something to do." It is Tessie's mantra. Even if it's not always true, she repeats it often, as if to convince herself. "Now, it's not so easy. I used to sew. But you know what I do now, if I have nothing else? I play solitaire." The two-way radio emits a scratchy roar. Tessie doesn't flinch. "Okay, I'm comin'," she jokes.

Would she like to be dropped off in back? "See, we had to go by the garbage," she quips, her shoulders rising and falling from laughter. To be viewed as an extension of detritus, Tessie can't help but point to the irony of arriving beside the mounds of refuse at the back door. Her friends will get a kick out of that one.

Walking in the back door, she passes the outdoor playground and proceeds down the cinderblock corridor until she becomes breathless again. "Wait, I have to take a rest," she says, next to the drinking fountain. It prompts another story.

"One woman in my neighborhood, she only wanted to die," she says. "One time, we pass by this water fountain and she says, 'Wait, Toby, I'll take the pill I have to take.' I say, 'If you want to die, don't take the pill if you want to die that bad.' She says, 'Oh no, I don't want to die that much.'" She laughs, which causes her to gulp down air. Suddenly, her ratchety cough returns.

"I talk too much," she says, blaming her cough on her story-telling. We continue down the hallway, carpeted in a dizzying array of blue and green patterns, the wallpaper a bold blue-and-white stripe.

In the meeting room, with its crystal chandeliers and gold brocade curtains, three long banquet tables covered with blue tablecloths are arranged in an L shape. From the kitchen, there is the unmistakable aroma of coffee and Danish.

Standing at the doorway, she introduces me to her friend Minnie. "This is Minnie, this is the best girl that I love." They kiss hello.

"How ya doing, *bubeleh?*" Minnie asks Tessie, who at these meetings is called by her given name from the old country, Toby. And so it has come to this. Tessie, now 93, feeling at her best among those who refer to her by the name her parents gave her, the name her classmates called her in school, not the one she embraced to fit into American life. Toby. The name she wants on her tombstone.

She advises me to take a seat. "Sit down, sweetheart, do you want coffee?" The mien of camaraderie is unmistakable. It is a cozy crowd, buzzing with anticipation. The fur caps. The painted eyebrows. The Zsa Zsa Gabor voices. The gold jewelry with the Hebrew *chai*—good luck—charms and Jewish stars. Names like Gertrude, Rose, Esther, and Sylvia are common.

A woman with a sweet smile, named Betty, arrives. Tessie holds her hand and strokes it. "She gave me so much courage," Betty tells me of my grandmother, who continues holding her friend's hand. Tessie turns to me and explains that Betty's husband died not long ago. "She gave me so much courage," Betty says again. "You know, you felt it came from her heart."

And I see this is why my grandmother *shleps* here as often as possible: to feel useful, as a hand-holder, a listener. Sometimes, there is sheer beauty in just showing up.

Tessie takes a seat, hanging her cane and the shoulder strap of her purse on the back of her chair. She waits for others to stop by and say hello, mostly because walking is difficult.

"I retain my water," one woman complains to Tessie right off the bat about how getting through the night isn't easy. "Okay. Three o'clock I wake up. What should I do? Should I play solitaire? No, I'm not gonna do what Toby does. You know what I'm reading? *Three Cities*, by Sholom Asch. By four-thirty what should I do? I get up at five-ten."

"*Oysh*," Tessie commiserates, a fellow insomniac during these hours.

⊲§⊳

"KOL OD BA-LEI-VAV PE-NI-MA, NE-FESH YE-HU-DI HO-MI-YA."
Each meeting of the Golden Age Club begins with the mem-

bers singing these Hebrew words of the Israeli national anthem, "*Hatikva*" ("The Hope"), which segues into "Oh say, can you see, by the dawn's early light." The words have the force of a gavel. Hearing Tessie join in a full octave below the sopranos, her voice off key but no less enthusiastic, it's hard not to wonder if this antediluvian display will simply die out when these people do.

Now, it is Andrew's turn to teach the group tai chi, an ancient Chinese discipline of movement. A tall man in his thirties with a short-cropped beard, he tells his audience that there is nothing magical about tai chi. Nothing mystical. It simply teaches us how to use our bodies efficiently. At any age.

"The single most important thing we do," he says, asking his audience to fill in the blanks, "and that is . . ."

"Breathing," the group replies in unison. Tessie looks unconvinced.

Everyone stands. He instructs the group to extend their spines. "Eyes closed. Keep your eyes closed."

Tessie is peeking. "Breathe in with your stomach. Relax your shoulders. Relax your elbows. Good. Good. Good. Very nicely done."

Grandma leans on the table. "I have to hold on or I'll fall," she tells me in a stage whisper. Then, she lifts one arm upward, her palm facing down and elbows relaxed. Turning to the right, Andrew demonstrates how to shift hands in slow motion, as if holding a giant ball, and lift one leg. Tessie grimaces. After about fifteen minutes of slow breathing and moving, I turn to her and ask how she liked it.

"I didn't pay attention," she shrugs.

BEFORE LEAVING, MY GRANDMOTHER AND HER FRIEND BETTY engage in a heated discussion about burial arrangements. Betty says she buried her husband Irving in his favorite suit. Tessie says she wants shrouds.

"*Nisht in a hindert yuren!*" Betty scoffs. Not in a hundred years! Tessie rolls her eyes.

Waiting for the bus to arrive, she and a woman with brightly rouged cheeks, named Gertrude, commiserate about the tai chi instruction. "They didn't like their physical training teacher last time he was here," Gertrude complains. "So what did they do? They got him again."

Tessie peers out the door for a moment. "It's so cold and windy out there," she says, still craning her neck for the bus.

"Yeah, terrible," Gertrude agrees, fastening the button on her blue blazer.

"I've gotta go take a look," Tessie says, wanting the bus to hurry up.

"Go ahead," Gertrude says, "take a look." During my next visit to New York, Grandma tells me that Gertrude passed away. Apparently, she fell in her home, alone, and was dead for several hours before her son discovered her. It is precisely what Tessie fears most, what we all fear most: being alone in the end.

But now, as the bus slides up to the curb, I watch as both old women, stepping out with their canes, brace themselves for the cold. What's remarkable, I think, is how they get through at all, their courage evident just in the simple acts of coming and going. Tessie extends a hand to help Gertrude onto the bus. Ever since she was mugged a year ago, Gertrude's been having trouble walking. When it's Tessie's turn, she announces her name to the driver.

He checks his list. "I don't have a Toby," he tells her.

"Tessie, Tessie," she says, impatiently. "I have two names. One I got in jail."

The driver looks shocked. "What'd you do to get there?"

She cracks a sly smile, almost coquettish. "Oh, you'd be surprised."

Gertrude is dropped off first, not far from the Long Island Expressway turnoff for the Queens zoo. As she waves good-bye from the front of the bus, Rod Stewart's voice comes over the radio: "Young hearts be free tonight. Time is on your side."

❦

BY ELEVEN-FIFTEEN, THERE IS ALREADY A LINEUP OF SILVER-crest residents in the recreation room, positioning themselves to be first in line for lunch, across the hallway. The smell of soup takes Pearlie back about seventy-five years, when she was first married. Before she and Moe saved up enough money to buy a house—five rooms and a porch for $2,500 in Mapleton Park—they lived with her parents. At the time, her father was working as a presser for Moe. Every morning, the pregnant Pearl would send her husband and father off to work.

"Moe always said that my father was never a good worker but he kept him because he was my father," she remembers. "I used to get very angry when he would say that. And I wanted to tell you, because my mother was kosher and she was so careful about money, she would prepare every day soup or meat or whatever it was for my father to take to work. He'd eat it up there in the shop. And when he'd open up his thermos, everyone was crazy from the smell. It made them hungry, the potatoes and chicken."

Pearlie strolls to the hallway to pay Nancy, who works at the reception desk, $3.50 for my lunch ticket. The dining room is an airy room with a cluster of round Formica-topped tables and chrome chairs. Its eastern wall is a large glass window that offers a ringside view of Fred Segals, the trendy collection of boutique stores across the street, with its parking lot filled with Range Rovers and Land Cruisers. On another wall, there is a colorful mural of outdoor scenes beneath the words "America the Beautiful," painted by one of the residents.

On the menu board, it says there is soup: chicken noodle and tomato. Blueberry pancakes, bacon and fried eggs, sausage, oatmeal. I sneeze, from a lingering cold, and Pearlie looks concerned. *"Mere zul zein for dina keppula.* Whatever should happen to you should rather happen to me," she says. The Yiddish expression imparts another memory. *"Keppula,"* she says, smiling at the Yiddish word for "head," "that's what Grandpa would call his you-know-what." She unpeels a cackle. So do I.

Pearlie retrieves two hard-boiled eggs, a little tuna, and two slices of white bread. Plus a banana, cottage cheese, and yogurt. Walking across the dining room, she takes everything off her tray and puts it on her place mat at a table near the window. "I always have nice people at our table," she says of her friends Dora, Mitsie, Natalie, and Nin. Exactly who sits where is, of course, a sure source of animosity among some residents. But Pearlie doesn't care. "I think no matter how mean or bad a person is, you can always find some good in them," she says. It is her fundamental philosophy, really.

There are very few men in here. "Yeah, men are a novelty," Pearl explains.

Do men tend to complain more than women as they get older? "I don't know," Pearlie says. "Let's ask the girls." She turns to her friends, acting the role of cynosure. "Do you think men complain more than women about their health problems?"

Dora looks glum. "I don't know," she says.

"I tell ya, we haven't got so many men to get opinions from," Pearl says. As if on cue, one of the few male residents, Alex, sits down. Natalie needs to ask him a question. "Which detective is it that did the nude thing in the shower? Is that *Law & Order* or *NYPD Blue?*" she asks.

"*NYPD Blue,*" Alex says.

"Oh, yeah," Natalie says of a recent trip she made to the Third Street Promenade, a block away from their building. "I was on the promenade yesterday, and I saw the fat guy." She means the television actor Dennis Franz. Naturally, celebrity sightings are not uncommon here.

"Did you tell him to lower his pants so you could recognize him?" Alex says, laughing.

"He looks exactly the same," Natalie says.

Alex, who says he decided to move into this building because he loves the salad bar and the quiet, is a big health-food devotee. Every morning, he downs one tablespoon of lecithin, four tablespoons of unprocessed bran, and at least four glassses of water. "I hate it," he says.

"How can you eat something you hate?" Natalie asks him.

"It takes time," he says.

"What he's eating is good for him," says Pearl, in a conciliatory voice.

"I know it, Pearl," Natalie says, sounding annoyed. "But I hate it. I drink a lot of eggnog. You bet. With brandy in it."

"She adds a little brandy," Pearlie says to me, apologetically.

"A little?" Natalie scoffs. "I pour it in!"

Alex tells me he can't believe I have three children, since he thinks I look like a teenager. This, of course, is why I love coming here. "I get so damn old everyone looks like a teenager. Even Pearlie is starting to look young."

"That's a compliment," she says, laughing. "You know why he's so independent?" she says. " 'Cause he's the only man at the table. That's why."

Alex changes the subject. "The curb came up and hit me without any notice," he says. "After I recovered from that, I ran after a bus and my hip gave out on me. Three or four days ago."

Pearlie smiles suggestively. "Got any marks on ya?" she asks. "Black and blue?"

Alex puts down his salad fork. "She always wants to know! I'm not gonna show you nothing, kid. You're not a nurse." He turns to me. "You gotta watch out for your grandma. I'm telling ya. The fires are still burning."

⌦

WEDNESDAY, DECEMBER 28, 1994: HAVING JUST OPENED TODAY'S mail, I was delighted to receive an anniversary card from Tessie. Her script has grown crabbed and spidery, but she still dots her *i*'s with little circles, still manages to send me a birthday card (with Aunt Cynthia's help) every year. She's also the only person who bothers to acknowledge our wedding anniversary. Could it be leftover guilt from not coming to our wedding? Or something else?

When I opened her card, though, there was a cryptic note inside. Beside the Hallmark poem and floral scene, Tessie wrote of her love for us and also advised Brock and me to "raise the children the best way possible."

"What does that mean?" I asked Brock.

"What do you think?" he said. "Jewish, of course." Obviously, we are not strangers to debates on intermarriage. Nor are Brock's parents. His maternal grandmother was excommunicated from the Catholic church for marrying a Protestant. So was his father, an Irish Catholic. When we were married by a judge, Brock stomped on a glass, in accordance with Jewish custom. He did it, he told me, for the emotional release: He loved the roar of an audience afterward, dramatically erupting with the words "*Mazel tov!*" Mostly, we spoke then of our love overriding everything else.

Still, like any married couple together for seventeen years, we have our moments. "There are two issues in our marriage," he announced to me not long ago. "G-O-D and D-O-G." I want both. He wants neither.

We call Tessie to thank her for the card, and I nudge Brock to ask her what she meant by "the best way possible."

She answers: "Talk nice. Respect your parents. Go to college." Then, she accuses me of trying to be cute for having asked the question.

PEARLIE CALLS TO THANK ME FOR GOING TO THE LIBRARY YES-
terday and picking up three books—biographies of Audrey Hepburn and Will Rogers and a memoir by Art Buchwald—all with
the oversized print that makes reading easier on her eyes. She says
she's already finished the Audrey Hepburn book. "She was really
very unhappy all her life, Joy," she reports to me sotto voce. "So
many affairs! All those movies did it."

I tell Pearlie what happened to me the night before: I went
downstairs to the kitchen for a roll of toilet paper and by the time
I got there, I forgot why. I called out to Brock: Why did I come
downstairs? He called back: "Two reasons: toilet paper and your
Alzheimer's medication."

Pearlie laughs her head off at that one. "You see, you hang out
with shit long enough," she says of my spending time with her,
"and you turn to shit."

In truth, though, Pearlie has come to relish her quasi–celebrity
status in the neighborhood. Since her picture was prominently
displayed on the cover of the *Los Angeles Times* Sunday magazine,
all sorts of people have stopped her on the street to say hello. In
fact, just yesterday, while waiting in the pharmacy for a prescription, a homeless woman told her that she reads Pearlie's words
when she's run out of her lithium as a sort of pick-me-up. "Even
the bag ladies read," Grandma reminds me.

Then she reads me the riot act. "Listen, darling, are you going
to take a nap today?" Sounds like heaven. "Do you realize how
many jobs you have? The children. The house. Your husband. Your
book. Why are you so piggish? So mean to yourself? You don't give
yourself a rest for a minute. And if you're not going to be good to
yourself, nobody's going to be good to you. Do you hear me, darling? Be a little selfish, Joyala. When you're good to yourself you're
good to your family. You hear me?"

MEN HAVE THEIR WAR STORIES, WOMEN THEIR BIRTH STORIES.
Women without them bear their own Purple Hearts in the battle-
field of love: fighting to survive. This, to me, is what war and

Tessie's treasures:
Bobbie, Mike, and Cynthia.

babies mean. Though the former is a
test of man and the latter a test of God,
both require getting through the pain in
order to find the joy. And hope. In fact,
I've often wondered if men create war
because, having no womb stories to tell,
they're jealous and in need of their own
glories.

In any case, when I ask Pearlie and
Tessie to recount their stories of childbirth, the gratification is immediate. I
think of my parents and their begin-
nings, forgetting for a moment how difficult their lives have
become. And I think of my children, wondering if I felt compelled
to have three of them because my grandmothers did, as if I were
somehow encoded to do so. Or was it something more magical,
like the number 3 itself?

This is one of my favorite things—to listen to my grandmothers
recount their stories of going into labor. The bond that binds us is
more than intergenerational. It is primal.

☞☜

How was childbirth for you?

TESSIE: I picked up a big tub of butter in the store. Sixty-four
pounds. And I had to put it on the counter and slice it.
And put it back. Then pick it up and put it back in the
refrigerator. I was already eight months. I wasn't pregnant a full nine months.

It was very busy Sunday morning. We took care of
the business and about eleven o'clock we close up and
go home and get dressed and go to Brownsville to visit
my parents. My mother's standing in the kitchen by the
table and cutting the dough for pierogi, like kreplach. I
was so tired. I sat down and all of a sudden my water
broke. Izzy goes down—there's no telephone—so Izzy
goes down to call the doctor. No answer. He finally

came in the evening, and my father put up a cot in the dining room and he slept. Every time I started screaming, he jumped up.

My mother was crying. She says, "They say the children from eight months don't live." So the doctor says, "From seven, yes. So why not eight? Don't worry. He'll be all right." It was very hard for me, because your father, he came like this—his elbow was up and his hand was on his head. So, the doctor had to push back the baby, straighten out the arm. That's why he had another doctor with him. So on that round table in the dining room they put me down. It was not in the hospital or so. Took two days. I must have been like a horse, strong, maybe. I don't know. I think I still smell the ether they gave me.

So, he couldn't come out. Maybe his head showed. I don't know. I wasn't there! [*Laughing*] So they pushed back and straightened out the arm and the baby started coming. But they used forceps to straighten him out, so he had marks here and here and here, on his head. And my mother saw him the first time when he came out. She says in Yiddish: "For this here my daughter had to struggle so?" My father fainted. Since his first wife died from childbirth, that was on his mind—that he was going to lose a daughter because he lost a wife. He started crying and he fainted.

The doctor had no scale to weigh him, but he says he weighed about eight pounds. Five pounds weighs the head and the rest is the body. He had a very big head. He must have been a strong baby, too, that he survived all that pushing and pulling and pushing and pulling.

PEARLIE: First, I must tell you about Jerry. He was born on my birthday. A real gift from God. He was the most handsome child you'd ever want to see. I went into labor because I ran for the bus: I was going to take title for our new house. But it was walking back and forth to that sewing machine that made him come out. That sewing machine, I'd hold on and push and *kvetch*. My mother and father were both there. I remember my mother screaming, "The men. The men. The men. They give you all the trouble!"

With your mother I was very sick. I had a hemorrhage. I had the baby at home. She was such a little baby, only about five pounds when she was born. Very tiny. And the doctor stuffed me up, on account of the hemorrhage. And I remember all my husband's relatives—it was Decoration Day—came to the house to celebrate that I had a little girl. Drinking and carrying on. The doctor walked in, and I had fever. The doctor got very angry and said, "I want all these people out of the house." He said, "Your wife is very sick and you've got to take care of her." He was so young, Grandpa. Like a little boy.

DeeDee, she was the easiest one, though I was afraid 'cause I had bled a lot when I was pregnant with her. The doctor thought maybe I lost a twin. After she was born, I got kinda sad. I had, like, crying jags. I don't know why it was.

Fabulous Mandel Broit

When I was small, we were very religious. Mama served it as a dessert with dairy or meat, and that's why it's made with oil and not butter. Also, I use oil 'cause it holds together nice. They charge six dollars a pound for it at the Promenade. But let me tell you what I do:

It's four eggs. Three cups of flour. I'll give you this here [written recipe]. So, two and a half teaspoons of baking powder, a half a teaspoon vanilla, and a half a teaspoon of almond flavor. If you don't like that, you can use one teaspoon of whatever. And a half a cup of sugar. The kids may like it sweeter, but with this almond you can get away with less sugar and a half a cup of oil. If you like it richer, ya gotta use three-quarters a cup of oil and three-quarters a cup of sugar. You also need a preheated 350-degree oven.

What you do is you gotta mix the eggs first. Separate them and beat the whites and then add the yolks. Then ya take the flour and put in the baking powder and little bits of salt if you like. If not, you don't have to. And you mix the eggs and the flour and the baking powder. Put in the vanilla or almond flavor, whichever you want. And the sugar and oil. Throw it all in. Mix it around.

And you've gotta have it so that you can kvetch it—to pull and roll it a little bit. It can't be very loose. Then you can use almonds, nuts, chocolate chips—whatever you like—and just throw 'em right in.

Now, see, the way I do it is I use just an old cookie sheet. When it's all mixed together, I put the almonds in the dough. Like, for instance, I take out, oh, about a handful of dough. I don't look. I just throw in a couple of almonds. I never bother with blanched. You just throw 'em in. And I knead it out: You make logs. About eight or nine inches long and three inches wide. Then I put it up and put it right on a greased cookie tray and flatten it down. Make sure the tray is oiled good.

When it gets a little golden brown, you take it out. You see, according to your oven. Some ovens need more, some need less. It's gotta be in about three-quarters of an hour. Then you take it out and slice it while it's hot. And if you like, you can put it back into the oven again to toast it. Yeah. That's optional.

If you want more explanation, just come over and I'll make it with you. Or I'll come to you and you can see how it's done. It's good to go with a solid recipe, so you have your guidelines. So take this, darling. And use it in good health.

CHAPTER 6

Kishen Tuchis: Kiss My Ass

*Shirley with Pearlie's handmade
parasol and costume.*

BENEATH PEARLIE'S EXHIBITIONISM IS HIDDEN A DEEPLY PRIVATE woman whose complex character was forged in the terror of watching a sister and two brothers die and a mother without the means or ability to protect them. Then, when it came Pearlie's turn to mother, she, too, stood helpless as her daughter Shirley—my mother—almost died. On the freezing night that she raced her 1-year-old daughter to the hospital, Pearlie vowed that this child would make it, no matter what anyone else said, this baby girl would know music and dance and joy.

"The worst thing in the whole world was when Shirley got sick," Pearlie tells me as I drive her to a reunion of the Dancing Dolls. It is a windy morning in December, the sun bright. Even though remembering back to the winter of 1928 is painful, Pearlie summons forth the details with the force of necessity.

"She got bronchal demonia," Pearlie says. It sounds like my mom was possessed by the devil.

"You mean bronchial pneumonia?" I ask.

"Yeah, bronchal demonia," Pearlie says, "and we didn't think she'd live." She wipes the sides of her mouth with a tissue. It is a part of aging she truly hates, this buildup of saliva. But she dabs at her lips so subtly, so matter-of-factly, that the tissue in her hand has become like a magician's scarf. "I said, If she goes, I'll never be able to live with myself. She was six months in the hospital. Can you imagine, six months in the hospital? Did you ever hear having one hundred and seven degrees temperature? It was late at night. Stella and Frank took us to the hospital. And the doctor, his name was Dr. Weinmuller, told me, he says, 'Only God could save your child.' "

Pearlie remembers cooking up homemade gefilte fish and batches of cookies and mandel broit and egg bread for the nurse at Brooklyn Hospital—Mary Giotti was her name, a very wonderful Italian nurse who loved Jewish cooking—to smuggle her in beyond visiting hours to see Shirley. My grandmother's dogged pursuit to sneak in chicken soup for my mother, taking the trolley to the hospital day after day, has a mythical cant about it. But what is indisputable is that there were no antibiotics to treat pneumonia at the time. Instead, doctors drilled a hole in my mother's side to remove the infection in her lungs.

Pearlie continues. "They used to open where the rib is and use Dakin's solution, a kind of purple medication that's like an antiseptic. They would put the medication in and then draw it out, and they would draw out the pus that way. You mother has, I think, a little mark over here from it." Pearlie points to her right side. "She kept on having fever, though. I begged them to let me take her home. They wouldn't. Then, all of a sudden, I got a call from the hospital and they said you better come quick, we don't think your daughter's going to last till the morning. And I came there, and your mother was black. Her face was all black and blue.

"And you know, every time I'd go there, I'd live by what Grandpa would say. He'd say, 'Oh, my Sherkela is going to be all right. She's going to be fine.' But this time, I looked. He looked at her. And he says, 'Uh, I don't know.' He says, 'I have my doubts.' And I remember screaming, carrying on. And she came over and told me the story, Mary Giotti. She told me that Shirley coughed at night. And when she got stronger, instead of dragging out the pus from the side, the pus deposited itself up here." She points to her chest. "And she was able to cough it up. That was her lifesaver." Soon after, a chicken pox outbreak hit the hospital, and Pearlie was barred from seeing Shirley for three weeks.

I think of my own daughter, who is roughly the age my mother was when she was hospitalized, and listening to Pearlie's story becomes excruciating.

Since the doctor advised that Pearlie and Moe "move seashore" (she invariably relates this phrase minus a preposition) because the fresh ocean air would do my mother good, they sold their two-family home in Bensonhurst and headed to a Brighton Beach apartment. "I was very, very much attached to Shirley," she says of my mom. "She was sort of my whole life. And I don' t know why.

"I couldn't put Shirley on a high enough pedestal," Pearlie tells me. She knows some people might think she's overdoing it when she says things like that, but they also don't know how it feels to have a child on the brink of death. Or one who dies.

Pearlie looks straight ahead through the windshield. Her voice grows emphatic, as she recalls how she surrendered her own singing and dancing ambitions by transferring her drive to Shirley. Every Saturday. "This day was Shirley's—always. It was drama and comedy. I took her to an English teacher. He was supposed to be a trained Shakespearean actor, but when he couldn't act anymore, he taught. He wasn't fifty. He was fat, he was big, he wasn't representative of a stage person. He would read. She would read from books. And they'd do a little acting out. And I got such a pride in seeing her get that kind of education. The way she spoke made me feel that she's going to be an actress.

"And from there we'd go to a teacher. Her name was Miss Horsey. Mabel Horsey. A black teacher. And she would teach her singing and dancing. And then I had another teacher for her, I forget, you mother will remember the name. I don't remember his name. He was an actor and at one time a dancer. And he taught her acrobats, he taught her these flip-flops, to go over. She made the most beautiful split. And tap dancing. And I kept that up until she was about twelve, because I had DeeDee and I couldn't take her. I couldn't *shlep* her to New York."

In fact, my mother later tells me over a tuna sandwich at her kitchen table that she does remember the dancing teacher, Sammy Burns, whom she recounts as being "a strange guy. Everybody who was in any of his classes had to come to him and kiss him before they left and he pinched our asses." Not that enduring such humiliations would cause Shirley to rebel. A good girl, she may have resented Pearlie's stage mothering but never would say so.

"There were no serious conflicts I can remember with Pearlie, because there was no fighting," my mom explains, her curly brown hair now flecked with gray. "We just did what was expected and I would—still do—rationalize why I chose to do something that happened to be what my mother wanted. But she couldn't at the time admit how she used relationships for her own good."

The "talkies" were just beginning. Through Miss Horsey, who acted as an agent for some of her students, Pearlie managed to get Shirley and Jerry into a low-rent version of an Our Gang movie, *The Dead-End Kids,* for which they were each paid about $10. In the short film, the gang digs a hole to build a pool, creating a giant, muddy mess. But since they're trespassing and have to make a quick getaway, the final comic moment occurs when Jerry's big butt can't squeeze through a fence. Pearlie proudly had still photographs from that forgettable film of Jerry's fat ass framed.

But the stage-mother routine—stitching together homemade hula skirts and dancing costumes, taking Shirley to diction classes at Columbus Circle, being away from home—wore thin on Moe, the cloakie who was now starting up his own manufacturing business. "Grandpa was so angry at me," she says of her time away from him. "He says, 'You dragged the kids, you don't know what to do with yourself.' He was very, very angry, which he seldom was. But I used to leave Jerry, I really neglected him, to take Shirley to New York."

She pauses, thinking. "Maybe that's the reason I have such a guilty complex. Maybe that's the reason why Daddy got to drinking," she says of Moe, "because I wasn't home."

This is the first time I've heard Pearlie blame herself for my grandfather's alcoholism, a topic she normally sidesteps. But now, she seems to be suggesting that by reaching beyond the traditional role of stay-at-home wife, she did him in. The layers of guilt seem endless. "A mother's full of sacrifice. If she isn't, it [the guilt] comes back to her. No matter what. You just have to do your best—your gut—for them. And you get paid back in a million ways."

Of course, there were also moments of lasting pride, especially when Pearl's mother, Annie, was on hand to appreciate Shirley's accomplishments on stage, singing and dancing to "Minnie the Moocher." "When Shirley was about five years old, we would go to her concerts, and Mama would see her, and she'd push everybody. 'That's my granddaughter! That's my granddaughter dancing!' Oh, she *kvelled* so, I can't even tell ya."

Inside the Senior Recreation Center on Ocean Avenue, Pearlie raises a Styrofoam cup to offer a toast. "Here's to health, happiness, and many more years of Dancing Dolls," she says, sipping coffee, unaware that because of illness and death, this would be the final gathering of the Dolls. "The trouble is, your thoughts are still young but your body says no."

Pearlie puts down her coffee to square-dance with her partner Elsie, holding her crocheted sweater like a skirt and curtsying. By turns, she is a coquettish girl, a vampy prancer, a burlesque queen, a swinging Florrie Dorrie.

"Last one," Elsie advises, linking arms with Pearl. "You want to do the hora?"

"Okay."

I look at my grandmother, sashaying around the room—lighter than air, really—clapping and grinning at her friends, and I'm struck by her elegance, especially as she dances with a wadded-up Kleenex in her right hand, a beatific smile skidding across her face. She is a dancing doll, a sobriquet that befits her more than any other.

Her friend Norma leans toward me and says, "The others know the steps. But they lack the grace. If there's one thing Pearl has, it's grace."

Tell me your philosophy toward marriage.

TESSIE: They say marriage is a terrible thing. It's like an onion: You cry by it and yet you eat it. But it doesn't sound so nice as it does in German.

PEARLIE: My mother always said, "You need to be a good actress to be a smart wife." She would save up dollars in her stocking, called a *knippel*. That's a Jewish word for a bundle. She loved diamonds and saved up for jewelry. When my father would ask her about one of her new purchases, she'd say, "Oh, I got it a looooong time ago!" See, you had to work around your husband.

I'll tell ya, if a marriage is strong, the children will feel secure. I believe in that very much. Children don't like when parents fight or disagree. It hurts them. They want to feel their mother and father have the best relationship, that they care for each other, they care for their family. 'Cause you can build anything out of love.

LATE AFTERNOON LIGHT IS FALLING ON TESSIE'S LIVING ROOM wall. The aroma of chicken soup, cooking on the stove, is thick and comforting. The green and fuchsia porcelain lamps in the living room cast a warm light as Grandma naps in her bedroom. Soon, she'll be up. I listen as her snoring comes in waves of snorts and deep inhalations. Steam heat hisses through the vents.

The girl in the photograph with the doll. She has froufrou hair—a sort of flip that looks more like car fins than a hairdo. A chiffon dress. Big eyes. Who is she? A granddaughter. A girl now grown with her own girl. Me.

"*Shayna maydala*, it's five o'clock," Tessie says, having just woken up. "Do you feel like eating or not?"

"I think I love you so much because you're the only person who calls me *shayna maydala*," I say. I mean that I feel safe here, nourished—and still like a child. *Shayna maydala* is Yiddish for "pretty little girl." Either God made grandchildren so parents could get it right the second time around or God made grandmothers so kids could get twice the love. Either way, I win.

"Never mind," she replies, padding into the kitchen in her mule slippers. I tell her she needs a taste tester for her matzo balls.

"Delicious," I say, spooning some soup and a piece of dumpling into my mouth. She scrunches up her face.

"That's why I love you," she says. "Because you say it's good even if it's not." Translation: She thinks the *knaydlach* are too hard.

I ask her if she can remember bringing my father home from her parents' when he was first born. "My father got me a horse and wagon," she says. "Sure. It must have been at least five dollars. Anyhow, I went home to Greenpoint. What an apartment—not even a coal stove. Okay, I never had anything decent. And I got up Thursday morning. The house was empty yet. Nothing in the house. And the baby was crying. Izzy went to open the store, and the baby's crying, and I sat down and I cried, too. I didn't know what to do.

"I had no telephone to call up, but my sister Sylvia—God bless her—she said she couldn't go to work. It was on her mind that I'm all alone in the house with the baby. And she got up and she told her boss she was going home and that's all. She came to Greenpoint, and when I saw her, believe me, if I'd see an angel I wouldn't appreciate more. We were so close, Sylvia and I. Even though we used to fight like drunken sailors, Mama said. She went to the store. She got some things. She shopped. And I felt so much better that I picked up the baby. I just didn't know what to do. Mama was always there. When the baby was crying, Mama was there. But now, he was crying and I was crying."

Tessie takes a drink of water from her glass measuring cup. "Okay, I'll put on the chicken now?" she asks me. "I ask you permission—and *gay pishen.*" Go pee. This is Tessie's idea of poetry.

I HAVE TWO SCRATCHY PHOTOGRAPHS OF TESSIE AND IZZY IN front of their grocery store in Williamsburg. Both are wearing white aprons and white coats. Looking jubilant beneath a sign that advertises, "New! Different! Delicious Manischewitz Matzo Cereal," Izzy stands in marked contrast to Tessie, her left hand cocked on her hip as she poses in front of a display of Carnation condensed milk cans. He looks hopeful, she despondent. It is their last store, one of four that never made it. The depression. Creditors. Not enough *chochmas,* wisdom, about running a business. Whatever the reason for their stores' failures, it came as little solace that Izzy would find work in Max's store, Title's Miracle Market, in Ozone Park in 1935.

But as a grocer lady—running a store that had absolutely no self-service—Tessie had little time for anything else, including being a mother to my father or my aunt, Cynthia. Mostly, my father was raised by his grandmother and grandfather, whom he called *Bubbe* and *Zayde.* They lived in a tenement building in Brownsville. Certainly, his worldview was insular enough that he spoke only Yiddish by the time he began kindergarten at PS 109, a source of both pride and shame for the young "Mechel." One of Tessie's favorite stories about little Mechy—Mickey to the neighborhood kids—was his encounter in the street one hot summer day, when a group of local boys spoke to him: Not understanding a word of their English, he replied, "*Kishen tuchis.*" Kiss my ass. I've come to see this expression as my family's watchword in facing a seemingly hostile world.

I imagine the depression years to be straight out of Dickens: the cramped quarters, darkened hallways, lack of central heating. And yet, what is phenomenal to me is that my grandmother remembers those days of struggle through a prism of humor. The summer my father was born, for example, in 1923, Tessie had a customer, Mrs. Indisky, who embroidered rompers with a red and blue cross-stitch for Tessie's new baby. "She had a lot of kids," Tessie remembers of her jolly customer. "She came into the store one day and she says, 'I tell my husband he should push it into the mattress, not into me.' In Polish she used to say."

And there was the couple who ran the bakery next door, he with a little red beard and she with the *sheitel*, a wig. "She was such an ugly woman, the wife—a real wretch," Tessie says, gnawing on a chicken bone. "But the husband said to me, 'Well, what do I care? At night it's dark anyway.'"

I laugh. "That's how they used to talk," she says of her customers. Though she worked hard, the store was also her salvation, her social touchpoint. She remembers selling canned coffee, loose coffee, kasha, cereal—anything in a box. Butter and eggs and all kinds of cheeses. A tub of salt butter, a tub of sweet butter, a

Swiss cheese as big as the table she's sitting at. Slicing every piece of cheese, the American cheese, the Muenster cheese. Selling milk by the quart to customers who came in with their own pitchers.

It is a wintry Tuesday night in the dining room alcove that adjoins the living room. On the wall, there are two still lifes, needlepointed by Sylvia. At the table, covered with an embroidered tablecloth, Tessie sits, as usual, in the wooden chair closest to the kitchen. And I sit beside the portable bar that's been stocked with the same three bottles of liquor for the past five years—

Izzy at Williamsburg store, ca. 1932.

Ballantine's Scotch whisky, Wolfschmidt vodka, and Old Overholt straight rye whiskey.

She passes me a plate of broiled chicken. "Would you like a *flegeleh?*" A wing from the chicken, she explains.

"No, thank you," I say, feeling that I've eaten enough for ten people.

"This is called finishing?" she asks, eyeing my leftover chicken breast. "If I would eat this, each little bone would be bare."

"Go ahead," I say.

"No, I'm going to have to gargle. You know, the neck has a lot of bones. I love it. I only eat chicken because of the bones."

THE ONLY STORE SHE ACTUALLY LIVED UPSTAIRS FROM WAS IN Hollis, then a neighborhood so new that the streets didn't yet have names. Their corner store in Woodhaven, she tells me, was trouble from the start because Izzy couldn't get along with the landlord. "He was a German—a real Nazi who was a baker," she says. "He'd buy bloodshot eggs. *Ach.*"

Grandma Tessie's stories about the grocery business abound. Back in the days when there were no ready-made containers, customers would bring in their own bottles for milk or cream. "There was a very nice lady, she had a little girl, Anna, about six years old," Grandma says. "She would come in: She wants a measure sour cream, two measures sour cream. With a little jug, a little container. So my husband would give it. The next day she came in again and again. And one day, her mother came in and she says, 'Tell me, why when I buy the sour cream the jug is full, and when my Anna goes, there's hardly any? Why don't you give her the right measure?' So Izzy said, 'I gave her the right measure, the same thing as you.'

"The next day, Anna comes in again. So Izzy would take a little part waxed paper with a little rubber band to cover it up. He follows her. On the way, she picks up the paper and she drinks the cream. And then she comes home with a little bit left. He followed her home, and he told her that she shouldn't accuse him that he doesn't give her the right measure, but she drinks the sour cream on the way home, the kid."

She smiles. "Oh, stories about the grocery business. *Oy oy oy.*"

It was in Williamsburg where they went bankrupt. No one

could pay the bills. Cynthia was an infant, and Tessie was caring
for Izzy's mother, Rose (Rezel), whom she set up in my father's
bedroom so she could look out at the schoolyard across the way on
Sackman Street in a newly renovated Brownsville building with
steam heat. Rose was dying of cancer.

"She felt she was burning hot, she was burning. The cancer ate
her bones. It went through the spine and all. It was horrible. I'll
never forget." Tessie would soak towels in the bathtub to put on
her mother-in-law's backside. And Kayla, her sister-in-law, would
visit and criticize Tessie for washing Cynthia's diapers in the same
tub she'd use to soak the washcloths for Rezel. Didn't she know
cancer was contagious?

Refrigeration had yet to be invented. Izzy would buy a thousand
cases of eggs and need to put them in storage. "So we would put
them in storage," Tessie remembers, "but we couldn't afford to pay
the storage money." And there were no buyers, it was such a poor
neighborhood. People were ashamed that they were receiving wel-
fare checks from the WPA. "Whatever it was, it wasn't," she says.

"We were really penniless. Mike used to say to me, 'Mommy, do
you have a penny for me?' He doesn't say he *wants* a penny, but if I
had. He knew that there is none. He understood." She remembers
that when her third child, Bobbie, was born—"it was an accident,
all right, it happens"—she thanked God for giving her a girl,
because she didn't have ten dollars for the *mohel*, the man who
circumcises a male baby eight days after its birth. "Whatever was
in the store, we ate. And then there was nothing left."

She shrugs. "All in all, I'm average born and average raised and
average went through hell. I accept everything. I take it as it
comes. And now, too." She leans under the counter for her
Rokeach soap and Brillo pad.

Looking back, she's come to regret her ambition because it
caused her to stand at a remove from her children. She likens herself to Shannon Faulkner, the young woman who waged a success-
ful legal battle to gain admission to the all-male Citadel but then
left after her first week there. "A decent girl wouldn't do this," she
says, not of Faulkner's decision to give up the fight but of making
waves in the first place. "It's not nice." Still, she identifies with
Faulkner's drive, because running the stores with Izzy felt adven-
turous at the time.

"Maybe that's why I'm talking like this now," she says of her criticism of women striving to be treated equally with men. "I worked like a man. I worked very hard when I was young. I didn't know any better. Women want to show off they can do just the same as the men? All right. Good luck to them." In this context, she means good riddance.

Had she never gone into business with Izzy, she says now, there wouldn't have been as many arguments between them. He'd criticize her for orders; she'd criticize him for not making a sale. At home, they basically got along, she remembers. Except Izzy would worry when my father slept by an open window. Tessie liked that he was breathing fresh air. "He'd say, 'Tessie, close the window. It's cold outside.' And I'd say, 'So if I close the window, will that make it warmer?'" She smiles.

I clear the rest of the dishes from the table. Grandma tells me, "My mother would say, 'With relatives you can eat kugel, but sometimes they'll eat faster than you.'"

What does that mean? "It's not good with relatives," she says. "Business is not good with relatives, especially a grocery. A partnership can put pressure on a relationship. I knew when to keep quiet and when to give him an argument when he's wrong." For instance, Izzy insisted she put a red bow on the roof of her baby carriage for good luck, a superstitious holdover from the old country. She didn't believe in the evil eye, but she did it anyway.

She begins scrubbing her white porcelain pot, which reminds me of trips she used to make to Cleveland, *shlepping* her kosher dishes, more than thirty years ago. "You see this pot?" she asks me, pointing to an aluminum double boiler. "That pot, when we came to this country, it belonged to my mother. So, it's more than seventy years old. Here, these spoons, my father bought for my mother as a surprise. They're silver-plated. The first Passover, he got from shul. There was a guy who peddled these things, so we had a set of spoons, forks, and knives."

Suddenly, her mind ricochets from the long ago to the future. "Eh," she says of her belongings, now scrubbing again. "You know what they're going to do after I'm gone? Throw it all in the garbage."

She smiles to herself. "See how nice?" she asks of the pot, now unstained. Sometimes, she surprises even herself with her accomplishments, the smallest ones, especially. "I didn't think I could get that so clean. But I did."

How do you learn to live alone?

TESSIE: You don't learn. You just take day by day and it comes and you accept it and you have no choice. And that's how you learn to live with it. Nobody's an expert.

PEARLIE: It's hard, but you do it. You sort of graduate into it. When I lost Moe, you get used to doing this on your own and deciding things on your own. You use your head a little more. I think it comes naturally. Nature sorta helps you out. It guides you when you know you have to depend on yourself. It's up to you to keep on *draying* [turning] the wheel. It makes you more independent. So, you do what you have to do, darling.

TUESDAY, JANUARY 3, 1995. THE DENTAL SITUATION VARIES FOR MY grandmothers. When I ask Tessie, for instance, if her teeth are her own, she rather buoyantly replies, "Of course! I paid for them." Pearlie is another story.

She's been worried because she hasn't been able to take out her upper set of dentures. When she finally managed to pry them loose, her gums were swollen and red. I offered to take her to the dentist.

It's rainy and cold out when I drive up, a half-hour early. It's important to Pearlie that she arrive early so she doesn't get jittery about being late. She emerges from her building with her trademark brown tam and matching brown sweater.

"Hi, doll," she says, barely brushing my cheek hello with a peck of a kiss. I escort her around to the passenger side of the car.

"Watch your *tuchis*," she advises as I strap her in her seat belt.

This is the first time I've ever seen Pearlie without her teeth in, and I finally see her for what she is—an old woman. She has a total of seven teeth of her own left, all on the bottom of her mouth. For three days, she's been getting by with only these teeth, eating mushy food. I swing the car into a parking lot behind the dentist's two-story building on Wilshire Boulevard, above the copy store on Seventh Street, just across from Lincoln Park.

As we sit in the waiting room, neither one of us is eager to pick up a *People* magazine for a hit of gossip. Pearlie launches into one of her existential treatises.

"There's so much fear, Joyala. The fear of losing your faculties. The fear of losing what you have been. It's so hard to take. You can't shake that fear. If not today, it's tomorrow. If not tomorrow, the next day. It'll come get you."

She dabs at her eye with a tissue. "I've changed my mind a lot about living. You've gotta struggle. You hurt your family. And there's nothing you can do about it. The fear is so horrible." In some ways, life's just a continuous horror show, isn't it? She's only uttering the monstrous truth.

"Don't say a word to your mother," she says. "She's got enough *tsuris* as it is. I wish I could make it easier. But really, I'm just a pain in the ass. I'm feeling what your mother is going through and what your father is going through. Those things hurt. Sometimes, I feel I shouldn't talk to them, because maybe she feels what I feel. And I don't want her to feel what I feel. You know what I mean?"

Not exactly.

"I feel bad," she says, "and I don't want her to feel bad. And I'm so afraid I might slip up. Lately, I haven't been talking to her too much. Because I'm afraid I might say something to her that might hurt her that I don't realize."

A mother's nightmare—to know your child is hurting and you can't do a thing about it. You can't protect. You can't advise. You can't comfort. A daughter's dilemma—to know your parents are going through hell, and you have to watch, absorbing the sadness but knowing anything you say sounds ridiculous. A granddaughter-grandmother bond is forged in the dentist's waiting room.

The trouble with Pearlie's teeth began with the earthquake, nearly a year ago. The jar in the bathroom that she keeps her dentures in crashed off the vanity table and she was panicky at the thought of being without them. Ever since, she's kept her teeth in at night.

"I'm afraid if the earthquake comes, I want my teeth." I can't help laughing. When the earthquake hit, I was afraid I wouldn't get to my children in time—and Grandma worried about her teeth. She fake-laughs. "It's funny," she says, "but it's a natural thing.

"It's hard with the teeth," she continues. "That's why I didn't touch them until I had to. Any little change is hard when you get to our age."

The most dramatic change, of course, has come with my grand-mother's inability to deal with her anxiety—mostly about my parents' health. It's like all her coping mechanisms have shut down. "I was all right until your mother," she says, meaning until my mother's cancer was diagnosed. "It took all the gumption out of me."

She knows she needs help, so—with much prodding from the family—she's made an appointment to see a psychiatrist.

"I feel very insecure," she adds. "When you get into the ninety bracket, it's like the end of the road, really."

AFTER LUNCH, PEARLIE WRITES A LETTER TO HER GOOD FRIEND, Ethel.

> Dear Ethel,
>
> It's so hard to figure one's life out. Here we are with such beautiful grandchildren and great-grandchildren, and God should only give us the strength to enjoy them. God has given me such a beautiful family, and I can't thank him enough. But that isn't enough. I am so worried about Shirley and Mike. Mike is not well and it scares me so. I wake up each morning with fear. It's been so hard to face the day. The fear is always there.
>
> Thursday, Joy took me to her house and I had such pleasure out of my beautiful great-granddaughter and great-grandsons. They are so smart. I can learn so much from them now.
>
> What bothers me, I can't do what I did before. Well, I guess that is ungrateful of me. God has been good to me in letting me live this long. While we can maintain our home and dignity, everything is fine. But once that goes, it is so hard to adjust.
>
> I love you always.
>
>   Pearlie

An hour later, the phone rings. "Listen, darling, I have a prob-lem."

What now? "I've been thinking," Pearl says. "Maybe I should hold off on the dentures. They're feeling good now." She's looking for my permission to cancel yet another dentist's appointment. Piece of cake. I tell her not to worry for a second and just cancel it.

"I think I'll wait for tomorrow and see," she says.

She asks what I'm up to. In truth, I'm staring at my blank computer screen, I explain, trying to get some work done before I pick up the kids from school.

"Don't work so hard!" she yells at me. "You hear me?"

How can I work so hard if she's yelling at me on the phone? She laughs.

"I've been worrying about your father," she says. "Your mother says he's been losing weight." It's true. Dad has dropped nearly twenty pounds in the past three months. Mom has been trying to fatten him up with Ensure and ice cream, her "guggle muggles," but she says she's the one gaining the weight.

"I can't even tell you how I feel," Pearl says of my father's illness. "I just can't take it."

"I know, Grandma," I say. "I feel the same way."

"Right away, I think about it and my stomach backs up on me," she says. "Maybe when you're younger, you can take it better. Look, I lost a son. And I was able to take it. And I was able to take care of Grandpa. And yet, now I can't. I don't want to be a little baby and cry. I should be able to take it. So, I thought I'd speak to my adviser, Joyala, 'cause you give me hope."

"Oh, great," I tell her. "It's the blind leading the blind." The truth is that I've become my grandmother's adviser only because she has the good sense not to bother my mother, who has begun attending I Can Cope support groups for cancer caretakers. And my aunt is probably unreachable by phone. My sister Shari isn't home when she calls her and my sister Peggy is at work in Austin, Texas. Clearly, I'm on the lower rungs of the food chain in Pearlie's constellation of trusted advisers.

"You're going through the same thing, aren't you?" Pearlie asks. "Whichever way you turn the dreidel, you can't find your way home," she says.

What does that mean? I ask. "It means you want it to be like before—healthy and happy—and you can't. Now, it seems all the ropes are loose." Which brings her back to the dentures.

"So when I call, I should tell him I'm going to wait, Joy?"

"What are you asking me for?" I ask, annoyed. "We've already covered this."

"Always, it takes time with the dentures."

"Just call up and say you have to cancel your appointment."

"Okay, smarty-pants," she says.

"You're such a pain in the ass!" I say.

"Pain in the ass is right," she agrees. "That's what I am, all right. I won't keep you anymore."

"Good-bye, Grandma. I love you."

"I love you, too. Love to the children. *Kineahora,* they're so beautiful. "

☜☞

IT IS, PERHAPS, THE GREATEST PARADOX OF GRANDDAUGHTER-hood that the very thing that drives your parents away from their parents is what brings you closer to them: One generation's wedge can be a bridge for the next. What infuriates my parents about my grandmothers makes me love them only more. What my parents see as controlling, I see as a charming eccentricity. What my parents see as intrusive, I see as a sign of affection.

Pearlie's desire to dance, which she foisted onto my mother at a young age, is, I think, one of her most lovely attributes. My grandma Tessie's congenital inability to compliment her *kinder* (children) is, I presume, a loving holdover from her parents' generation—to praise a child or call attention to him is to tempt God's wrath. Better to say nothing and keep the evil spirits away. Pearlie's penchant for jewels and sparkles, which my mother rejected as nouveau riche nonsense, is a sign only of her diamonds-are-a-girl's-best-friend giddiness, which I share. Tessie's informing my father that she could read his thoughts by looking at the lines on his forehead was, I think, a sincere if misguided way of keeping an impressionable boy off the streets and out of trouble.

Phrasing it politely, my grandmothers get what they want. More than survivors, they're fomenters—out to agitate, even if only from the confines of their kitchens. Family members alternately describe Pearlie as manipulative, maneuvering, and finagling. Tessie is similarly referred to as tough, strong-willed, and a know-it-all. But in truth, I see them slightly differently. I like to say they're shrewd, operating in a social milieu where women still must be cunning to be taken seriously. They dare to dream and are ready to confront their most basic fears. For Pearl, it's a primitive fear of abandonment and death. For Tessie, it's a more public fear of embarrassment and disapproval. But dreamers are not necessarily the greatest mothers, either.

Simply put, I would not want my grandmothers for mothers. God forbid. In fact, if my grandmothers raised me, I undoubtedly would have gone mad long ago. When I walk into Tessie's apartment—thirty minutes after I said I'd be back from an appointment in Manhattan—she opens the door with hands on hips and lips pursed, and I know the critical vein will spill open. "I was so worried!" she says, walking away from me and bounding into the kitchen to check her lamb stew. Translation: You should have called.

Pearlie, too, expresses her concern in odd ways. "Joyala, I called to tell you to keep an eye on the baby," she says, as if I wouldn't. "Yeah, I just saw a news report of a baby that walked into traffic on the street. Can you imagine?" Or: "Listen, Joy, I called to tell you I just saw a report on the news about dangers in the bathroom for babies. The electric wires. The slippery floors. Oh my God, you must be careful." Has she always been such a nervous Nellie?

So, when I think about my grandmothers' lives as mothers, I develop a whole new appreciation for my parents' insistence on breaking free and carving a realm for themselves.

And yet, I also feel torn, piecing together the puzzle of their lives. My mother remembers Pearlie steaming open love letters from my father when they were dating; when I ask Pearlie about this, she vehemently denies it. Then reconsidering, she asks of my mother: "Maybe she wrinkled up the letters?" My father remembers Tessie purposely leaving him in a crowded Brooklyn street to test his survival skills as a 5-year-old; Tessie has no recollection of such a moment. "Lying," my dad once told me, "was a way of life in my family." Whom to believe? Or is this just an example of how memory grows more selective as we age?

There is, however, consensus on some issues. Pearlie lived vicariously through my mother. Tessie, by her own admission, was never one to cuddle or show affection physically; instead, she treated my father as "a pal" more than a son. Both were demanding, though Pearlie would rhapsodize about her children's triumphs one moment and send them off to summer camp the next. My mother, for example, was made to sleep away at the age of 5, presumably so Moe could have Pearlie to himself for the summer.

In any case, I always had the impression that, for my parents,

the best thing about Brooklyn (read, Pearlie and Tessie) was leaving. You don't have to close your eyes to see the pretty girl with the
ready laugh and the brilliant guy with the sparkling blue eyes saying "So long, suckers," and meaning it.

Though much has been made about the repetition of mistakes
in a family over time, the obverse is also true. Whatever it is that
makes you loony at the mere mention of your parents—the bile—
can turn into something else a generation later. This, I've come to
believe, is one of the miracles of evolution. It's like the centrifugal
force of love: The further children pull away, the greater the tug
grandchildren feel to be reeled back in.

✁ ☞

I'VE INVITED MY FATHER TO MEET ME FOR LUNCH. "DO YOU
have an agenda today?" he asks me, as we sit down in a booth by
the window at Junior's Deli in Westwood, halfway between his
house and mine.

"Not really," I say.

"Oh, come on," he says.

"I'm going to cry," I warn him as the tears stupidly fall down my
cheeks. I can't help but notice how thin he's grown. Despite
attempts at normalcy, like the tasseled loafers, his maroon cardi-
gan hangs off his shrunken shoulders like an oversized cape.

"Are you going to talk and then cry or cry and then talk?" he
teases me.

Since July, my father's battle with mesothelioma has worsened.
The tumor that has invaded the lining around his lungs is, basically, incurable. And the prognosis is bad, about eighteen months
from the time of diagnosis, according to the medical literature.
This is his third cancer. There was his colon cancer my senior year
of high school. There was the prostate cancer in 1987 for which he
still takes medication. Now, this latest cancer is the result of
asbestos exposure, probably from forty years ago. Our moments
together are infused with the knowledge that everything happening could be the last time—Thanksgiving, Chanukah, New Year's.

The last time my father and I shared a meal alone together was
a few weeks before my wedding. He called, asking to meet me for
dinner, and I was terrified about what he wanted to say. Was he ill
again? Was something up with Mom? No, he wanted to spend

time with me because, he said, he didn't really know me. And, he was about to give me a wedding, saying good-bye.

Now, sitting in this deli booth together, it feels like we're beginning to say good-bye in another way. Just the two of us, face-to-face. Usually, our time together is spent with Mom and Brock and in the company of my children. At the moment, we both order a cup of soup and half a sandwich—pastrami for me, corned beef for him. But he barely touches his food.

"I'm writing this book about your mother and about Pearlie, thinking about their lives and interviewing them," I say, "and I realize the person I most want to talk to is you." I watch the tears slide down the creases edging his blue eyes, onto his cheeks. The only time I ever saw my dad cry before this moment was at the funeral of my baby son, when he told me there is no greater sadness in life than a parent losing a child.

He hates being in the position of sounding like "a chronic *kvetch*," he tells me. But when his friends ask how he's doing, it makes him sad. He's frightened that though his lungs are okay now, the tumor could end up squishing his other organs. Or metastasize to his bones. He's been reading medical journals. The outlook isn't good.

But when he talks about my writing about Tessie and Pearlie, he begins to weep. "Don't be afraid to write the truth. To write about what's personal," he says, his voice cracking. "You have a way of writing so simply, but also emotionally. Do you know what a gift that is?" My father has always been the greatest supporter of my writing life.

I ask him to please consider telling Grandma Tessie about his illness. I put myself in her position, and I'd want to know. Despite the loneliness. Despite the feelings of helplessness. Despite the sadness it would cause. As a mother, I'd still want to know if my son was sick. Maybe she can hear it in his voice now, anyway.

"De Nile," he tells me, wiping his tears with a handkerchief, "is more than a river in Egypt for my mother." We crack up together. Still, he promises to think about telling Tessie, who still believes cancer is caused by aggravation. He asks the waitress to wrap up the rest of his sandwich for my mother.

In the following weeks, just as my father begins chemotherapy, he informs his mother about his medical treatment in the most cursory way, saying that what he has is not serious. It is a lie. Is he protecting her? Or himself? The truth, he believes, would be too cruel. He asks me to act as a kind of intermediary, filling her in on the blanks of his condition when I see her next.

After his second round of chemotherapy, he sends me an e-mail missive.

> *Subject: Re: Greetings*
> *Date: 95-01-26 22-55-24 EST*
> *From: MJH 427*
> *To: Joyala*
>   *The second day of chemo was something I don't want to go into. Hope Mom told you about it. I now have bronchitis in addition to having gone through a couple of very unpleasant side effects. My mouth tastes like I ate a doorknob. Tomorrow is the third shot. I am medicated like a* culta hevnick. *Tell Trevor I'll explain what* kishen tuchis *means online. Please tell Brock I'll have to miss the Stupid Bowl Party. I am contagious.*

"HOW'S DADDY?" GRANDMA TESSIE ASKS ME THE MINUTE I walk into her apartment.

I haven't called my father Daddy since I was a little girl, but hearing Grandma Tessie say it causes my throat to lock up. Slowly, carefully, I explain the facts, minus the grim details about prognosis. I tell my grandmother that my father had fluid drained from his chest cavity, so he's breathing more easily. But the tumor has grown. It's not in his lungs, but in the pleura, the lining that encases his lungs. This is why he's started chemotherapy. I leave out the part about the doctors at Sloan-Kettering saying his chances of improvement from chemo are 1 in 10. It's a very rare form of cancer, with about two thousand cases diagnosed in the United States every year.

"So where did he get it?" she asks. I tell her that the risk of developing the disease increases each year up to forty to forty-five years after the first exposure. We're not exactly sure what the exposure was or when it occurred, since my father quit smoking cigarettes in 1963, the year that the Surgeon General first recognized a link between smoking and cancer. But my father was one of millions of smokers who chose Kent cigarettes with the "Micronite" filter, which, in fact, was ringed by a layer of asbestos from 1952 to 1956. It was a filter advertised in the *Journal of the American Medical Association* as being "healthy." My father remembers the filter well, because it was the same color as his father's eyes—blue.

She absorbs the information, though it's difficult to say how much she really understands. How much she *wants* to understand.

"Is it serious?" she wants to know.

"Yes," I say, betraying my father. Out of nowhere, tears stream down my face. "It's serious." I apologize for my tears and reach for the red playing cards on the table, shuffling the deck. Already, I'm feeling guilty for saying too much, even if it is the truth. Was it wrong of me to have told her?

"On the contrary," she says, picking up the cards I've dealt. "Look, you get used to the *tsuris*. Even when you have joy, you even enjoy the joy though you have the *tsuris*. I don't know how to explain it. But you get used to it." She thinks for a moment. "I've got to go first."

Initially, I assume she's talking about picking up the first gin card, and then I realize she means that she wants to die before my father. She sounds like she's in a race to the finish.

"But don't talk now," she says. "Let's not talk about it. It's enough that I think of it." I know that the subtext of all my visits to Tessie is more basic than words, anyway. I come here in my father's stead. Whether as an emissary or go-between or advance man, I'm a poor substitute, in any case. The truth is, both my grandmothers would prefer the company of their own children. But we make a good show of it, anyway. We just "slink along," as Pearlie says.

I can't help myself from asking one more question of Tessie, though. "When was the last time you told Dad that you loved him?"

"He knows," she says. "I don't have to tell him."

Mike's bar mitzvah, July 1936.

We play gin rummy in silence. Until she sees the king of hearts. "Oh, you gave me a king," she says, slyly. "Ha ha ha." Then, she picks up another card. "I knew you were waiting for this," she says, taunting me.

I pick up the six of clubs. "Now this time I'm going to lose," she says. "Why did you take it, the six of clubs?"

Her focus seems unshakable. I ask her where her inner strength comes from. She doesn't answer. I want to talk life. She wants to play cards. I ask again.

"Well," she says, peering out over her cards, "I hope every day for better."

"You hope every day for better?" I ask.

"Sure," she says. "Otherwise, you couldn't exist. Knock on wood, and you got to hope. No matter what religion you observe and what you think, you still have to have hope. I don't think I ever lost hope. When you don't have today and you don't hope that tomorrow will be better, so why—"

I hand her a two of hearts. "*Oy oy oy oy oy*," she says, looking at her cards. "What can I give you? What can I give you? Here, make gin and take me out of misery."

She gives me a six of hearts. I'm at a total loss as to understand what cards she's collecting. I hand her another one.

"Gin!" she says, smiling.

"You slaughtered me," I whine.

"Am I not entitled?" she asks.

GRANDMA TESSIE'S

Wondrous Chopped Liver

You think I'm made of chopped liver? I haven't made it in, oy, I don't know how long. I used to make real good chopped liver. Is this open, the tape recorder? Oy, I better not say it. No no, the thing is this. In Yiddish, they say *meshit* and *memisht* when you pour it in: Mishing is mixing and shitting is just pour it in.

Let's say if I expect ten people so I buy a pound of liver. Beef liver, but a good one. Nice and fresh. And I broil. You must have it on a big fire.

You dice about two or three onions. Sure. Chopped liver is very good with a lot of onions. So you dice 'em up. Cook 'em in vegetable oil. You stew the onion, first without any grease, just with salt at a small light. And it stews slowly.

Don't grind the liver when it's warm, otherwise it gets greenish inside. You must only grind it when it's cold. I had my experience already. I paid for it. And you make about three hard-boiled eggs. And you mix it up while you grind. See, I have an electric grinder. If you want, maybe I'll will it to you. I have a meat grinder, just like a regular butcher meat grinder, but a small one. I used to make hamburger meat with it, and chopped liver.

In the meantime, the onion you mix in with the grinder. Salt and pepper. That's all. You put it in the dish, you mix it up with a fork. There's nothing to it. It's only time. But it isn't an exact recipe. Not too much oil. Let's say for a pound of liver, you use a half a cup of oil. Even that's too much. That's the only time you put in the oil is to fry the onion. The onion gets salt. Very small light.

I used to make a lot a lot the chopped liver.

CHAPTER 7
Bren: Fireball

In velvet evening dresses, Tessie (top right)
and her sisters (clockwise) Gussie, Sylvia, Rose,
and Leah, for a hospital fundraiser.

MY GRANDMOTHERS BAKE IN THEIR HEADS.

This is partly because when you bake in your head, there are no dishes to wash, no grocery shopping to do, no worries about forgetting a cherished ingredient. Though it is a concession to being old, this head cooking, there's nothing like focusing on a favorite recipe, sort of like an old friend, to pass the time. Some people relive past glories. Others quietly mull over regrets. But Tessie and Pearlie fantasize about food.

"Cookies, I have very good recipes," Tessie tells me one afternoon, as we share a piece of her marble cake, which she proclaims to be too dry and therefore "tastes like doit."

I gobble it up with coffee. "What kind of cookies?" I ask.

"Not too rich. Only with margarine, a stick of margarine."

Anything else? "On top of each cookie, a cherry or a chocolate chip."

While she daydreams, I sneak up behind her to wash some dishes. "Get out of here," she yells at me. I ignore her entreaties. This is part of our domestic dance: her having a conniption every time I wash a dish, and me telling her to pipe down. And though I try to convince her that I'm perfectly capable of mastering the particulars of her kitchen setup, she refuses my help unless I move in, stealthlike, and commandeer the sink.

Whenever I'm in Tessie's kosher kitchen, I feel like she's put a voodoo hex on me. Since she adheres to the Jewish dietary laws of *kashruth*, meat dishes cannot be eaten or prepared with dairy dishes. But I can never remember which cupboard is for *flayshig* (meat) and which is for *milchedig* (dairy). Or which utensil drawer is for meat flatware and which one is for dairy. In fact, I invariably mess it up so badly that she finds endless excuses to keep me away from washing or drying her dishes.

"You're not in my union!" she says, trying to push me aside. I know she thinks that since I don't keep kosher I have the cooties. "Get outta here. It's been nice knowing you." I keep washing, anyway.

Just to make sure I understand how I've bollixed the whole thing up, she asks a question. I know it's a pop quiz. "When you took out the potato peeler yesterday, from which drawer did you take from—the first or the second?" she asks. " 'Cause I got to know if it came out of *flayshig*."

I begin to stammer. "I took it out from the . . . which side did I take it out from?" I'm stalling. "I think it was, aaaah, the right?"

"The right is this," she says, showing me that I've messed up again.

It's the same when I actually sit down to eat. I can't help myself. I have a long history of misbehaving. There was, for example, the *goyisher* boyfriend incident, when I first brought Brock to meet her, and he promptly requested mayonnaise to slather on his turkey sandwich on rye. Twenty years later, I'm still hopelessly confused. Just the night before, I found myself eating her broiled lamb chops and a baked potato and then asking for butter for my potato.

"Butter!?" Grandma asked, like I had committed a heinous crime.

Surely, keeping kosher is one of the reasons Tessie has lived so long. For one thing, she rarely eats out. "Who knows, when you go out to a restaurant, how long they keep it and what dirty hands they touched it." Besides, being kosher is often a wonderful way to bypass bad cooking. "It's very convenient for me to give the excuse I'm kosher if I don't want to eat someplace," she explains. Also, she resists junk food. "I eat plain," she likes to say.

But, there is one exception: chocolate. "I don't eat chocolate," she says, correcting me. "I nosh. To nosh and to eat, there's a big difference. To eat, you sit down to eat. But if you nosh, you just grab a candy. Like my doctor said, 'Everybody's cheating.' No matter what. You put them on a diet, everybody's cheating. So, I cheat."

In fact, she comes from a long line of noshers, including her father. Before milk was pasteurized, it had to be boiled. Tessie's mother didn't like to serve it raw, so her father would snack on the thick skin from the fat of the milk. Remembering him, her voice drops and grows near reverential. Then a rush of memories. His long white beard, stained around the mouth with brown patches from tobacco. His proclamation to his daughters: "All for one and one for all." His arrival in America when he was 55, already considered old back in the 1920s. His giving her a *zetz* (whack) in the old country, when he thought she misplaced his initialed spoon. "My father was born too soon," she tells me. "He thought about big things and always came out short." Even now, as she summons his memory, she seems haunted: Did she do enough to win her father's love?

⊲⊳

GRANDMA PEARLIE'S BATH TOWELS FROM SIXTY YEARS AGO ARE still in pristine condition. The towels are black with pink flowers and monogrammed PMF, for Pearl and Moe Feldman. She remembers buying them at one of the first bath stores to open in Bensonhurst. How is it possible for them to remain so lovely for so long?

"Joy, you must understand. Joy," Pearlie explains, "these weren't used. They were more on display." I wonder: To display a towel for more than half a century rather than use it. What kind of person would do that? Sentimental? Cheap? Bourgeois? I look at Pearlie, now wearing her flannel Lanz nightgown and shearling booties, and she smiles, taking me in with her chocolate brown eyes that were once hazel. What the towels mean, really, is what Pearlie means, too: How far the human heart reaches to spread lovingkindness—maybe the highest form of wisdom—and wraps itself in a fold of comfort.

Does she feel attached to anything else, like the towels? I ask.

She retrieves a purse from the bottom drawer of her bedroom chifforobe. The purse is a fantastic white shoulder strap, lined and stitched together with tiny white beads. "You use a thin crochet needle," she explains of her beading technique. "You have to string the beads. The beads come in, like, bunches. It's all handmade.

"Grandpa used to get so mad," she says of her handwork. "He was jealous, because I was giving time to this. He would say, 'What do you need it for? You're just using your eyes up.' He said, 'Don't do this. Come over here, and let's enjoy ourselves.' "

She hands me another beaded purse, this one a lovely black velvet with a tasseled cord. "I was going to make a hat of that," she says, "but then I thought, No, I would do it practical. So I decided to make a bag out of it."

She returns the purses to the bottom bureau drawer. Holding on to them—to their beauty, to her sheer creative brilliance—she seems to be keeping something else, too. It's as if the handbags represent a sort of minirebellion against my grandfather and his insistence that she stay at home and be a good wife. Or possibly a reminder of her own inner reserves of talent.

She thinks for a moment. From her vantage, looking out the fifth-floor balcony door, she can see the Getty Museum under construction on its hillside perch in the Santa Monica mountains. "You know, you go into a marriage and you think everything is going to be lovey-dovey," she says, offering me a plate of her homemade Toll House cookies. "But you don't know enough about each other. You got to really study each other to know what makes him happy and what makes you happy, too. Because you're a person, too."

How do you do that? "It's hard, Joy. I got so involved with bringing up the children and myself. Trying to maintain a nice home and having a nice social life with people, entertaining. I forgot the important thing between a man and a woman."

Namely? "What they like, what they dislike." She forgot herself in the equation, in other words, deferring to him. "Like I tried to share Grandpa's business life, and he thought it was lowering a woman's status, to let her work. That was his idea. Women should not work. A woman was there to keep the home and to have children and to make him happy. But I felt maybe I could do more."

The emotional juggling act for Pearlie was not about the demands of work versus children. It was about the conflicting opinions of her husband and her mother. When Pearlie told Moe her period was late in 1931, he wasn't pleased.

"They used to do everything under cover then," she says of their search for a secret abortionist on the Lower East Side. Even though the depression caused the abortion rate to increase substantially, the practice remained illegal. Nearly 1 million pregnancies resulted in abortion in 1930, representing 40 percent of all conceptions. By 1936, the incidence of abortion had risen to one pregnancy in three. Still, abortion was the official cause of death for thousands of American women each year. Pearlie was actually risking her life to be a good wife.

"They took me in this little room where the doctor was. And he said to me, 'This is going to hurt you a little bit, but before you know it, it'll be over.' And I remember him putting in some kind of knife and going zzzzzzzzzz, like that." She had a second abortion a few years later by her confinement doctor. In 1938, despite her continued used of a pessary to prevent conception, Pearlie became pregnant again.

"I went over to my mother's house, and I said, 'Mom, Moe wants me to have an abortion.' He didn't want to have any more babies. He thought by having children, it took away a lot from a husband and wife. That you had to give a lot of time and love, and he didn't want to share so much. He wanted to keep what he had. So she said to me, 'You'll have that child.' She said, 'Don't listen to your husband. Have it. And you'll be glad all your life that you had it.' She said, 'When you'll be sending that baby to school and college, you'll always feel young.' And I did. And that's my Deedala."

And Moe? "Oh, he accepted it. He accepted it."

⌐◄╣ ►┐

A Theological Bubbe Discourse

What is your idea of God?

PEARLIE: I'm not that much of a philosopher. But I know that you pray, "Please God, I hope this one is better" when you're in despair. When you need help, you always go to God. Like, when your mother was sick when she was a little baby, I prayed to God. I prayed to God for

Jerry. I prayed to God for Moe. I prayed to God every day for all my children and grandchildren and great-grandchildren. God should be good in giving everything they deserve.

And God is a mystery to me. Absolutely. Like the question of how the universe began, it's also a mystery: Was you there, Charlie?

Maybe because I wasn't educated enough in the Jewish religion. These people who have studied the Bible, their attitude is quite different than mine. My interpretation is, things happen. I was born and I was raised and I will die like everybody else. We're no different. I think intellectual people look a little deeper than that. You can't make no contract with God.

TESSIE: I don't know. I don't ask. I don't want to butt in.

I'll tell you something: It's good to believe in God. Because if anything goes wrong, then you have someone to blame.

No jokes. I do believe there is a God in this world. I do. Yeah. You have to believe in something; otherwise you have no one to turn to. When the bullets were flying and you used to say, "Oh dear God," if we lay down on the floor it shouldn't hit us, who would I have said "dear" to, instead of "dear God"? Who was I talking to? I believe. Like what's his name, Martin? Yeah. Martin Luther King. I have a dream.

What do you think happens when you die?

PEARLIE: I think that nothing happens. Nothing. You just become nothing. Like before you're born you're nothing? I think when you die it's the same thing.

TESSIE: They bury you. And that's that. You want to make yourself a name, you got to do it while you're alive. After you die, you're dead. That's what I believe.

TESSIE RISES IN THE DARK, IN THE HEART OF QUEENS. SHE swings her legs over the right side of her bed and sits for a moment, gathering her thoughts. Silently, she invokes what she calls her either-or prayer: "Either I can be on my own or good-bye, Charlie." It's 6:07 A.M. and the temperature is 37 degrees.

"You up?" I ask.

"I'm not down," she replies, snapping on her bedside lamp, its china base shaped like Marie Antoinette. In the past few months, the sleeping arrangement has changed so that I now share Tessie's bedroom, sleeping beside her in a twin bed.

Her soft white hair stands in tufts on the back of her head. On the left corner of her dresser bureau, she keeps a folded hanky because this is the spot she must grab hold of to make her way to the kitchen; the handkerchief is intended to keep the dresser handprint-free. Atop her refrigerator, which she stills calls "the icebox," there is a black Emerson radio. Holding on to the doorframe for support, she rounds the corner into her kitchen and clicks on the CBS morning news with Charles Osgood. She likes to listen to the radio to make believe somebody's talking in her house. The sound of voices is comforting. Sometimes, she doesn't really even listen. But it goes, so she's not alone.

"What are all those thousands of people going to do?" she asks, listening to a news report about proposed AFDC cuts while peering into the light of her old General Electric refrigerator. "Where are they going to go?" She shuts off the radio, which prompts her to remember the day she first laid eyes on one, in November 1933.

"When Bobbie was born, and I came back from the hospital—I went by myself, came home by myself—my husband made me a little surprise. He bought me a radio in honor of the baby. It was a big deal to have a radio that time. Not everyone could afford it. And Fanny, Mrs. Stahl's daughter who lived upstairs, came down and showed me how to open it." (She says "open" when she means "turn it on.") "And she wrote down numbers, like for WOR. That's how I learned to use it. In the beginning, I was afraid to touch it."

The following month, for Chanukah, Tessie was making potato latkes while listening to The Jewish Hour, a Yiddish radio program. She set the plate of potato pancakes on the table just as the radio announcer said, "Come, kinder, the latkes will get cold." "I got so scared," she says now, laughing. "I thought he was looking into my house."

By nine-thirty on a Tuesday morning in February, she is writing out a check to pay her monthly telephone bill. "If I press my arm on the table, very tight, then I can write," she explains of the arthritis in her hand. "Very slowly. Like a first grader." The index finger of her right hand is misshapen, almost clawlike. She calls it her "telephone finger," reasoning that its crookedness was caused by dialing her black rotary phone all these years. Jamaica 6- ——. Hers is the only phone number I bothered to memorize by way of its exchange, not the number.

The phone rings. "It's Cynthia," Grandma announces before picking up the receiver. "Who else?"

Every morning, my aunt Cynthia checks in on Tessie from work. It is Cynthia, nearing retirement herself, who brings Grandma her food, makeup, nail polish, and meat from the kosher butcher. Not to mention birthday cards for grandchildren and great-grandchildren. There are even some days, depending on street parking, that Cynthia makes an early-morning food delivery on her way to work, leaving a bag of fresh rolls and deli for Tessie before she wakes up. Without Cynthia's generosity, my overnight visits with Grandma would be impossible.

As usual, their conversation focuses on making arrangements for her upcoming hair appointment. Tessie's hair, now white and wispy, is a constant source of attention. Mostly, I remember her blue-rinse period, during which she didn't want her gray to go yellow. Before that, there was her skunk period. It dates back to her father's death, in 1934. "My father died and they came to tell, so I got gray," she says. While in mourning, she wore a black kerchief over her head for a week. When she removed it, she discovered that her black hair had suddenly become streaked with gray.

She pushes her glasses up on the bridge of her nose, which has accordionlike flesh now from the weight of her glasses after all these years. The front-door intercom buzzes. "It's my boss," Tessie says of Lucy, her Haitian-born home attendant. "She's early today."

In fact, Lucy is scheduled to work from nine to one, Monday through Friday, but usually she arrives before ten and leaves before noon—a mutual arrangement that seems to be a constant source of discussion when Lucy is out of earshot.

She walks in, as she does most mornings, with a weather report. "It's cold!" she says, her booming voice breathless. "Yeah. Cold!" She hands Tessie her morning copy of the *New York Post* and asks what she needs at the store. Tessie says she'd like more bottled water.

"If I get lost—" Lucy says.

"I'll call 911," Tessie replies. This is part of their daily repertoire. "Every morning!" Lucy says, laughing. It takes her a minute to lock the door, her red talons are so long.

After her father died, Tessie convinced her mother to move in with her family. "If I had to do it today, I wouldn't do it again," she tells me. "My mother wasn't happy to stay with me." It upset Charna that Izzy worked on the Sabbath, for example. And despite her keeping a kosher home—storing all her dishes in the basement and using her mother's instead—"it wasn't good enough for my mother." Even my father's violin playing was curtailed at home, in deference to Charna's period of mourning.

But with Charna there, Tessie's home became a stopping point for the extended family. She lived directly across the street from an El train that ran all the way to Liberty Avenue. Below the elevated station was the freight yard where the Ringling Brothers Circus would unload elephants and horses and tigers in the middle of the night. But it wasn't the exotic animals that interested Tessie nearly so much as the interfamily squabbles and disputes, her long-standing reputation as a sedulous confidante having preceded her. And like a resident shrink, it was Grandma who came to be seen by her children as the Miss Lonelyhearts of Brooklyn, holding on to everyone's secrets. In seeing her power, no wonder my father would be drawn to the world of psychoanalysis.

In my father's family, Tessie was the symbol of continuity. She liked the idea of being in the center of things, probably because she was a middle child. And having her mother there suited that need, because everyone came Sundays, no matter what, to visit *Bubbe*. The men played cards. The women gossiped. The kids played ball across the street at the freight yard on Junius Street. Or peeked into the fridge to snag some of *Bubbe's* pickled herring. And if they were lucky, they could buy sweets over at Oscar Boxer's, the candy store down the street where you could also make a telephone call.

Tessie and her sisters were a formidable crew. "None of us was too bad looking," Tessie tells me. "I mean, we didn't have any, like, deafs or blinds or whatever." Gussie, the oldest sister, was short, like Tessie, and loved hunting for bargains on Pitkin Avenue. Tessie saw Leah as being "all buttons and bows," vain enough to dye her hair and insist that her birth date be omitted from her tombstone. Sylvia, whom the dentist used to call *payanka,* or "princess," in

Polish, was quiet and independent and thin. Rosie, perhaps the most beautiful sister, was not a good shopper.

Tessie remembers: "If I bought a new hat, she'd ask to see it. She tries it on. 'It's beautiful,' she says. 'Go get yourself another one.'" In retrospect, Tessie thinks that maybe Rose, who died of Alzheimer's, had succumbed to the illness before anyone realized.

"We were all very different," she says. "I could get along." And what about Max, her older brother? "With Max, I was the boss," she says. "He never did anything without asking me."

She eyes Lucy, who is now reaching out the kitchen window for a mop, stored outside on the balcony. "One time, across the street where we lived was the railroad tracks. So Mike would play football with the boys from school. And Sunday I used to cook dinner because we were all together. And it was almost two o'clock. We had to eat. And Mike is still playing there. So Izzy goes over to him. 'Mechel, Mechel,' he calls, 'time to eat.' And Mike says, 'But we're about to score a touchdown.' And Izzy says, 'Touchdown, shmouchdown. Make it tomorrow. Now come eat.'"

On December 15, 1936, Tessie Horowitz became a United States citizen. Looking back, she's not sure why she waited sixteen years to finally fulfill a girlhood dream. She had completed an application form five years before but was pregnant with her daughter, Cynthia. "I was ashamed," she says. "It wasn't nice to go in the court with people and be pregnant. You know me, stupid." On the photograph attached to her naturalization paper, No. 4142644, she bears a world-weary expression. And the courthouse clerk mistakenly listed her eye color as brown, rather than gray.

But it was her life within the Jewish community, more than her abiding sense of nationalism, that mattered most. "Tessie Horowitz was well-known in Brooklyn," she says, pushing up her glasses with her forearm. It is not a boast, just a remembrance.

She is standing at the kitchen sink, cleaning a chicken. Behind her, there is a wall hanging with the inscription: "If you give a man bread, you nourish him once. If you teach him to plant, you nourish him forever." The plaque takes her back to her *shnorring* days. Tessie, with her sisters, raising money for any number of Jewish organizations—the local hospital, the theater, the Hebrew day school—in the name of *tzedaka*, giving charity to the poor, even as her husband was earning only $20 a week.

For Tessie as for other immigrant mothers, it was the practice of bread-giving, not breadwinning, that stood as the fundamental value of goodness. Yet the social basis of American culture lay in winning, taking, making it in a world where money was the reward for good behavior and hard work. Therein lay the roots of the conflict she seemed to face every day. To be American meant to equate independence and freedom with upward mobility, with leaving the community behind in order to become a success. She'd tolerate it for her son, not for herself.

She runs the tap water over the chicken skin, plucking feathers with a giant carving knife. "Years ago," she continues, "there was no Social Security. When a man retired or was thrown out of his job or became ill, and he was a religious man, a kosher man, he had no place to go to a hospital 'cause he didn't have money to pay. This is what we used to take in. We'd give the hospital thousands of dollars. For what did we give money? They accepted the poor people who we recommended."

She smiles. "My friends, my girlfriends, when they saw me

Tessie's naturalization paper, with the wrong eye color, 1936.

come they would run across the street because I always asked, 'Would you like to buy a theater ticket or a carfare ticket or—what else did we have—a raffle ticket?' And they didn't want to spend the money and they didn't want to give. Gussie, my sister. I went with Gussie. She'd say to me, 'Cross the street. Ida Leventhal is there.' She saw us on this side, and she went on the other."

I laugh. I can easily conjure up the image of these two barracudas storming the streets of Brooklyn. "Yeah, that's how I was appreciated."

Her glasses are splattered with water. She cleans them with a tissue. Neither her husband nor her children were thrilled by her works of charity. "Of course, I would see about their homework. And make sure they got to school on time. Mike never missed a day of school in his life. He was not a day late and never absent. One day, he said, 'Mother, it's ladies free in Dodger Stadium.' He wants to go to the Dodgers game. He'll take me out. How many times he asked me I should go with him to a game. I had other better things to do than go, for my pleasure."

She continues, her storytelling bearing a lyricism of its own. "I went in the subway. You know how the subway goes Saturday night, when people were coming home from theaters, from shows, from parties? And I had a big tin can, a *pushke*. And I would go to collect money from passengers. We were ten, twelve women in one train. With big bands on our coats, Beth El Hospital, and everybody would put in something. Put in a quarter or a dime. A dollar. It depends what. Some people make believe they're sleeping. So I go like this—shaking the can in their face. Anything for the hospital? The money—woke them up! And naturally, if the guy was with a girl, he wouldn't show the girl that he don't want to give. So he would throw in half a dollar, a quarter, whatever. We'd make quite a few hundred dollars that way."

She had other fundraising techniques, too. Once, she traveled all the way to Hoboken to pick up a couch for the *rebbitsin,* the rabbi's wife.

"There was a guy, his father was a carpenter in Kozowa, and he used to do fancy carpentry in Hoboken, the son. I knew where to go for the *landsleit.* He had a furniture factory. And he had promised the rabbi's wife a couch, but it didn't come soon enough. So what do you think I did? I took another man, a *shoiket*—that's a chicken killer—who was my father's friend. I said, 'Yosel, we're going to Hoboken.' The couch came next week."

She credits her mother's taking care of her children for her volunteer life. "I said to my mother, 'If I have a *mitzvah,* Mother,' I says, 'it's on account of you and you're going to get it, not I.'"

She thinks for a moment, making a connection between her do-goodism and her longevity. "Maybe that's why I lived so long," she says. "Because I tried to help other people. I never was fresh to my mother. No, I don't think so."

THERE ARE CERTAIN THINGS MY GRANDMOTHERS SHARE WITH me that they wouldn't dare mention to my parents. Funeral arrangements, for example, are a favorite of Pearlie's. She refers to this as her "transportation question." "Joyala, I hate to talk about this, but I have to, Joy."

It is Pearlie's ninety-third birthday. As we sit and talk, two more birthday cards are quietly slipped beneath her door. She's received fifteen cards, including one from the White House. DeeDee's husband, Elliott, heard that anyone over 90 could get a personal greeting from the Clintons, so he sent away for one on Pearl's behalf.

She launches into future plans, which basically means facing her own death. Since my mother has been preoccupied with my father's

Women relegated to the kitchen for the Passover Seder on Junius Street in Brownsville. Tessie (second from right) with sisters (from left) Rose, Gussie, Leah, and Sylvia and sister-in-law Ida.

illness, Pearlie has been feeling abandoned. More and more, she worries about her mental slipups, about her need to move to a nursing home. She has one in mind, over on Fourteenth Street.

"When I think about it, it gets me noy-vuss," she says, still haunted by images of her father and husband in nursing homes. "But this is a good place. Not fancy. I danced there many times with the Dolls. It's not too shabby. They treat the people very nice. And I might be able to get a private room with a private bath. That's important. When they get old, people get crazy and they pee and shit all over the place."

She instructs me to write down the name and phone number and address of the nursing home, Crescent Bay Hospital. "When your health is good, your spirit is good. The less you bother your family, the better."

Pearlie opens the deep wooden drawer of her desk in the living room and pulls out several gray Fannie Mae zippered bags. In them, she shows me her blue Naugahyde Home Federal Savings pouches, which contain her Social Security card, banking information, medical FHP card, and funeral papers. She shows me this, for the fifth time in as many months, because she wants to make sure someone in the family knows how to get her body to its proper burial site.

I assure her that one of us will travel back to New York with her body when the time comes. "I have the money for that," she says. "Take a free trip on me!"

She sits, silent, in the gathering dusk, then says with feeling, "Grandpa's people—they enjoyed life. They'd enjoy to its finish, too. My mother-in-law, she'd say, 'Kinderlach [little children], don't feel bad when I die. Drink a little schnapps and get together. Everybody's gotta die sometime. So, don't take it seriously. Eat and enjoy yourself!' And the family did! They'd eat herring and drink vodka and dance and carry on."

More silence. "Listen," she says, "don't feel sad if I go. God has spared me. He's been really wonderful to me. I mean it." This is the first time she's spoken of her own letting go. "You figure if you're not here anymore, you don't feel that pain." She's referring to my father's current bout with chemotherapy—his withered body, his ashen complexion, his eyes ringed with fear—and my mother's corresponding helplessness.

She changes the subject, asking after my daughter Lucy, for

whom she recently bought a doll stroller. "Oooh, I just love that doll of yours," she tells me. "She's a real *bren* [fireball]. I get all my wisdom from your little girl. From Lucy Anna."

Just the day before, Lucy and I gave Pearlie a ride home from my house. Pearlie couldn't believe that her great-granddaughter, at eighteen months, could belt out the lyrics to a song, called "Run Baby Run," by Sheryl Crow. My grandmother actually slapped her thigh in disbelief and joy. And in those sweet moments she was delighting in my baby daughter's exuberance, it occurred to me that maybe this was all the mystery we'll ever need to know—the pure joy of song, of music, flashing from one generation to the next. From one *bren* to another.

There is an injunction in the Talmud: When a man faces his Maker, he will have to account for those pleasures of life he failed to experience. From that standpoint, Pearlie will have little accounting to do, presuming the injunction applies to women, too.

❧

WHEN TESSIE AND I PLAY CARDS, I SOMETIMES FEEL LIKE A character in a David Mamet play. Our dialogue is cryptic. Clipped. Short. And yet, there is always something brewing beneath the surface.

"*Oy oy oy,*" she says, fanning the cards I deal to her from a Jumbo Index deck. I turn over a jack of diamonds. "I got trouble. You shouldn't know from it. Oh, I don't want the jack. Do you?"

"No, thank you. You may go."

"Okay, I'll go. Where to, I don't know, but I'll go."

"Okay, so go."

"I'll give you—what shall I give you? I don't care."

"Of course not. Want a five of hearts?"

"Yeah."

"You do?"

"Thank you."

"You're welcome," I say.

"What shall I give you?"

"I don't know. Better be good."

"Better be good. I have to give you something."

"Give me something. I'll take the eight. Here's the king."

"Oh, another. *Hoo-ha!*"

"*Hoo-ha?*"

"*Hoo-ha!*"

And so on.

It's nine o'clock on Wednesday night in February. Tessie and I have been playing gin for the past hour. I want to play one more hand before going to bed. But this time I've challenged her to play for the Queen of the Universe title. Whoever wins becomes Queen of the Universe.

"Of the entire universe?" she asks. "Pish-posh."

"Yes, not only this galaxy but the next galaxy as well," I say.

"You're an odd kid," she says.

"Thank you," I say.

"I have a good card for you," she says, discarding. "Here. I aim to please." She sees I don't want it. "Nah?"

I hand her a jack. "Another *yankel?* Here, take an eight."

I don't want it.

"What should I give you? A nine. Oh my. Oh my oh my oh my oh."

I pick up every card she gives me now, a technique which I use to fluster her.

"I've got time," she says. "I ain't going anyplace." She slyly looks at me, dangling a card before my face.

"That's not my card. Why do you tease me like that?" I ask.

" 'Cause I don't need it!" she says. But then she picks up another, and "That's it."

I scream.

"Stop!" she says. "People will think a murder is going on!"

I congratulate the new queen, bowing on my hands and knees. She chuckles, as if to humor me. But the entire exercise is simply a diversion from telling her about my telephone conversation with my mother, earlier in the evening.

"What did Mommy say?" she asks. I tell her that Mom's worried that my father is continuing to lose weight, down some thirty pounds now. She inhales deeply. "Well, I believe in God and I think we have a very good God," Tessie says. "I hope that he's going to listen to me. And a miracle can happen."

I thought she didn't believe in miracles. "There can be miracles—as far as health is concerned," she says. "I don't believe exactly that it happens, but it could happen."

Who's to argue? "You can't be a *chachem,*" she says, using the paradoxical Yiddish expression for someone who is either a fool or a wise person. She means a wise guy. "You can't be too smart. You got to let it be. That's for sure. You've gotta have *chachma* [wisdom]." Suddenly, my mind snaps. I imagine a chorus line of Jewish grandmothers with spatulas, singing, "You've Gotta Have *Chachma*," just like the lineup of ballplayers in the locker room who sang "You've Gotta Have Heart" in *Damn Yankees*.

I eat another slice of marble cake. "Okay, let's go," she says, seeing that I've finished.

Go where?

"*Gay shlufen*." Time for sleep. No doubt, I need it.

⌐◻⌐

OVER IN AISLE 3A, GRANDMA PEARLIE SEES THE CLEANSERS. "Get me one can of Comet," she says, directing me. I'm pushing the shopping cart. She's holding her grocery list: vegetable oil, margarine, sweet potatoes (3 pounds for $1), salmon, chicken, eggs, toilet paper. She used to clip coupons. Now, she doesn't bother.

To be 93 years old and shop for your own groceries is like living inside a bad driver's-ed film: everyone moving too fast, carts that are funky and brakeless, dodging the oncoming traffic with the ferocity of a gnat.

"With bleach?" I ask.

"Yeah, for the bathtub," she replies. She also needs baby shampoo.

"You want two-in-one tangles?" I ask.

"I don't have enough hair to tangle," she replies.

Waiting in the checkout line at the Vons Supermarket on Wilshire Boulevard and Euclid Street, she stands amidst the *National Enquirer*s, ChapStick dispenser, razors, candy, and Bic lighters. My eyes drift to the headline in the *Sun:* Gorilla Has Human Baby.

The bagger asks if she wants paper or plastic. "Double plastic," Pearlie says. She turns to me. "I'm just so glad I can do the shopping, even."

One of the fundamental distinctions between my grandmother's generation and my parents' is their sense of duty about caring for—and living with—elderly parents. Ever since Pearlie moved to Los Angeles, my mother has seen it as her job to escort Pearlie to the doctor's office. And my father has been sending a monthly check to his mother for more than forty years. But Pearlie and Tessie took it a step further and insisted that their aging parents move in with them. In some ways, they considered it an honor to be the caretaker. Tessie's mother lived with her for twelve years until her death. Pearlie moved her family in with her parents, ostensibly to care for her mother. Then, after Anna's death in 1943, Pearlie's father Sam moved into her home in Manhattan Beach for three years.

Whether it was a moral obligation or familial duty—or simply a means of seeking their parents' approval—I wonder why they were the ones who took their parents in. And now, do they secretly desire their own children to follow suit? Even if their words speak of "not being a boyden"?

"See now, I had to give up a lot for my parents," Pearlie tells me, waiting in the parking lot for the white-and-blue WISE shuttle van that will take her back to the Silvercrest. She smiles at her friends Joe and Jo, who are also waiting to be picked up. "With my mother, she had high blood pressure, terrible pains with rheumatics and arthritis. And I would take her always to the doctor. I gave up my apartment where I was and I moved in with them because my father couldn't give her the attention she needed. And it disturbed the life, married life."

How so? "Once you're married, your family's good to come and visit, but not to live with, you understand. Because a parent wants the best for the child. And when they see either the wife or the husband not being just the right way, it's a double hurt."

A double hurt? "See, my husband thought I was being used more than the other children, because I was helping my mother. There was nobody else to do it. My brother Maxie had three wives. My sister Stella was in business and she didn't have the time."

It's strange how time can soften the edges between sisters. Or how, in looking back, she's come to distill her competition with her sister into who was smarter, who was prettier, who was nicer. "My sister had a funny thing about me. She was under the impression I was the good-looking one, and she became bitter toward me," Pearlie says. "But I wasn't as bright as she was, either." Recollecting Stella now, Pearlie adds, "We thought we weren't close, but we were close."

But Moe felt gypped that Pearlie took on the responsibility of caring for her parents. "He felt there were other children in the family, too, see. He'd call me the *kaporeh heendle*. That means: Why must you be the one to have all the responsibility? Like, if something happens, you blame it on someone else. It's like the one to get the bitter end of it, the *shlub* [yokel]."

Kaporeh heendle is Yiddish for "whipping boy," the innocent victim who takes the curse, like a scapegoat. Some very Orthodox Jews on Yom Kippur will say a prayer and wave a chicken (the *heendle*) over their heads so that the chicken can take away their sins. For Pearlie, there was only one way to handle the *kaporeh heendle* label—a painful symbol of the clash between her roles as dutiful daughter and dutiful wife. "I'd laugh it off and make a joke of it," she tells me. " 'Cause I knew it hurted my mother, it hurted my father, it hurted Moe, it hurted me."

AFTER INGRATIATING MYSELF LONG ENOUGH, I FIND MYSELF peering inside Pearlie's closet. "You're gonna be amazed when you look," she says, self-critically, sliding open the door on the left side. "It's terrible, terrible."

In truth, the narrow closet with two sliding doors is a treasure trove. It's not the neatnik factor, or lack thereof, that intrigues me so much as her sense of priority, her expeditious maintenance of order. The way Pearlie squirrels things away is a testament to her remarkable creative powers. Or her desire to keep living. Her "filing system," as she calls it, includes storing towels under the couch ("that's my other closet"), shoes under a rollaway bed, capes on the back side of the chair next to her bed, coats on her bathroom door hook. There is order in her chaos.

"Your mother said to me, 'Mom, you have to throw things out,' " she says, laughing. This, I find hilarious, given my mother's pack rat nature. But Pearlie doesn't want to get rid of much, because everything seems tied to a memory she'd rather keep. "I know I don't do it, and I know I should do it. And yet I can't."

She walks back into the bedroom. "This," she says, pointing to a rack of clothes, "is my place for pants. And over here, I've got suits. Not cotton. Whadyacallit suits? Yeah. Polyester." On the closet floor, three giant cardboard boxes are brimming with her handmade sweaters.

"We're not through yet," she says, cackling. She opens the right closet door. "And these are jackets. DeeDee sends me jackets. They're very nice to wear, these here. Dresses I don't wear. And yet, I can't throw them out. I think maybe I will wear them sometime. They just hang around, ya know. But I don't wear them, because I'm often cold."

Though initially reluctant to show me her closet, Pearlie now has become a tour guide of her entire bedroom. She opens the accordionlike wooden doors of her dresser bureau—the one she and Moe bestowed on my parents in the 1950s and that came crashing down on her legs in the earthquake last year—to show me her costume jewelry.

"Wait a minute, I want you to see something else," she says, pointing to the capes my grandfather made for her, now hung up on one side of her bedroom door. And in the top drawer of her white lacquered dresser, next to her bed, she shows me a box within a box. In it, there is a gold cigarette lighter, which she hands to me. It belonged to my grandfather. The lighter is thick with the intoxicating smell of lighter fluid, which brings to mind the gleeful way Grandpa Moe would click open the lighter and puff on his cigar.

But the lighter is also replete with its own secret history—the graft, bribes, and payoffs of Moe's business life. "The unions were being formed, and you couldn't hire anybody without a union card," she explains. "And if you hired somebody they weren't union and they were on lower wage, you had to keep it under secret."

"This," she says of the lighter, which on closer inspection is engraved with the initials MS, "was given for the union people."

Like a bribe? MS was a union official? "That was the name," she says. "Morris something. I don't know his name." In other words, my grandfather ran a nonunion union shop. If that sounds like a contradiction in terms, it is. But gangster activity was pandemic in the garment industry at the time. The first choice many New York clothing manufacturers had to make, outside the high-fashion field, was whether they wanted a racketeer as a partner, a creditor, or a competitor.

"It was supposed to be a union shop," Pearlie explains, "but if he took in somebody that wasn't in the union he had these guys cover up for him, see. I remember he had one guy—his name was Phil—and he used to give that Phil so much money it used to kill me. I just couldn't see it. For nothing. And he said, 'Well, he protects me.' "

What did Phil the Protector do? "At that time," Pearlie continues, "the union took over, and if you didn't get protection from the union, they'd come in and shoot you. Or you'd walk in the street and they'd shoot you. It was that kind of time." In fact, Moe always suspected that one of his own business partners had been "knocked off," just like MS. "And that's why Grandpa had this fear about himself, that he never knew when somebody would come in and kill him. And that's why he started drinking."

She switches subjects. "Did I tell you about the time Grandpa was operated on, on his throat?" she asks. "It was during the 1940s. They told him he mustn't talk for a week. And I brought him a little notepad to write everything down. The first thing he says when I get to the hospital is, 'I love you.' And I said, 'You're not supposed to speak.' He says, 'Ah, bullshit.' " She laughs at the memory.

Beside her bed, Pearlie keeps a collection of framed photographs. There is the picture of Jerry in his Army uniform, incredibly dashing with his clear-blue eyes and superwavy hair. "Besides being handsome, he was so good," she says. "He used to call me *Mamenyu,* that was a pet name. And he was crazy about Shirley."

☜☞

IN THE SUMMER OF 1943, TESSIE AND PEARLIE, WHO WERE 41 years old, sent their sons off to the Army. Gasoline was being rationed, and Izzy convinced Tessie to store their car. "Izzy said, 'I'm not gonna drive for pleasure when my son is in the Army. Maybe they'll need that little gas we use up. It might help him make it to Japan.' "

Both Mike and Jerry wound up stationed at the University of Michigan with the Pacific Military Research Section, studying Japanese to become translators. (My father would later sign my report cards in Japanese, which embarrassed me no end.)

Pearlie, in one of her many missives to Jerry, went on a fishing expedition on behalf of Shirley: Did Jerry know any "nice Jewish boys" in his unit who might be suitable candidates for Shirley? Shirley was then a 17-year-old Brooklyn College student, starring in a production of Chekhov's *The Seagull.* Pearlie enticed him with a package of cookies and some other bait—a fetching black-and-white photograph of Shirley decked out in a candy-striped, two-piece bathing suit, à la Lana Turner. The picture sparked

Mike's interest. Whether I have my uncle Jerry or a photograph or the chocolate chip cookies to thank for my existence on earth, I'm not sure. But in any case, it was Pearlie's masterful maneuvering that brought my parents together.

"Your mother fell hook, line, and sinker," she says of my parents' first meeting after corresponding with each other. "And I liked Mike right away, too." Actually, my mother would later tell me she thought my father looked a little nerdy with his crewcut. But when they met again, and his hair had grown in and he wore his uniform, she was smitten. This was during the period that Pearlie allegedly steamed open my mother's letters.

I ask her again about it, and this time she issues a nondenial denial: "I don't know," she says, closing her closet, "unless I decided to forget about it."

She continues: "You fight for your children more than you do for yourself. I mean, you want things to be good for your children more than if it pertained to yourself. So, the fear—in case they have sex and they don't get married. The aftermath and disappointment and feelings you have, those things a mother and father feel very much. And I think the same thing with a son. It's very important for him to meet the right one. And how do you know it's the right one?"

Tessie, on the other hand, warmed to Shirley slowly. Her mother, Charna, referred to Shirley as *"lachen diggeh,"* the laughing one. And she wasn't exactly thrilled by her son's reports of

Shirley (left) on the beach at 17 in the photo Pearlie used to snare my father. Two Army buddies (right), Mike and Jerry.

Pearlie sexualizing her chicken offerings. "When Mike came back from the Army, your grandma Pearlie was smart enough to know how to keep him," Tessie tells me one morning over coffee. "She would ask him, 'Do you want hot sauce with my cold breast or cold sauce with my hot breast?' She knew how to work it. How to get him to come again. And Moe, too. He'd say to Mike and Shirley, 'Don't break the couch. I just fixed it!' Or he'd tell Mike, 'Keep your legs crossed, you son of a gun!' "

Though Tessie was not ecstatic about Shirley—she seemed too short and couldn't speak Yiddish—Izzy adored her. Ultimately, Tessie would rise to my mother's defense, too. When her sister-in-law Kayla, the neurotic, compulsive neatnik, suggested that Shirley wasn't worthy of Mike, Tessie was overheard saying, in Yiddish, "Kayla isn't worth Shirley's shit."

The in-laws continued sniffing one another out, though. Moe thought of Mike, a budding psychotherapist with a degree from City College, as a threat. Not only was Mike taking his daughter away, but Moe also worried that Mike was psychoanalyzing him, which he undoubtedly was. He referred to his future son-in-law as a *fumphiologist*. *Fumpha*, in Yiddish, means "to ridicule."

But he was also proud. Moe took Mike to his favorite tailor on Thirty-eighth Street, Manny Walker, a very fine men's clothing store. He had an account there. This is where Moe would buy suits for the salespeople who sold him goods under the table, bribing union officials to leave him alone.

"So he takes me into the store," my father tells me, one day not long after he's lost all his hair from chemotherapy, "and he says to Manny Walker, the owner of the store, 'Hey, Cockface, come over here.' So Manny says, 'Oh Moe, how are you?' 'Cockface,' he says, 'I want to introduce you to my son-in-law, Dr. Horowitz, and I want you to give him two of your best suits.' "

"Yeah," Pearlie later concurs, "he'd call people funny names all the time."

She chuckles softly. "Did your father tell you how Moe checked him out in the shower before he and Shirley were married?" In fact, he has. Countless times. Pearlie repeats the story, anyway. Moe walked in on Mike when he was showering and then walked downstairs, extending his right arm and flapping it at Pearl, as if to imitate a giant penis. My father had passed Pearlie and Moe's *schlong* test.

BEFORE DAWN BREAKS, I'M AWAKENED BY THE SOUND OF FLUT-
tering cards at the dining room table. And I notice the hallway
light is on.

Grandma Tessie is eating her favorite kosher cookies, chocolate
wafers from France—Gofred Aron Chocolat, with the Hebrew let-
tering on the box. I check out the ingredients printed on the wrapper and notice a fat content that could keep us glued to these
seats for a week.

She motions for me to take a cookie. "They're waiting for us to
buy some more," she says, meaning I should keep eating. She sips
her cup of Sanka.

There really is no point asking Tessie why she's awake, playing
solitaire. It's clear that she's obsessing, worried about my father.
The word "cancer" terrifies her. It makes her think of her mother
and the end of her life. The depth of her grief, sometimes, is so
vast that it seems to grow unmentionable over time.

Tessie isn't sure, but her mother, Charna, either had colon or
stomach cancer. But she refused surgery. "She said, 'I was born a
whole woman and I want to die a whole woman. I don't want to be
cut up.' And the family doctor said, 'It's going to be very hard.' And
she stayed with me. It was hard on me. She was in pain, and I
claim that it's hard on me? In comparison, it was nothing for me
what she went through."

She munches on the wafer cookie, remembering. "You know,
the nurse used to take maybe a pinch of rice, and cook it in a little
pot, to feed her something. She couldn't eat. And then it was on a
Friday night, I brought over the candlestick. I lit the candles, only
my mother should *bentsh licht,* make the blessing over Sabbath.
And she hardly said it. Okay, and I put it back again in the dining
room, fine. Then about eight o'clock, we got a telegram from Mike
that he's coming home from Japan.

"And I went over to Mama the first thing. I says, Mama,
Mechel *kim ta hane.* So she said, *Aleft is Gott.* Thank God. That
she couldn't finish the prayer for the candles. But this she could
say. *Aleft is Gott.* And that's all I heard. No voice anymore. That
was the last voice I heard from her. She was close to seventy.

"Sunday morning, the doctor came and he prescribed something. I don't know what, but he did something to take her out of misery. Which I don't believe a doctor would do it: a pill that would put her to sleep. That's what Gussie said. But I don't believe it was so. March 8, 1946, she died. The next week, right after the *shivah*, Mike came home on a Friday night. And the first thing, he walked in—he had a key, he always had, my children always had a key—he came in and went straight to her bedroom. 'Where's *Bubbe?*' he asks." Tessie said nothing.

She didn't have the heart to tell her son his grandmother had died.

"I think I had an almost nervous breakdown—to go wash the floor in the living room where the Jewish burial society washed my mother's body." This is a remarkable admission, one I've never heard mentioned in my family. Grandma Tessie, the stalwart, the *shtarker,* suffering from mental exhaustion?

The memory of her mother's death brings back her father's, too. "I wanted to go in to see him, to see his body. But they wouldn't let me in, the men who were washing his body and putting on the shrouds. And I said, 'Let me see him. He's still warm.' And he said, 'No, you're not supposed to drop even one tear on a dead body. You can cry but don't go near him.' The president of his organization, he said to me, 'The Jewish people don't cry. You got to accept what God does.' And he wouldn't let us in."

The Jewish people don't cry? "I mean, you don't have to. Because it depends. Not on Saturdays. Would you believe that Saturdays you're not in mourning? I used to wear black earrings after my father or my mother died. But not on Saturdays."

What about the nervous breakdown? "Mama died, she slept in the living room. When she died, the rabbi came up to see me, and the hospital bed was there. And I had called up the company that they should take out the bed. It was a hospital bed. So I could take it out. So, they put it on the floor."

They put what on the floor? "The body. The body. They took the bed out and my mother's body was on the floor of the living room. And the women washed it. They cleaned it. They put on the shrouds. I had a French curtain at the door. One woman stayed by the door, she wouldn't let in anybody. But I didn't have carpeting. I had linoleum, those rugs, like carpet. And I knew that I wash it, I see my mother laying on the floor. I didn't see her but this was in my mind.

"And I washed once. I washed twice. I felt that I was going to— I couldn't do. And I got sick. I was very sick after that. Imagine, to have her for twelve years and to see her—she died in my hands. I heard her snore—that was the last thing. And I thought, you know, she sometimes used to wet the mattress, so the nurse took a lot of newspaper and put on two linens on top. And I thought she's snoring so much, maybe she's not comfortable. And that was her last minutes. And then, when the heart became a muscle, that's when it hurts. So I put my hands under her. She was still warm, but she was dry. And she made such a noise! She was snoring, like, so loud that I was sure that people across the street could hear her. And Izzy was sleeping and the two girls were sleeping. Mike was in the Army. And I just stood there. As I held my hands under her, it stopped. That's when she passed out [on].

"Then I went over and woke up Izzy. And I said to Izzy, 'Mama snored, it was terrible. And I stood there. And now she stopped snoring.' He goes over to the bed. He puts his ear to the heart. He said, 'Mama is dead.' But he said to me, 'Don't scream. Don't scream because the children are sleeping.' And I kept quiet. I was so hardened up already. I didn't say boo until the morning. And that's how she passed out."

And what about the nervous breakdown? "I got out of it," she says. "My sisters and all, we were talking and going. I got used to it. I got used to it. I had to take care of the children. It was a responsibility. A home I had to take care of."

So why do you call it a nervous breakdown?

"I said almost."

"Okay, your almost nervous breakdown."

"Don't ask. I couldn't even think right. And if I had to go, like shopping, I didn't know what I went for, what I bought or what I did. Took me three years to come back to normal. Wasn't so easy. And then Mike came home and he was—a different—you know, we used to talk about it and all. I got it out of my system." The depth of her sadness was not just about her mother's death. It was also about watching her son leave home.

My father was just setting out to begin work on his Ph.D. in psychology at the Menninger Clinic in Topeka, Kansas. Not that Tessie upholds the values of shrinkdom. I ask her what she thinks of therapy. "It's okay," she shrugs. "If you haven't got the brains yourself, you pay for it."

Rich Noodle Pudding

I never really used a specific recipe. I just shitaron, pour it in. So I hate to give it to ya, unless I really know exactly. Plus, it's very rich. You don't want that. You do?

Okay, so you cook up your wide- or medium-sized noodles. Say, a half a pound or a pound. Drain it well. And you throw in one measure sour cream. That's one cup. You throw in about four eggs. You throw in cottage cheese. I used to take about a pint. You can take less if you want. If you want, you can take just the white of the eggs. If not, it's too much trouble, you just mix in the eggs. If you like it sweet, use three-quarters a cup of sugar; if not, half a cup. And you just mix them all up together, the cottage cheese and sour cream. The whole works.

Then you grease your pan real well and you bake it. And you bake it for about three-quarters of an hour. At 350 degrees. And you see, until it gets nice and brown. Not dark brown. Very light. You can tell.

And then you take it out—add any kind of pie topping you want to put on it. Canned strawberries or cherries or pineapple. Or cut up an apple on it. Whatever you want you can put on top. It makes it very delicious. But it's very, very rich. If it's in season, you don't even have to cook the strawberries. You can put plain strawberries on top. Or if you like, canned huckleberries on top. Or the kids love the cherries. Peaches are nice on top, too.

So, you have to take the pudding out and put on top the fruit. I used to lay it in lines. And then I'd throw the juice over it, and put it back in the oven for twenty minutes. And then it gets a nice color on it and sort of seeps into the pudding. Very rich. Yeah. It's supposed to be a secret recipe, from Helen's mother's sister-in-law. But ya know, it looks so beautiful when you soive it.

CHAPTER 8

Mensch: Honorable One

Pearlie and Moe, Mike, Shirley, and baby Steve, Brooklyn 1949;
Tessie and first grandchild, Steve, in Topeka, Kansas.

THE FABRIC OF MEMORY IS A TWISTED, IF DELICATE, WEAVE OF truth and fiction. How we remember, how we come to believe certain memories—based on family myth or the slapdash way a photograph is framed—is certainly as much a reality as the event itself.

It is often said that the very old remember best what happened from childhood, as if there is a biological loop that brings our brains back to the beginning. But I don't think so. I think the very old look to what they *need* to remember, otherwise the regrets and sorrow would crowd the mind in a paralyzing din. Always, there is longing. Mostly, it seems, for connection.

Why, in looking back on their lives, do my grandmothers mostly recall moments of sadness (though their rules of politesse dictate that they assiduously avoid such discussions) more than the pleasure and joy? Or is holding on to the pain a sort of primal reminder of that which is precious? My parents' wedding in 1947, for example, is a subject neither Tessie nor Pearlie can discuss without a sense of longing. But longing for what? For their babies to never grow up? For Tessie, it was wishing her mother were alive for such a joyous event. For Pearlie, it was the sadness of bringing her 72-year-old father from a rundown nursing home to attend the wedding. "He stayed for the ceremony and part of the supper. But he was too sick, and the nurse took him home again. When I saw him go, I just cried my eyes out."

Or when my brother Steve was born in Kansas in July 1949, you'd think Pearlie and Tessie might recall the delight of what it felt like to become a grandmother for the first time. But no. Pearlie can recount only the fight she had with my father over a gross-looking pickle in the refrigerator: She wanted to throw it out and he wanted to keep it. Tessie talks about bringing one of her famous strudels to the airport for Pearlie to take to my parents in Kansas.

So, when my aunt DeeDee offered to let me read through Grandma Pearlie's letters—thousands of them to DeeDee from the 1950s to the present—I was ecstatic. Here, while sifting through the giant, cedar-lined trunk and cardboard boxes in DeeDee's basement in Freeport, Maine, I'd finally be able to separate fact from fantasy, to transcend memory in favor of archival truths. That, at least, is what I'd hoped.

What I discovered, instead, during a giant Maine snowstorm in February 1995, was a completely different story. I came to understand that Pearlie—and here I felt like I was making the most amazing connection of all—is a gifted writer. Prodigious. Prolific. Profound. True, her grammar isn't great and her sentences run on forever. But the style is only a reflection of the breathless way she recounts the details of her life, in person. Pearlie, in other words, has always had a deep-seated need to articulate her feelings on paper, to unpack her heart.

"Writing helps me a lot," she tells me later of her letter writing, perhaps one of the greatest art forms, though sadly, it seems to have grown anachronistic. "When I feel blue, I can express myself with a pen and paper. Because what we say we forget after a while. But if it's written, it's there for you to see. You can't erase it—it's there in pen and ink—you can't.

"See, if anything, I think I'd be an author if I had a choice to do it over again." I discover that Pearlie wrote about me at the beginning of my life. Now, toward the end of hers, I'm writing about her. The synchronicity pleases me.

But there is something else, too. The letters—the tiny envelopes from the fifties, the blue aerograms of the sixties, the slightly off-kilter letters of Grandma's black Royal typewriter, the four-cent Abe Lincoln stamps, the skewed and sprawling penmanship of Pearlie's handwritten letters—offer up only part of the whole. Like any good writer, Pearlie knows instinctively to hold back. The collection of letters to her daughter reveals her attempts at protecting a child from the truth, at masking her husband's excessive drinking and failing business. The letters, in other words, document the anatomy of a cover-up, amid the precepts and unsolicited advice on bloomers, love, and marriage.

July 17, 1955

Dorothy Feldman
Youth Hospitality Tour
Bonn University, Germany
Dear DeeDee,

DeeDee if your bloomers become too messy soak it in a little lux. I know it is hard living out of a trunk so the heck with it if it isn't just so. DeeDee if it gets too hot just wear your braziere. The heck with the clincher. You went for a good time so have it.

About the boy situation. Be careful but isn't that silly to tell you. As if I don't know my darling is a lady at all times.

Of course not to talk to strangers that is passe to tell a daughter of the 1955 stage.

Love and millions of xxxxxxxx
Mom and Dad

August 3, 1955

Dorothy Feldman
Youth Hospitality Tour
Palazzo Pitti
Florence, Italy
Leader Miss Ann Harris
Dear DeeDee,

Well the Horowitzes with all the little Horowitz's arrived Saturday night and are all fine. My how they have grown. You should see the smallest one Joy how she plays Simon Says and Davey Crockett. She sings so loud you wonder where it all comes from as she is so thin. Stevie is a nice kid but has to keep himself busy all the time and Shari is a glamour gal and

goes around putting on lipstick and powder and jewelry. It is
much easier this year as they are not so destructive.

Love you trillions xxxxxxx
Mom

October 22, 1958

Miss Dorothy Feldman
Smith College
Wallace House
Northampton, Mass.

Dear DeeDee,

   Gosh, your mother is such a stinker: When it comes to
romance I want everything for My DeeDala—character,
money, and a nice guy. Am I asking too much? But then
again, I feel I have a wonderful daughter. Believe me,
DeeDee, if you should settle with Elliott I know he would
make a wonderful husband, but then again, as long as there
isn't any rushing—like you say—play the field but try and win
a good home base.

Love millions of xxxxxxxx
Mom

Nov 7, 1958

Dear DeeDee,

   Joe Kent asked me if I would do her the honor of being her
guest at her Garden club luncheon. It is supposed to have all
the oof oofs of Manhattan Beach in that club, and you know
Mrs. Golden how stiff she is. You know the one that lives next
door to Rabbi Neustein? Actually, she was very nice. Sylvia
Christenfeld is president of the club, and she was very very
nice. You know DeeDee, it's strange but sometimes you find
the person that people don't like and mark them as a stinker
you yourself by being pleasant and nice to them—they'll act
the same way with you. Well, to describe the meeting is just
like any other first. The girls eat their lunch, which is prepared by the hostess, they call the minutes and then they had
a fellow I noticed he was wearing a marriage ring on his finger
and they called him doctor. Well, he teaches biology and
botany at Brooklyn College and if you ever saw a fairy that's
him. He came in with a red plaid bow tie and a red plaid scarf

to match and he told us how to raise orchids. It took him four years to raise one plant and it produced two orchids. I also learned that in putting flowers in a container, the right way is to make sure it comes out like an L. But personally I don't like it so regimented. It reminds me of children that have to be brought up just so. At one time I thought of joining the garden club but one meeting of it was enough.

Oh yes. Do you remember Mrs. Willner who lived on Beaumont Street? At first she didn't recognize me as she said my whole personality has changed so. I got thinner and my hairdo.

Love and trillions of xxxx

Mom

Saturday November 8, 1958

DeeDee Darling,

Saw Gigi with Daddy and it is a beautiful picture. So light and gay and Leslie Caron to me is like Shari grown up. I think our Shari is so much like her. She looks like her and the expressions and mannerisms are so much alike. Daddy enjoyed it very much too. Today Daddy took me out to Hempstead to the chinks I had dinner there and got my glasses back.

This week at the gym we entertained for some old people from the old age home and you should see how their faces lit up. I felt good when I saw the pleasure they got out of it. We danced different dances Israly [sic] dances and you know that new dance the Pasadova. It is great. Tomorrow I am invited as a guest to a very swanky house here in Manhattan Beach for the garden club. You know DeeDee I just realized why you like art so. First of all, Daddy is creative in his own way in designing and I think I am a bit creative myself. Not that it always turns out good. Last night, I took apart an old frame of a hat that had a few mink tails, took off ¼" from the inside of my seam on my lace dress and made a beautiful hat. It looks almost like a dache. It reminds me of a rich girl dressed in poor clothing.

My tenants downstairs are wonderful. I found out that she is an Italian and he is Jewish but that don't make any difference as they are very nice. The dogs don't bother me at all they are very quiet.

I don't know, but by now I should be used to you being

away but it gets worse each time you go away to school and miss you so much. Gosh am I becoming a mother holder onto daughter I hope not. Love you trillions and take care of yourself dress warm.

Love and millions of xxxxxx
Mom

☜⚑☞

What do you regret most in your life?

TESSIE: Well, I didn't shoot anybody. I didn't kill anybody. I didn't hit anybody. Maybe I didn't do enough for my children, but otherwise, I don't think I would do much different. I don't envy money. I don't envy anything. But I envy education. To me, it's everything.

PEARLIE: You can't put it in the book. Turn off the tape recorder and I'll tell you.

☜⚑☞

To KVETCH OR NOT TO KVETCH: WHAT A SILLY QUESTION. Given the choice, neither of my grandmothers wants to discuss life's sorrows. It is bad form.

"You know how I like to talk: I don't like to *kvetch*," Tessie says. "No matter how I feel, I'll never show it."

"Why make other people sad if you don't have to?" Pearlie wants to know.

My grandmothers are not wallowers. In recounting their life stories, their omissions and distortions are usually about loss. That's because it's not nice to *kvetch*. This, I think, may be the pivotal reason they've lived so long. Never underestimate the value of denial. Glossing has its rewards.

But over the months we spend together, I push them to the darker times, too. Bringing alive these memories is both exhilarating and defeating. Sometimes, Tessie says, a memory should be just that—past tense, left alone in the far recesses of the heart. Pearlie talks about the blessing of time to diffuse pain. But by blunting our heartaches, time also has an odd way of enabling us to romanticize grief.

"As I get older, it's like, where have all the years gone?" Pearlie asks. "It's like my life becomes a memory instead of a reality. Talking to you about it, it becomes a realization. Your questions bring back memories that hurt me, too. I didn't think they would. It's like opening old wounds."

Heard over and over, my grandmothers' memories manage to lend a kind of stability to life, and there is little enough of that these days. Even their sad memories, retrieved at my urging, seem like an immortal part of them. They, in fact, contain such a richness of life that in their midst death itself seems impossible. Which may help explain why I keep coming back to Tessie and Pearlie: The power of memory offers a passion greater even than love. For it is in the blurring of fact and fiction, past and future, life and death, that truth can emerge.

So even when we talk about how illness and death have intersected their long lives, there is nothing morbid about it. Indeed, when they drop their stoic pretenses long enough, my grandmothers show me that it is out of the wreckage of loss that life can take its most unexpected, sometimes joyful, turns.

☞

"GRANDMA?" I SAY TO TESSIE.

"Yes, sweetheart."

"What gives you your greatest pleasure?"

"Who told you that I have great pleasure?" she asks, rhetorically. The tone in her voice suggests that I've just asked the world's dumbest question. Still, I persist. "The greatest pleasure?" she asks, mulling it over as she sips hot water from a white ceramic coffee mug. This is part of her early morning ritual, drinking hot water before figuring out what she wants for breakfast. Time had it when she'd add grapefruit juice to the hot water, but she's recently discovered that the juice irritates her throat, causing her cough to worsen. "When I heard your mother is okay. I was very scared. I hope it's true what they tell me." Her suspicion about whether she's being fully informed—or lied to—is a recurring topic.

I assure her that my parents have been straight with her about Mom's recovery. There's been no recurrence of her cancer. "Thank God," she says. "That to me is a very, very whaddyacallit—a lucky happening. But there is always in the corner of my mind to doubt.

Maybe they're not telling me the truth." From pleasure to pain in an instant, this is how most of our conversations go.

She retrieves a canister of Quaker oatmeal from the cupboard and asks me to open it, because she doesn't have the strength in her fingers to pull off the plastic ring on top. What happens when no one is here to help? "I pull and I pull, that's all."

I ask if there is a part of her life she'd like to talk about that we haven't yet discussed.

"I personally wouldn't like to talk about anything," she says, peeved at the question.

Nothing? "What's gone is gone," she says. "Maybe you remember the good things; you try to forget the bad."

She runs the tap. "What's there to talk about?" Her voice is thick with bitterness. "The way I was marrying off my children, two daughters, without a husband? What kind of wedding could I give? Just a wedding."

Remembering this period of her life, in the early 1950s, is difficult. "So I didn't make her a big wedding," she says of my aunt Cynthia. "You're not allowed. The children were allowed to hear music, but . . ." Her voice trails off. She is referring to the Jewish practice of mourning in which Orthodox Jews are expected to abstain from exhibiting pleasure in public—dancing, for example—for up to one year after a loved one has died, to honor the memory of the deceased.

The discussion is making her edgy. "I don't want to think of it. I really mean it." October 1951 was, perhaps, the saddest time in Tessie's life. At 54, Izzy, a longtime smoker and coffee lover, suffered a heart attack. For three weeks, he was lying in an oxygen tent in Jamaica Hospital. "I came upstairs to his room in the hospital and he was laying in the expensive room, the whaddyacall."

Intensive care? "Yes," she says, handing me a bowl of oatmeal. I gather the spoons. She eats straight out of the pot, like she's on a camp-out. She says it's because she's too lazy to wash another dish, but the relaxed table manners are clearly a by-product of so many years living alone. She holds the pot handle and looks down at her trembling hand.

"See, my hands are shaking?" she asks. She shrugs. "Look," she explains, "there are moments that you're happy you're alive. There are moments that you wish you weren't here. You take it as it comes. You play by ear."

*Tessie and husband Sam Weinreb,
a milkman from her shtetl.*

Reluctantly, she ventures back to the past. "Nobody could go visit him upstairs in the hospital. You stayed in the lobby. And let's say only Cynthia or I could go up. But then you come down and you tell the news, how he is. I said to him, 'So, there's a lot of people downstairs.' And he is laying in the oxygen tent, and I don't want him to use it up, the oxygen. I thought the less he'll talk to me, he'll live longer. I was afraid to use up a breath of air, of his air, to talk to him."

The doctors suggested Izzy try a new drug, cortisone, which Tessie thinks hastened his demise. Toward the end, he was given a blood transfusion, which didn't take. "When I came up, I saw this. And the doctor saw that I see that the blood doesn't circulate. It doesn't help. So they said, 'Would you please go down for a few minutes? We have to ministrate some.' I went downstairs, and Gussie was in the lobby. In the waiting room. Ten minutes later, the doctor came down to tell me that he is gone."

So you never really said good-bye? I ask. "Who says good-bye to anybody?" she responds. Another stupid question. "I brought Sam to the hospital it was nine-thirty at night. Twelve o'clock he was dead. What do you mean, say good-bye? Who would say good-bye?"

❧ ☞

I WORRY BASIC BIOLOGY, ESPECIALLY NOW THAT I HAVE A daughter. We are witnessing such dramatic evolutionary changes within the span of just three generations, like the age at which puberty begins, that I wonder whether my daughter's becoming a "woman" will occur when she's still a child. Girls are menstruating earlier and earlier; news reports suggest this could be due to hormones in cow's milk. Will that mean shorter life spans? Is my grandmothers' longevity related to late onset of menstruation or menopause?

The medical issue of women taking hormones—estrogen, in particular—during and after menopause has especially hit home. Estrogen has become the most commonly prescribed drug in the United States. But some studies are now suggesting that my mother's breast cancer might well have been caused by taking estrogen for nearly two decades. Was she a medical guinea pig? How did Tessie and Pearlie get by without taking anything in their menopausal years?

So, I decide to ask my grandmothers some questions.

Gamy Girl Questions

How did you learn about getting your period?

TESSIE: I felt very, very blue, green, yellow. I felt terrible. I was so downhearted. And my mother said, "Don't be sorry." I was already fifteen years old. And Mama was worried, too, but she wouldn't admit it. And then she says, "All right, tomorrow we're going to the doctor." But about this I didn't like the idea. So that morning I got my period. I never got it regular. You just put a *shmatte* and that's all. My mother didn't say anything.

PEARLIE: My mother slapped me across the face and said, "Now you're a lady." I didn't like it at all. It was such a mess, and oh, why do we have to go through that? And I said to her, "Why do the ladies only have it? Why do the boys get away with murder?"

I got it very late, I was about fourteen when I got my period. Mother used to give us cloths, old cloths. She used to boil them and give us old cloths, and it was so uncomfortable. You had to make, like, a sandwich in private and tie in onto something. I'd tie it into my shirt. And you used to wash them out, and oh, it was smelly and the whole damn thing. It wasn't easy, living then. It's a better life today. When people say, Oh, the good old days . . . I don't think the good old days were so good. I think today is a much better life. People live better, enjoy life better.

When did you go into menopause?

TESSIE: I was fifty-three years old already and I was still getting my periods. Maybe that's why I lived so different. I was hemorrhaging all the time. I had no flashes. No change of life, blah blah blah. I had to have a D&C twice to stop it. Mike took me in Cleveland to the blood man. He said I'm okay. I sent him pure silver cuff links, engraved. *Oy,* was he happy. I remember my mother used to get hot flashes. She opened the door and got fresh air. No jokes. I didn't know why she does it. She stopped menstruating like thirty-five or thirty-seven years old.

PEARLIE: I was about fifty-eight, fifty-nine, sixty. Yeah. I went through it like nothing. I used to get the flashes, you know. I didn't feel good. So, Grandpa took me to one of the biggest professors at Mount Sinai Hospital in New York. I don't remember his name. But he said to me, "Look, don't do anything. Just lie down, put a cold compress to your head and your chest. Take it easy. Relax." That's what I did. And I didn't have any problems at all. For how long did I do that? About two years.

Since I'm living here, I hoid this about estrogen— that it causes bad side effects. I kept on telling your mother, and she'd make nothing of it.

AS TESSIE PREPARES A DINNER OF BROILED CHICKEN AND baked potatoes, I steer the conversation back in time, trying to understand the underpinnings of her stoicism. When did she allow herself to cry, to mourn for her husband?

"By myself," she says, flatly, scrubbing a potato. "I never cried in public."

Why is that? "I don't like pity. I don't like sympathy. I want to be independent. I'd make believe it doesn't matter. But my neighbor told me many years later, she said she'd go to the incinerator with the garbage and she'd pass my door. We lived in a big building, in Jamaica. You remember? Yeah. One time, she heard me cry so terrible. She didn't know that Izzy died. I had nothing to do with tenants. So she didn't dare to come in.

"Aunt Gussie was with me all the time. She was a big help." Grandma places two potatoes beneath the dome of her stovetop potato cooker, an old aluminum contraption that looks like a miniature flying saucer, which she's jury-rigged with a hanger to replace a broken handle on top. The kitchen appliance, despite its appearance, produces the most delectable baked potato I've ever eaten.

"My landlord came for the rent in Jamaica yet. He said, 'Why don't you get married?' I said, 'If God wanted me to be married, he wouldn't have taken my husband. He could have lasted for me.' I thought my world was over when Izzy died. But then I married Sam. I just got married to get rid of everybody else."

She tells the story of her decision to remarry, only half-joking. It was Sam, the jolly fat boy she used to play with in her shtetl back home, she married. Sam, the *mensch* who counseled her children how to behave while sitting *shivah* for Izzy. Sam, the milkman, whom Izzy used to feel sorry for because he had lost his wife many years earlier. "Sam, he was five years older than I," she says. "He was never big, that's beside the point.

"Sam's sister wanted to be my sister-in-law," Tessie says, turning over the chicken in the toaster-oven. "I gained a lot of friends from their family. Gussie talked me into marrying Sam. She said under one condition: I gotta be your maid-of-honor. She used to tease me. We had fun. Plenty of times I went with her to doctors and hospitals and all. She had a goiter. She had to be operated. Her children I took care of."

But it wasn't just her sister's promptings that led her to marry Sam. Sometimes fate intervenes. Though she had worked as a cashier in her brother's store after Izzy's death, Tessie couldn't stand people's sympathy and condolences. For six months, she studied bookkeeping and was on her way for a job interview at Rokeach, the kosher-food manufacturer, but she lost her watch on the way. It was the only valued piece of jewelry Izzy had given her. She took the loss as a sign—to forget work and marry Sam, instead.

He drove a horse-and-wagon milk truck for Borden's, delivering bottles of milk from 1 A.M. until 10 A.M. Mondays was collection day. But Sam, a short, stocky man who smoked Tiparillo cigars, suffered a heart attack a year after he and Tessie were married. Then, he stopped work altogether.

Their ten-year marriage enabled them both to begin a second life together. After my aunt Cynthia was divorced, Tessie and Sam helped to raise my cousin Ned. Grandma took Ned on field trips, volunteered in his classroom, prepared his dinners, treated him as a son. And she became a stepmother to Sam's children, Sanford and Thelma. Sam and she traveled more, visiting her son and grandchildren in Ohio and then California. When the Beatles played "I Want to Hold Your Hand" live on a Sunday night *Ed Sullivan* broadcast in February 1964, I screamed for Paul in the company of Grandma Tessie and Grandpa Sam, who offered a rousing review: "*Oy.*"

"Many a times I'm sorry I remarried," she confides now. I'm not sure if she's telling me this for my benefit, seeing me as a proxy for my father. "I liked Sam. He was good and all. But I felt that I'm ignoring Izzy, like I adjusted to somebody else and it didn't mean anything, he didn't mean a thing to me. But he did! And the children. I think they must have thought to themselves how come that I forget their father."

Clearly, she didn't forget him. It is Izzy next to whom she'll be buried. "I felt guilty that I remarried," she says again. "I was ashamed."

She checks the potatoes. "Another thing, who the hell needed a man? And for what?"

❧ ☚

IT IS LATE MORNING ON A TUESDAY IN WINTER. I'VE ORDERED a car to pick me up to take me to the airport. Tessie is sitting on the armrest of her chair, peering out through the venetian blinds onto the street below. There is a soft snow flurry.

"It's *gurnisht*," she says in response to a question about her life. "*Gur* means 'a lot.' *Nisht* is 'nothing.' See, they made one word out of it."

It's hard for me to accept that she really thinks her life story is worth nothing.

"Me with my story," she says. The words are biting.

I play the cheerleader. I tell her how interesting her story is to me, how much she's lived in her lifetime.

"Oh, I lived a very long life," she agrees, watching me as I button my coat. She wears a housedress, her stockings rolled to her knees. "So what? It wasn't my idea to go through to make something, invent something or so. I was compelled to go this way. That's all. It isn't my due. It just happened."

I try again: Life just happens to everybody. But how you live it—how you choose to accept or not accept, to survive it or not—counts. Doesn't it?

"So you have a choice?" she asks. "I had to do what I had to."

There is silence. Our partings are like this: She turns morose and I look forward to getting out, to seeing my children and husband, to overcoming my sense of claustrophobia in this apartment, her depression.

"In the spring and summer," she says, staring at the street, still searching for the car service that will pick me up, "when the trees have their leaves, you can't see so much far. But now, the branches are so bare. You can see all the way for three blocks. Yeah, you can see far. Quite far."

✂ ☞

WHEN I RETURN HOME, I CALL PEARLIE TO SEE HOW SHE'S doing. "Mother, she's gotta hide her feelings," she says of Mom's worries about my father's chemotherapy ordeals. "But it's harder to hide your feelings than let them out. I'm finding that out."

Though she sounds like a therapist's dream patient, Pearlie has just quit seeing her shrink, after only three sessions. "She sorta lisps," Pearlie confides. "And she's got an accent. I don't think she's Jewish." Basically, Pearlie thought the therapist's focus on breathing exercises was just plain silly. She thinks she needs all that touchy-feely hokum about as much as she needs a hole in the head.

Still, she gets panicky at the thought of going out. Her feet are "numby," her vision isn't great, and her self-confidence is going down the tubes. "I don't know why I'm so damn nervous," she says. "I just feel *grizhy.*"

Is that Yiddish? "No, it's my own word," she says. "It means I'm not here and I'm not there. *Nishta heen* and *nishta hare.* It's sort of like mish-mash, but not quite."

What's really bothering her, she says, is her future. "I'm worried about my transportation when I die." Here we go again.

Of course, Pearlie won't need transportation when she dies. What she means is that she's worried how her body will be flown to New York for the burial. Who will go with her? How can we be sure we can trust the mortuary to get things straight? What happens if she goes when DeeDee is traveling in Europe?

Her insurance company was changed to Pafco from Guardian

Life. "These places go out of business overnight," she says. "Look at what happened to the money in Japan and England. It can all go down the sewer.

"The uncertainty of everything is bothering me." Amid her anxiety, there are also flashes of clarity that are breathtaking. "Look, Joy, I'm a realist," she continues. "I know my age. I know my health. Ya gotta figure this age is limited. So I need to deal with this. I don't want to leave the whole family in a dither—how to get rid of the old lady.

"When I'm dead—to be a burden, I hate it."

I tell her she's taking this burden cliché to demented proportions: She's a burden only when she talks about being a burden.

She continues. "You have to be blown up, so it don't smell, the body," she says, back to her current obsession. "They have to take you to whaddyacallit. Not the beauty parlor . . ."

The mortuary? "Yeah. And from here it has to be prepared for shipment. So then I'll be laying with my dear little husband, Moisheleh."

I tell her she needs to get her mind off this stuff. She needs a project. "I've got a big enough project," she says. "Me!" And all she can do is worry about my father. "When I came home from seeing your father the other day, I wanted to cry," she says. "Why does God be so mean like that? Your father has had cancer twice before already. But we can't make our own rules. Acceptance is a hard thing. Very hard. Very hard. Life can be cruel, Joyala."

She says it was the same with Grandpa Moe. He knew he was dying, but he didn't want to own up to it. "You've gotta accept," she said. "It's the hardest thing in the world. I think it's harder for Mike, because he's in his right mind. Sometimes it's better not to have a mind than to have a mind. It's so complicated, isn't it?"

What's complicated is trying to make sense of this discussion. "Who is so sure of their lives?" she wants to know. "With the earthquake, it really shook us all up. When you come down to it, we live day by day. Really."

She's sounding very philosophical. Most people don't even deal with these questions because they generate too much anxiety. Facing down the final truth. "You can't open it up," she says. "When you open up the can, it stinks!"

The next day, I make a round of phone calls and discover that Pearlie's burial arrangements, through a Los Angeles mortuary called Malinow and Silverman, are up to date. I speak to a nice fellow, named Randy, who tells me that since certain aircraft, like the DC-10s, can only "take two human remains per flight," his company usually has fewer cargo problems if he flies the bodies he's arranged for burial on the red-eye flight. He especially likes American Airlines.

As for escorting a body, Randy tells me that families usually don't do that anymore because to buy an airline ticket at the last minute is prohibitive in cost, usually $1,200. Even with the 40 percent bereavement discount rate, it's still $800.

I report all this to Grandma, who feels reassured, I think. "So, Joyala, do me a favor and take care of that cold," she says, hearing my snuffles over the phone. "Anything hot—except your husband. And kiss the children for me. I can't get over that Lucy Anna. The way she sings. Ooooh. And your boys, I'm telling ya."

Her doting. There's nothing that compares.

FRIDAY, MARCH 10, 1995. I CALL GRANDMA TESSIE TO WISH her a good *Shabbes*. She sounds awful. Her voice is weak, and she's still got that horrible frog in her throat.

"That frog wouldn't leave me," she jokes. "He moved in and he's staying put. Pretty soon I'll have to charge him rent."

I put Gus on the phone to say hello and watch him giggle at Tessie's jokes. When he hands the receiver back to me, I ask her what she's told him. "I told him he could sneak in your valise," she says, knowing he's been after me to bring him along on an upcoming visit to see her. "He could creep in there and you wouldn't even know."

She asks how Dad is. I tell her he's had his third chemotherapy session this week. The doctor switched from a mix of cisplatin and Adriamycin to ZP-16, a poison used to kill lung cancer cells. I don't tell her he's lost all his hair and continues to lose weight, appearing ghostlike now, with hollowed-out eyes and yellowing skin. The last time I saw him, he self-consciously wore a panama hat. Gus said the fedora made him look like Indiana Jones. I see my children now as shock absorbers for my parents' pain—and mine.

"Let's hope for the best," she says. "That doesn't help, either."

What, hope?

"No, my mood," she explains. She coughs uncontrollably. I can hear her unwrap the hard candy she needs to quell the cough. It takes more than a minute before she can resume speaking. "If something happens to me, it'll be from the throat. This I know. I don't function right. I don't go out. My legs don't carry me. I sit in the house all the time. All I can do is go from the kitchen to the bathroom.

"No matter what I do, no matter what I say, no matter what I think, I think only of my son. The way he tells it to me, he thinks I'm a baby. All right, he wants me not to feel bad. I make believe I believe him. And I don't. It keeps me, like, boiling inside. It's not good when someone you love is sick and you can't help. *Ach.*"

So what does she do?

"I'm a big nosher," she explains. "What do I do? I eat chocolate."

IT IS NIGHT. PEARLIE HASN'T BEEN SLEEPING WELL BECAUSE her stomach keeps backing up on her. Though her doctor has prescribed Ativan, an antianxiety drug which she calls her "happy pill," she tries not to take it regularly because she's afraid she might fall asleep and never wake up. Her eyes are puffy, her face is drawn, the color in her face has all drained away. The combination of her sleeplessness and our taped interviews is taking its toll.

"He gave me something to take, to get the shakes outta me," she says. This business of accepting one's limits is throwing Pearlie into a state of existential panic. Her preoccupation with death—or fear of the unknown—is keeping her up nights. Every night she gets into bed now, she wonders if this is it. "I figure if I kick off, it'll be hard."

Though my interviews with her are generally a diversion from such thoughts, on this night I lead her into difficult terrain—the subject of my grandfather's drinking, a verboten topic in my family. In the parlance of today's self-helpism, Pearlie would be branded an enabler. That is, she enabled my grandfather to drink.

"Exactly, exactly, exactly," she says now, more than eager to reflect on her life forty years ago through the lens of the 1990s. Back then, when Moe was acting like Jackie ("How sweet it is") Gleason and drunkenness had a tinge of debonair urbanity about it, Pearlie couldn't acknowledge the depth of her shame.

There is great conviction in her voice. "See, people will never get better unless they go for treatment," she says. "It never gets better. It's a sickness. We'd fight about it all the time. He'd get very, very angry and defensive, and ohhh. But it progressed. It got worse with Grandpa." But her letters to DeeDee offer a veiled reflection of reality.

Feb 7, 1959

Dear DeeDee

Yesterday I went to NY and brought in a few coats for Daddy from the stores which he liked very much. Boy they are getting to know my face. You know I think I missed my profession I should have been an actress. I walk in so nonchalant, but like Gleason says: One of these days!

Love and XXXXX,
Mom

April 30, 1959

Dear Dee,

Well, you know DeeDee this Thursday is our wedding anniversary so I got tickets for West Side Story. *I met Kate Lavander and she had discount tickets. I know Daddy likes good seats, so I asked for the best in the house and they gave me mesannine. They were $6.90 for the two seats.*

Gosh DeeDee, sometimes life can be so wonderful and it also can be so confusing and complicated. Life is so queer when you are a young girl you dream of your young prince someday and then when you find him you dream of a marriage and to be a good wife, then you hope to be a good mother, then when your children marry you hope to be a good mother-in-law then you hope to be a good grandma and it isn't easy. Well enough of this serious part of life.

Love you millions,
Mom

May 5, 1959

Dear DeeDee,

Why should you wait for the end of July for your engagement? If he is serious with you and you with him you are actually not pinned but engaged anyway. I can see pinning with kids at 16 or 18, but not at this stage. DeeDee, if you decide to get engaged when you come back this Summer, let him know about it. It's a shame but we women hate to admit that we are cunning but we have to be.

Try and work it out in such a way that he himself will feel that he will want to give you an engagement ring. At first I thought well maybe you shouldn't have told him that you want a diamond ring but now I am glad. I know Ethel's daughter wouldn't have got her diamond ring if she didn't let him know. Now here's a poor boy and his parents are just in mediocre circumstances and they sent her a beautiful ring. What is the idea of shlepping around without a certainty?

DeeDee are you drinking plenty of water? Don't forget as it is so important. I know you how you forget. Keep a rubber band on your hand so you don't forget.

Well anyway I think I hocked you enough a chinik, so DeeDee darling don't be mad at me for telling you my thoughts because Daddy tells me to mind my own business, but I know that if you would get engaged he would like to see Elliott make at least an effort to get a diamond ring and if they give you a birth stone can you imagine Daddy living it down?

Don't work too hard DeeDee.

I love you trillions and trillions.

Mom

Pearlie turns to me. "I remember one time, I was helping Grandpa in the shop. The night before he came home, he had gone to the horse races. While he was there, he must have made a lot of money. At the track, he used to go into the saloons there and have a drink, and they would give him tips for the horses. His lucky number was seven. But somebody watched him, and they went and bonked him on the head and he fell down and he didn't know nothing. But he was very good to the taxi drivers that used to take him there. And he always made sure they got a good tip.

"So, one of the cabbies saw him sitting there, and he got him in the car and he brought him home. And I'll never forget, Joy, when he brought him home he had a black eye. Over here was swollen, right here on his cheekbone. And I was so embarrassed. And I thought, My God, somebody from the street must have seen him—the neighbors! And they all have so much respect, gave him so much respect. How could he do something like that?

"He came in and I was just—I took my hand, and I almost broke my wrist knocking my hand on the table and saying, 'You can't do that to me! I don't deserve it! Why do you do it?' And he would just laugh. He was stewed. 'Oh, Pearlele,' he says, and always with sweet words and trying to apologize in a million ways. And then the next thing I know, he went upstairs and he fell asleep. He didn't know nothing till the next day. Next day he was like a different person.

"It's so hard to live with somebody that's like that because one day they're nice, and the next day you can't talk to them."

Waves of anger alternated with the impulse to cover up for him. "So then I felt so sorry for him. I felt so sorry. Just like a child that gets hurt, you want to kiss it and kiss the spot that hurts. He had to go to work and what was he going to tell people? After all, he has to meet the wholesalers and people where he gets his orders from. He says, 'What am I going to do?' So, I had to think of a way to cover up. I said, 'I'll tell you what. You wear my sunglasses so nobody will see the black under your eyes. And if anybody asks, you tell them you took down a bolt of lining from one of the big shelves and hit yourself in the face.' I was covering up for him, see."

Was that a good thing to do? "No, it wasn't," she replies. "I was very angry with myself for doing it. But it didn't take away the fact that I loved him." What was particularly painful was seeing her son Jerry covering up for Moe, too, trying to be his father's protector as they churned out car coats at M. Feldman & Son, Inc., on West Thirty-eighth Street. Even the phone number brings to mind shades of Willy Loman: Lackawanna 4-3893.

A car coat advertisement from Moe and Jerry's business, offering coats for $10.75.

She reels off the horror stories. How Moe began drinking at eleven in the morning, hitting the bottle of Seagram's he'd keep under his cutting table. How he'd drive drunk on trips to Maine to visit DeeDee. How he and Jerry would come home from work early because Moe would be stewed. The snowy night Jerry drove Moe home when the roads were icy and the sidewalks slippery, with Moe unable to walk and Jerry helping him but falling, too, cutting his chin and lip and needing stitches. Then, Moe—drunk as a skunk—driving him to the doctor. "I was so mad at Grandpa, I could have killed him," she says of that night. But she never learned how to drive, so she couldn't help, either.

"I was terribly terrified," she says. "I was never secure with Grandpa, you know?" The admission is so startlingly real that it seems to suck the air out of the room. And I feel all the more connected to her, thinking of how much of her energy was consumed by just holding on.

February 1960

DeeDee Dear,

I just received your special delivery back and don't worry as far as the wedding is concerned. You see we expected the mortgage money within a week or two and until that money comes through Daddy is a little tight in business and he is doing nicely and in order to fill in some orders he has to buy goods and his credit is so limited that they won't give him without cash and that is the reason we need this money. You see DeeDee, this is the money we figured on using for the wedding but by the time the wedding rolls around we will have the mortgage money so don't worry. If it was anything I certainly would let you know so don't worry, darling, everything is working out very nicely. In fact I think it is a wonderful chance for Daddy to come back. He has been so good I am keeping my fingers crossed.

Take care of yourself darling. Want to get this letter off to you. Love you trillions and trillions.

Mom

April 1960

Dear DeeDee,

Well, I just sent out the invitations that you wanted me to without the answering card.

*I have been going in every day with Daddy and it is working
out very nicely. I find it very interesting and I get a kick out of
Daddy showing me off. I know Daddy likes me sexy, so I wear
sweaters and snug skirts and it puts Daddy in a good frame of
mind and DeeDee I can't tell you how much he needs me
now. We go out to lunch or sometimes I bring lunch from
home for the two of us and it brings a man and wife in so much
closer contact. Daddy has been pretty good and I think it will
turn out all right. Of course, we had to raise a $1500.00 mort-
gage on our house as I don't think Daddy would have been able
to continue in the business without it and I hope it comes
through and I think we will be able to weather the storm.*

*DeeDee did you take that new corselet with you? I hope
you hung it up so that the steels don't bend.*

I love you millions.

xxxxxx Mom

To the outside world, they were living their high-flying years:
the summer trips to Grossinger's, dinners at Lundy's, dancing
at Delmonico's. As Pearlie baked stuffed cabbage for the sisterhood at the temple and joined a local garden club, she'd continue
writing letters to her daughters. Shirley would throw them away.
DeeDee saved hers. "If I had a good week or a good day,"
Grandma tells me, "I was so pleased and happy, I just took it for
granted that it was going to be that way—scared all the time.

"The worst thing in the world was for him to go into business
with Jerry. And Jerry really didn't want to go in, but to please his
father, he went in. Jerry spoke Japanese very well, and he wanted
to make some use of what he was taught. But Grandpa said,
'Look, what did I work for all these years? I worked to build up a
business; I want my son to have it.' That was his talk. And I was
skeptical, and I said, 'Jerry, I don't know if it's so wise for you to go
in with Daddy.' 'Cause I knew Daddy's habits, and—Jerry was so
good, he covered up for his father. Which wasn't a good thing."

As Moe's drinking escalated, the father-son business faltered.
"That business," she tells me, "was not for an American boy to go
into that kind of line. You had to be a finagler, you know. Like for
instance, you made a coat and it cost $7, so it had to sell for $12 or
$14. JCPenney was a big customer, especially in Boston. We
would supply the downstairs basement store. He knew the buyer

there. So he had to give that buyer a good buy, otherwise they wouldn't do business with him. Grandpa didn't have a solid trade name or anything like that."

It was a constant source of strain, trying to get away with selling inferior goods. "He'd have to bullshit the buyer, saying, 'Sell it in the basement. The material is good. The lining is good.' But if you put on the coat, he didn't use enough material. So the coats would stay open like that." She gestures with her hands, showing a wide expanse between her fingers.

May 1960

Dear DeeDee,

Everything is working out very nicely here. Since I have been going in with Daddy he is much steadier, but DeeDee, to be truthful, I feel it very hard but I wouldn't dare to tell Daddy. You see it is terribly hard to work and keep a home going nice at the same time and I am just finding that out. Sometimes when I go to the gym on my way home I do my shopping for the house and I have been taking lunch for Daddy, and as I found in the beginning he took me to lunch and I was eating way too much and I couldn't watch my calories. And that is the same with Daddy and this way he eats what is good for him and I make him get off his feet and rest awhile and he seems to like it so far but in the morning I have to get up earlier than Daddy as I have to wash the dishes away after breakfast, have lunch packed and then I also have to look nicely dressed, because buyers come in and then I go to the bank for Daddy and you know it is a different kind of respect when you look presentable. And believe me, DeeDee, I keep going all day. I clear all the files for Daddy—they sure were in a jumble—answer the phone, clean the showroom and cutting room, hang coats, take them off. Help Daddy at the cutting table and Daddy is working hard but he seems to be different now. He is better since Jerry isn't there and I think it is because not so much money is being drawn from the business but one thing I know he insists that I go to the gym once or twice a week, but when I do I see he reacts a lot like when Jerry used to be there and I know how important it is for me to be there with him. And so I am and you know Daddy. Sometimes, if I don't do one thing, he objects and starts to yell so I say, "Okay, boss, I am leaving." So he gets scared and changes his tone and we laugh it all off, but again, Dee Dee, if he is a good boy I just don't care how hard I work. It is better than the other way with the aggravation.

Take good care of yourself darling and try not to kill your-self working so hard as you have to make a very pretty bride.

Love you trillions and trillions. xxxxxxxx

Mom

May 14, 1962

Dear DeeDee,

Helen said the picture of the man that was large at top with the little thin legs, well, she said she thought you had Daddy in mind.* I don't want to go into too many details but maybe she wasn't altogether wrong. Daddy wants to be a big man but in reality he is only a little man and I think maybe that's where all his difficulties lie.

Elliott looked so good and he looked so happy. I think get-ting his EdD was a big load off his mind. Take care of your-selves, darlings. You left your little gray sweater in my house.

xxxxxx
Mom

Jan 30, 1962

Dear DeeDee,

Things are about the same here. Jerry, Helen and the chil-dren were over the house last Sunday for dinner and every-thing is just fine. Again.

We may get a big order on the skirts, but nothing is defi-nite. They wanted to know if we could handle it at the same price and they expect a big order if they decide on it. I hope so as the additional business would help.

I wish Daddy could stick to his diet, but it isn't that he eats so much if he would only not drink the scotch. You should see Nat showed Daddy he had a glass full of scotch and he has it

---

*Inspired by James Joyce's *Portrait of the Artist as a Young Man* in college, DeeDee made a woodcut of Daedalus holding his son Icarus, who flew into the sun on wings of wax. In fact, the portrait of Daedalus resembles her father, though DeeDee says she had no idea she was drawing her father at the time. The irony of having depicted the father holding the dead son who tried to please him is not lost on DeeDee: The woodcut presaged the actual event by some twenty years.

filled with Coca-Cola and whiskey, and he takes nips of it.
What can one do with these men? They are like little boys
that don't want to grow up.

Love and millions of xxxxxxxxxxxxxx
Mom

⊲⊟⊳

AS SHE RECOUNTS THIS PERIOD OF HER LIFE—AND CONTRARY
to the current outpouring of codependency literature—what grips
me when Pearlie speaks about Moe's alcoholism is a simple fact:
how much she loved him. It is not just her steadfast loyalty, her
unconditional love for her husband. More, I think, there is a certain nobility in her devotion. Divorce in those days was unthink-
able. And women were expected to define themselves through
their husbands and children. It is little wonder that my grandmother would cling to any shards of goodness—her children and
my grandfather on his better days—she could grasp.

There is not a trace of victimhood in her story, only affection for
a man who tried to be more than he was. The fact is, she stayed
with him. "Oh yeah," she says. "I would never leave him. No matter what."

She clears her throat. "My whole life revolved around him. I
think today, it's a different kind of world. Women today do what's
right for themselves. They love their families. But I think they do
it in such a way that makes them happy. To work out their lives in
a good way."

She laughs, thinking of herself back then. "No matter how
angry I'd be, sometimes I'd have to laugh. We never got to the
point where he ever hit me or anything like that. I would want to
do that to him."

Really? "Yeah, yeah," she says, laughing softly. There is a long
silence. She fidgets with a piece of yarn on the afghan covering
her recliner chair, reconsidering her words—her anger, especially.
It is as if she's opened a Pandora's box by discussing my grandfather's drinking, and she wants to shut it quickly. She counters
what she's said with memories of Moe's generosity, how good he
was to her, how he'd give her anything she wanted, how he'd
always bring her his winnings from the track.

"And I'd like to face people with the idea that we were a nice

family," she says. "I couldn't bear to think that anybody would
think that we weren't a nice family."

Pearlie rises and walks to the kitchen, pouring herself a glass of
water from the plastic pitcher she keeps for easy access. To get
away from my grandfather and his endless excuses, she decided to
begin work as a salesgirl at Martin's department store. Since she
felt unappreciated working for Moe and didn't want to sit at a
typewriter all day, she took a job in Brooklyn, downtown on Fulton
Street. She was 67 years old when she resumed her working life. It
made her feel like she was just coming into her own.

"I always liked to keep myself active, my mind going," she
explains. "I feel it's like a motor. If you stop it, it gets decayed on
you." Plus she loved being with people. "Martin's carried only better merchandise," she remembers. "Wonderful suits. Imported
knit suits from Italy, France. And I was in the better department
there—the higher-priced department. They would have these knit
suits, three-piece outfits. A dress and a jacket and pants to go with
it, and a blouse. You'd get a whole outfit."

She continues: "I was working in the large sizes," she says, "and I'd
pick out all the dresses for the women. They would be so ashamed
to get undressed, but they never were ashamed with me, because I
always covered up and gave them pep talks. I'd say, 'The body isn't all,
and you have a nice disposition. You have a nice face. That's
important. And you have a nice way with people.' I didn't make them
feel that their fatness was their whole life. Instead, they thought there
was another part of their body that was good and fine—their mind.
I always tried to make them feel good.

"So they'd come in and only ask for me. And the manager would
be so angry because we'd get commission on these sales. So she
tried to uphold the other salesgirls for the customers."

She smiles to herself. "I liked working there. I was considered a
mensch. Whatever I did, they liked me. And then when Grandpa
started getting sick, I stopped."

❧ ☞

HERE IS MY JOURNAL ENTRY FOR SUNDAY, MARCH 19, 1995:
Visited Mom and Dad yesterday. He was working in the garden
when we arrived. Dirt on his fingertips, showing off his beautiful
pink azaleas. The yellow daisies, potted and treelike now. It made

me happy to see he's regained enough strength to be puttering outside. His courage and Mom's—where does it come from?

But much of this is part of the Things Will Get Better Show, our perverse dance in defiance of death. I'm not sure why we have to play this particular charade, but we do. Dad, looking wan and exhausted, even came to the Boy's Club for Trevy's basketball game Friday night, against Mom's orders. Trevy scored a three-pointer—swish. Brock, Dad, and I cheered like wild, and the Cheshire cat smile that crept across Trev's face as he looked our way made life seem just about perfect for a flash second.

Mom is, I think, in shock. "Look, things are bad now," she tells me. "But they'll be over and he'll feel better. I really do believe that." I want to scream: *Who are you kidding?!* She thinks the chemo, which has zapped all his energy, is going to work? That his current cadaverous look is temporary? I want to shake her, but I know that would be like trying to wake her from a bad dream that isn't really a dream.

On Saturday, I stopped by to visit with Pearlie. We were going to take a walk, but the wind was starting to kick up, so we made it halfway around the block and came back.

Bought myself three books: *Everyone's Guide to Cancer Therapy* (revised second edition), *How We Die: Reflections of Life's Final Chapter* (by the Yale doc Sherwin Nuland), and *For Those Who Can't Believe* (by Rabbi Harold Shulweis, who I interviewed several years ago and admired). And for Dad, *Remarkable Recoveries.* Plus something he asked for, called *The Intelligent Eye: Learning to Think by Looking at Art* by David Perkins.

I also called Tessie. Right now, it feels like everything's out of order. She prays for the natural order of life: Parents die before their children. It is a simple plea.

"I spoke to God many a time," she tells me, "and I said, 'If you need someone up there, let me go before my son.' "

The Horowitz family in Cleveland, 1957.

"Ya Gotta Be Crazy" Gefilte Fish

❦

It's a good recipe, believe me. But ya gotta be crazy to do it. And another thing, I still got that wooden bowl. And the knife for it. But if you got half a brain, you get ready-made and it's good. In a jar. And it's clean.

But, okay, I'll give you the recipe. We worked on it together, Bobbie and me, don't ask. We did it little by little.

First, you need a deep wooden bowl, special for chopping fish or meat or whatever. You can grind the fish, like with a meat grinder. Years ago, there was no such thing to buy ready-made ground meat. But it tastes better when it's chopped. You can use a wooden board, but it'll spritz all over.

If there's one crazy person to do this recipe, I'll give them a medal.

6 pounds fish	Freshly ground pepper
(whitefish, pike, carp)	½ teaspoon sugar
3 eggs	3 tablespoons matzo meal
6 large onions	¾ cup cold water
2 quarts water	2 large sliced carrots (optional)
4 teaspoons kosher salt	

Wash and fillet the fish, reserving the head, skin, and bones. Combine the head, bones, and three sliced onions with water, two teaspoons salt, and pepper. Bring to a boil while preparing fish. Let simmer until fish is ready to be added to the pot.

Chop or grind the fish with three onions. Add eggs, salt, pepper, sugar, matzo meal, and cold water. Chop very fine. Moisten hands with water and shape into patties. Place in boiling fish stock. Be sure that each layer of patties is covered with water before placing the next layer into the stock. If necessary, add more water to cover fish. Cover pot and bring to a boil. Lower flame and cook for two hours. (Lid should not be tightly closed during this period.)

Fish must be cool before it is removed from pot. Strain the liquid into a dish. Pour liquid into a jar. Refrigerate stock to jell. Serve fish with jellied stock, if desired. When you be here next time, I'll give the pot and the bowl and the chopper. Whatever you like. Oooh boy, I wish I could get rid of it while I'm alive.

CHAPTER 9

Shvartzehs and *Faygelehs*: Blacks and Fairies

Pearlie dancing with my husband,
Brock Walsh, at our wedding.

SOMETIMES I WONDER IF MY GRANDMOTHERS ARE, IN FACT,
my guardian angels.

It sounds deluded, angels with Brooklyn accents and varicose
veins and puffy ankles. But that's the point, really. Each wrinkle,
each new juncture of decrepitude, is like a badge of honor. By
going the distance, my grandmothers have earned their wings.

Optimists with no illusions, they hint of their origins in unsus-
pecting ways. Take, for example, the time right after my mother's
surgery for breast cancer. Aunt DeeDee offered to take Pearlie
back to Maine for a little R and R, but Pearlie wouldn't budge. "I
wouldn't be happy," she told me. Meaning she wanted to stay to
protect my mother? "Yeah, isn't that funny?

"What am I doing? I'm just a pain in the ass to her, really. But I
feel without me, things will not be good. Isn't that a funny feeling?"

Tessie, too, offers celestial cues. When my daughter Lucy was
taking her first baby steps, Grandma took great delight in watching her great-granddaughter crash on her bottom. This was not a

streak of sadism but a show of faith. Just as Lucy would pick herself up, Tessie repeated the saying she heard from Uncle Sam
from Bayonne: When a baby stumbles, the angels put their arms
out to cushion the fall. As for her own divine beginnings, I
recently asked Tessie how she'd be celebrating her birthday. "I
wasn't born," she replied, obliquely. "I was issued."

That being said, it makes it all the more insane to rationalize
the presence of angels in one's life when they aren't all goodness
and light. Because while my angels may look like Mother Teresa,
they sound more like Archie Bunker. This is a problem. Or, as
Tessie likes to put it, "Whatever."

⊰▌⊱

BEING THE DAUGHTER OF A SHRINK, I'VE ALWAYS HAD A RATHER
abnormal stake in appearing Normal, with a capital N. Never mind
that I was a strange kid, spending hours in the living room studying
my father's medical textbook with its freakish photographs of
women with goiters. Or that I realized I had found a soul mate in
my best friend Amy when we confided our mutual obsessive-
compulsive behaviors, furtively clicking our bedroom lights on and
off a specified number of times at night. Nervies, we called them.

And yet, having been given the name Joy ("Soul of Joy" is the
Hebrew translation), I felt a certain pressure to sprinkle pleasure
everywhere I went, like fairy dust. To be normal and happy—isn't
this an inherent contradiction? Aren't misery, jealousy, and rivalry
the true hallmarks of the normal human condition?

In the context of my grandmothers, what's normal takes on an
embarrassing layer of political incorrectness. Tessie can be ven-
omous in her repudiation of those who she presumes find her unde-
sirable—non-Jews, especially, and blacks, in particular, whom she
refers to as *shvartzehs*. Pearlie's pronouncements about what is not
normal often revolve around homosexuals, otherwise referred to as
"fairies," or *faygelehs* (fags).

For me to confront these racist and homophobic leanings is not
only unpleasant but painful. But if I can figure out the core of
their tendentious ways, maybe I can begin to understand the limits of being normal.

Let's not kid ourselves. Mine *is* a normal American family. We
have our fair share of alcoholism, manic depression, suicide, and

Alzheimer's disease. Maybe more than our fair share of cancer. Divorce and intermarriage are less common. When it comes to the desire to avoid emotional imbroglios, the difficulty expressing feelings, the secrets bottled up but ready to spill out, my family is as regular as could be. But is it really normal to be prejudiced?

My grandmothers' particular brand of prejudice—normal for their time—makes me cringe. I don't mean to sound smugly self-righteous, but I can't help myself. Having been born the year before *Brown v. Board of Education* (which Clarence Thomas now wants to dismantle) and having come of age during the glow of the civil rights movement, maybe I'm overly sensitive to their language. But for two people who have experienced discrimination of another kind—anti-Semitism—you'd think they'd be extra sensitive to *any* form of hate. Fear, though, doesn't work that way. Sometimes, racism and tribalism can seem like interchangeable parts of a whole.

Or are some words not as loaded as I think? Maybe it's as simple as this: My grandmothers are a product of their time much as I'm a product of mine. And before you know it, their time will be over. Mine, too. Just as they grow despondent over the fact that half of all American Jews intermarry, so do I worry about the impact of affirmative action coming unhinged. I'd *like* to believe this to be a generational issue that may, in fact, improve over time. But the war in Bosnia and the rise of ethnic cleansing, the racial divide in America and the widening militia movement, cast serious doubt on this eventuality. Tolerance, if anything, seems on the wane.

I used to argue with Tessie and Pearlie, back when I was a student at Radcliffe College in the 1970s and I'd stay with them for Thanksgiving vacations. I remember my fights with Tessie, whenever she'd use the word *shvartzeh,* which I took to be the Yiddish equivalent of "nigger."

"Grandma, don't say that!" I'd say, in disgust.

"Why, what's wrong?" she'd reply, predictably. "*Shvartz* means black." In fact, the word *shvartz* does derive from the German word *schwarz,* meaning "black." But the way in which it's been used over the years, as a sort of cryptonym for black employees, is not unlike the way Jews use the word *faygeleh,* which, according to Leo Rosten's *The Joys of Yiddish,* is "a discreet way of describing a homosexual—especially where they might be overheard." Indeed, both words are offensive.

But the truth for Tessie, and for others of her generation, is that *shvartzeh* is really code for something else: a growing sense of encroachment. Her once predominantly Jewish neighborhood isn't so Jewish anymore. The faces here are Pakistani, Indian, Haitian. And the light-colored stone of her neighborhood synagogue, Young Israel of Briarwood, which is steps away from her apartment, is covered with gang graffiti. What *shvartzeh* really means is *other*. It means, beyond her control. It means dependency.

And these days, it mostly means Lucy, her home attendant. No one sees, talks to, or listens to my grandmother more. Together, they offer a sort of daily seminar in getting along: tolerance, with an edge. It seems the best we can hope for.

On a drizzly spring morning, Lucy puts the vacuum cleaner away in the hallway. Then, as she does most mornings when she's completed some light housekeeping, she pours herself a soda and takes a seat at the dining room table, covered with cloth. Tessie holds court from her recliner chair, discussing the origins of antipathy and her fatalism about the future, based on Americans' not appreciating what they have.

Simply put, she says, the melting pot is too squished. "I say I hope it will never happen in this country. But in another fifty or one hundred years, there will be a revolution in this country. You and I won't be here anymore. Maybe even earlier. There are too many different people in this country."

But America has always stood for being a land of diversity, I say. "You know there were one hundred and seventy-six million people altogether when I came here," she says. "Now there are three hundred million, who knows how many? We have so many people, and it's gettin' so much, they'll have to make a revolution."

Lucy nods. "Let's say she's from Haiti," Tessie continues, pointing to Lucy. "I'm from Europe. Strange people, you don't expect them to like each other. They like their own. That's how you start to hate the others."

Because you don't know each other?

"That's it," says Tessie.

"She's got experience," Lucy says with admiration. "That's why I always listen carefully. She's got a lot." A mutual respect. A mutual distrust, too.

So, beyond the words there is the reality: a new friendship between two unlikely women. Lucy, with her gold-capped teeth and braided cornrows and ankle bracelet. And Tessie, with her false teeth and hair-sprayed locks and swollen ankles. Between them is a bond that is sure and true. Even the prejudice is a sort of rock of reliability in an uncertain world.

"She make me feel good," Lucy says of Tessie. "She strong."

"Without my professor," Tessie says of Lucy when she's out of earshot, "I wouldn't get out of bed." Before Lucy's arrival each day, my grandmother must get up to wipe off the sink counter and clean her dishes. Lucy is not permitted to touch them. Like me, she has nonkosher cooties.

☙❧

FOR PEARLIE, THE PARAMETERS OF PREJUDICE HAVE MORE TO do with her homegrown assertions about happiness.

JOY: Are you a person who has prejudices?

PEARL: No.

JOY: None at all?

PEARL: No. I have no prejudices. I can't see black or white hateful of each other. I do think that it's easier, though, for people to marry, like, if they're black, to get a black person. For them, it's easier to get along. Although I predict that later on in years to come, it won't make any difference. I see it coming now very much.

JOY: We recently talked about people who are gay, and you told me you think it's more hurtful to the parents than to the person who's gay. What did you mean?

PEARL: You want your child to be so ideal. The proper thing. And do the proper thing and be the proper thing. You want them—you don't want your child to be a lesbian or a . . .

JOY: Homosexual?

PEARL: Yeah, right, a fairy. I remember I read *The Well of Loneliness* years and years ago when I was a young girl. The woman never got married and there was a lady with a man's feelings. I felt so sorry for her when I read that book. I cried and cried. I said, How could a person live like that? She didn't want anybody to know and she tried to hide her feelings. Most of them are really—

very few are happy. Although I heard this producer that
is a millionaire they had on TV the other day. He
openly says that he's a whatchamacallit.

JOY: You can't even say the word?

PEARL: Right. I don't know. Maybe I'm not right, but that's
the way I feel. Or this tennis player. Look how she has
to pay for the fact that she's . . .

JOY: Martina?

PEARL: Yeah.

JOY: What do you mean, "Look how she has to pay"? She's
done extremely well. She's amazing. She's changed the
whole game of women's tennis.

PEARL: Yeah, she's done well, but she's not happy. I feel she's
not happy. They're always hiding something. They're
hiding under a cloak, like.

JOY: You're not making any sense. People who are gay are not
happy because they're hiding their sexuality, but when
they come out, then you think it's wrong? So you think
it's bad when they're hiding and bad when they come
out?

PEARL: No, I don't object to them. I say it's wrong for them to
be bringing children into this world. They have to have
a baby with a man, but when they deny it, they're trying
to hide away from it. It's not right. It's against nature.

JOY: Scientists now are saying that homosexuality may be
biological: It's not like you have a choice—either you're
born that way or not.

PEARL: I don't believe that's true. I really don't believe it's
true. I'm from the old-fashioned people that believe
that you should stick to your own. Stick to what you're
born with.

JOY: Well, if you stick to your own, then you're going to be
homosexual, right?

PEARL: I don't mean that. I mean stick to what has been. I
don't believe in these . . . because it never works out
right.

JOY: What do you mean, "It never works out right"? There are
some gay people that fall in love and they stay together
for years.

PEARL: That I don't understand.

JOY: What's to understand?

PEARL: I can't see it. I can't see it.

JOY: Ever?

PEARL: Ever. I can't see it. I think it's a poor relationship. You're going against standards. You're fighting, you're fighting, you're always fighting. You're fighting yourself, you're fighting the world. I mean, all these people, look how hard it is for them.

JOY: But some people feel like it's harder for them that they're fighting not to be themselves by pretending to be something they're not.

PEARL: Well, I think it's up to them. I think that's the way they choose to live. But I don't think it's the right way. They're always trying to bury their feelings. I don't approve of it. I'll tell you the fact. I don't approve of it. To me, it's all a mess.

JOY: What's all a mess?

PEARL: The whole thing is wrong to me. I can't see it. I think it's something that you get into your mind and your body, and you build up around it, and you become that way. It's just not normal.

JOY: So you are prejudiced.

PEARL: I think I must be. I don't like to admit it. I could be wrong in this, but that's the way I feel.

Room for doubt. In a rational world, that's a start.

I'M GETTING READY TO LEAVE FOR MANHATTAN ON A BRIGHT spring morning.

"The jacket is too big on you," Tessie says, zapping on her TV to watch her soap opera. She handles her remote control with the authority of a Wild West sharpshooter.

"It's supposed to be sort of boxy," I tell her, updating her on fashion trends.

"Yeah, but . . ." Tessie stops, midsentence. She can't help herself. "But the shoulders are not supposed to hang down." She looks exasperated, pressing the mute button on her remote control. "This is a size for me, not for you."

I laugh. I've come to see her nudging as a sort of plaint of loneliness. It's her way of getting in her last licks, her riffs on love that
are most common just as I'm about to say good-bye. "I think that
I'm easy to criticize," she says, half-apologizing.
    "You mean you criticize people easily?"
    "Yeah."
    "You got it from your mother," I suggest.
    "My mother was like that," she agrees.
    "I wish she taught you how to be nice to yourself."
    "I am. When I'm hungry, I eat." I crack up. She thinks for a
moment. About how the critical gene moves onto the next generation. "I must have been very critical to my children. I demanded
the best, and it wasn't so easy." To me, she seems affectionate.
    "Am I?" she asks. "I don't know that I'm affectionate. I like to
do favors. I don't like to, like, cuddle with somebody." Perhaps, it
is precisely because she is constitutionally incapable of doing so
that she advises me to compliment my children more.
    "I know it makes them feel good. But I couldn't. Even though I
know it, I couldn't do it. I was very proud of them. Let's say my sister would come in. I'd show her Mechel's report card or Cynthia's
report card. I had all their books, their yearbooks. All their medals,
the little Arista pins. All their little papers." She pauses, pondering
how holding on to her children's mementos is a poor substitute for
holding on to them, physically. "It's not necessary," she says, of
saving these keepsakes. "They should have been thrown out a million years ago."
    But there is something that deeply moves me about my grand-
mother's filing system, especially when she retrieves a piece of my
past. Thinking about how she is at once affectionate and with-
holding, I ask why, exactly, she didn't come to my wedding. It is a
topic we usually sidestep.
    "I couldn't afford it, to begin with," she says, dodging the point.
I tell her that's ridiculous. "I figured you love him? Take him and
marry him. You wrote me a beautiful letter."
    "I did?"
    "And how." She walks into her bedroom to find it for me.
    When I first met Brock in the fall of 1973, I fell in love instantly.
His blue eyes, his dimples, his soccer gams, his wild red hair that
he wore in an Irish Afro he called a "salad." He claimed to have
looked me up when he visited Los Angeles that summer but mis-

spelled my last name, thinking it was Harawitz. Was it possible that a WASP from Poughkeepsie could be so unfamiliar with such a Jewish-sounding name? I was intrigued.

Then I heard him sing, and I was a goner. In those days, he used to perform with a band at Passim's in Harvard Square, playing acoustic guitar and crooning Dylan's "Just Like a Woman" or his own song, "The Music Box." When I overheard him practicing in one of the music rooms at Adams House one day, I drifted in and liked what I saw: this adorable guy pounding at the keys and singing at the top of his lungs, his eyes closed, with total joy and abandon. He wore corduroys and a sweater vest and his shirt-sleeves were rolled up. I'd never seen anything so beautiful in my life. I found myself projecting that image thirty years into the future. Even at 19, I knew this was the man I'd marry.

After graduating in 1975, we moved to Los Angeles and lived together in a funky Spanish bungalow in the Hollywood Hills. We thought it palatial. I began working as a copy girl and then wrote sports for the *Los Angeles Herald-Examiner,* the now defunct Hearst daily. Brock got a gig playing rhythm guitar and singing backup vocals for Andrew Gold and Linda Ronstadt, who was then in her cutoffs and Cub Scouts uniform heyday. We were engaged at Hussong's Cantina, a Mexican bar where Brock gave me a ring—a cigar band, the perfect anti-Establishment statement for hippies like us.

Just a week before our wedding in 1977 at the Hotel Bel-Air— we had swans, a string quartet, Linda Ronstadt singing "Doo Ron Ron," a lineup of hora dancers snaking around the room with Brock and me hoisted in the air on chairs, plus our first dance to "Straighten Up and Fly Right" by our friends, the Cheese and Crackers Orchestra—Mom blurted out she wasn't happy that Brock wasn't Jewish. I was infuriated: Wasn't it a tad late for her to be making an issue of this? In truth, she was only expressing the unstated feelings simmering from both sets of our parents. Brock's family wasn't thrilled that I wasn't Christian, either.

Grandma Pearlie, though, couldn't have been more embracing. Widowed just a month before, she led off our wedding processional. "I was so happy you found a man you loved," she told me later. "I couldn't do anything about Grandpa. He was gone. So, I had to live through another era of watching my grandchildren getting into higher fields and accomplishing what they wanted and

meeting nice boys or girls and getting married. That was the next
phase of my life, like a period connecting my first life with my second life.

"When you are nice to people, you are always nice to yourself.
You should remember that."

Niceness wasn't the issue for Grandma Tessie. She had moral
standards to uphold. Three years before, a precedent had been set
when my brother, Steve, married his college sweetheart, who is
not Jewish. Tessie was a no-show at their wedding. She would not
let her feelings for my brother get in the way of her rules about intermarriage. If Steve's wife, Debby, wouldn't convert, Tessie wouldn't
budge.

Still, I was haunted by her absence at my own wedding and
angered at her callousness. Just as on occasions when she'd refuse
to sit at the dinner table with my family—a sign of her disapproval
of our nonkosher practices—I took her rejection personally and
came to resent her Old World views. Couldn't she allow her love
for me to outweigh her religious principles? Wasn't it clear that
Brock and I would stay together forever?

Though she would allow Brock to call her Grandma and confided that she even liked him, she'd offer her blessings only if he
converted to Judaism. But to put him to a test—if he cared for me
enough he'd adopt my religion as his own—seemed like a loveless
proposition, a silly testament to another era. Another sensibility. At
the time, he and I shared the cynical, if historically accurate, view
that religion primarily serves to perpetuate war and divisiveness.
How could I ask him to embrace a set of guiding principles that
suggested that I was Chosen and he was not, because of blood-
lines?

Now, after rummaging through a desk drawer, she hands me a
typewritten letter on *Herald-Examiner* stationery. I'm stunned and
flattered that she knows exactly where to recover a piece of our
mutual history. Then, I cringe at the sight of my signature with the
lowercase *j*, an affectation, à la e. e. cummings, of the 1970s.

December 2, 1975

Dear Grandma,

I hear you're heading out this way in a few weeks. Hooray!
It will be terrific seeing you again, only this time in Califor-
nia. Your visit will mark a reconciliation of sorts. Not that you

approve of your grandson marrying a non-Jew, but that you've
come to accept Steve and Debby's marriage as a reality to be
dealt with as best you can. That means a lot to me.

I'll always respect your values just as I hope you'll respect
mine. I don't expect you to agree with what I believe, but it is
important to me that you at least open your heart and try to
understand how I feel. It's very hard for me to describe my
feelings now, because I know that you disapprove of my being
with Brock since he's not Jewish. That makes it impossible for
me to share with you my excitement about our relationship.
And that saddens me, too. Instead of being open with you, I
feel that I must hide my true feelings—that I love him and
want to spend the rest of my life with him. I don't expect you
to greet him with open arms, but I do at least hope you are
aware of how strongly I feel about him. I love you, Granny. I
only hope you'll try to understand a little of what I've written.

joy

"Look," she says to me as I finish reading the letter. "I love him.
He's a doll. He's wonderful. So, I accept. Forget about it." In the
span of twenty years, a heart can be pried open. I think of Tessie
being escorted by Brock on a turbulent flight back east, their
plane precariously circling New York during a blizzard as they
played gin rummy and giddily promised to one day run away
together. This is when he became her "lovah boy."

"Besides," she adds, "your children are Jewish to begin with."

According to Grandma Tessie's logic, which follows the ancient
laws of matrilineal descent, the children of a Jewish mother are
automatically Jewish, whereas the children of a Jewish father are
not. "The mother carries the child," she says. "It is through the
mother that a child comes into the world."

Despite recent changes dictated by Reform rabbis, who have
upheld the children of Jewish fathers to be Jews in order to
accommodate the growing number of intermarried couples, Tessie
dismisses such proclamations as heresy. In other words, even
though my brother's children studied the Torah and were bar and
bas mitzvahed, she refuses to acknowledge them as Jews. Her
mind is as closed on this as her attitude about *shvartzehs*, the us-
and-them distinctions taking on a life of their own.

The underside of love is not a pretty picture.

And my marriage? "The first shock is terrible, but you get used to it," she says. "The truth is, I was very heartbroken. But even my own child, I couldn't control, especially my grandchild? I have no right to even criticize."

"Look," she adds. "A sore heals, but it leaves a scar." She refolds the letter and then cranks up the volume with the remote control button. "My *Young and Restless* are gonna die," she says.

"They are?"

"If I don't watch 'em."

Remarkable Challah

⊰⊱

It's really no recipe: Just throw in. Let's say three, four eggs. You got a lot of challah from that. And I'd put in boiled water to dilute the yeast. Two packages of yeast in, say, a half cup of water or so. And flour. First you put the flour. Just put in a lot of flour. At least three cups or more, maybe. No, four. Four is better. So you leave the yeast to dilute in the warm water, with a little sugar. A drop of sugar. And then when it starts to rise and starts to blister, you see, it comes up like that. Then you put in the eggs. You put in a little oil. About a quarter of a cup of oil in the water. And if you like, you can put in a drop of sugar. If you want, you can put in a little honey, maybe half a cup. Some people put in honey. I never put it in.

Then you just keep on kneading it like this. Now they have the regular bread machines. DeeDee has a bread machine. And they come out wonderful, too. But this here, you knead it like this here, and you add more water, more water, till you feel you had enough. And then you just knead the dough, like this.

How long? Well, until all these flours absorb and it's dry. And that has to be on a floured board. And then, you put the flour again and you cut it up. And put it in a big plastic or whatever-you-can mixing bowl. But it has to be a big one. And you just cover it up and leave it near a warm place to rise. About an hour or so. Because don't forget, you have two packages of yeast in there.

After it's risen, you take part of it and again you knead it and you cut it in three parts and you make strips, and then you make a braid. You can make it round or however you want. And you can brush the top with egg yolk or the whole egg. You can put on poppy seeds, too, is nice.

My mother would take seven challahs, and she'd have, like, a white sheet. And she'd throw it—the white sheet would be on the bed—and she'd throw them over on the bed. You know, to cool off. But seven challahs. One for each day of the week.

CHAPTER 10

Koyach: Strength

Tessie and Steve, the football star.

PEARLIE'S DOCTOR, MICHAEL LUTSKY, DOESN'T KEEP HER WAIT-
ing long.

He is a deeply tanned figure in the doorway, dressed in a striped
oxford shirt and flowered tie, with a stethoscope slung around his
neck. He sits down on the small, brown vinyl–covered stool next
to Pearl, who is sitting on the examining table with her pants
cinched at the waist by safety pins. Leaning forward, his blue eyes
on Pearlie, he asks her how she feels.

"I have no desire to eat, Doctor," she tells him. His manner is
laconic, his voice quiet. He seems the sort of man who prefers listening to talking. She ticks off a list of medical concerns: Her
stomach feels awful. She belches a lot. She doesn't sleep for more
than two hours at a stretch at night. She gets sharp pains in her
shoulder blades. Privately, she tells me she thinks she's "going
cockin'." This is her term for dying. It is, of course, not an unrea-
sonable concern, at 93.

"These symptoms sound gallbladderish," the doctor says, studying her medical chart and reviewing her most recent ultrasound
results. He advises her to consult a surgeon about having her gall-

bladder removed, because gallstones could cause a more serious infection. Gallbladder surgery, he explains, is done with a little scope; patients are up and out of the hospital within a few days. It's really a minor procedure.

"See how lucky I am I got Dr. Lutsky?" Pearlie says to me. "I've been *draying* myself a *kop* [making my head spin] for no good reason."

He smiles, jotting down notes in her chart. And he recommends that she stay on a low-fat diet—only nonfat milk, no ice cream, chicken, fish, vegetables that don't cause gas, and fruit. In truth, she's practically been living on bananas and white bread for the past few weeks. She takes out a variety of prescription bottles from her maroon handbag for his perusal: Cardizem for high blood pressure; Axid, an antacid, for her hiatal hernia; Ativan for anxiety; Zoloft for anxiety; Ambien for sleeping.

"Let's deep-six this," Dr. Lutsky says of the sleeping pills, tossing the brown prescription bottle into the trash. He also hands me the Zoloft to discard. The antidepressants and sleeping pills were prescribed by a psychiatrist, who also advised Pearl to continue seeing the lisping psychologist she can't stand. But she trusts this doctor, who recommends she continue with the therapy, advice she'll ignore.

"It's always a good idea to talk things out," he tells her, softly. "It's a good idea."

✥

THE LAPAROSCOPIC CHOLECYSTECTOMY PEARLIE WILL UNDERGO is technically simple: Four small incisions are made in the abdominal area, which is pumped up like a balloon with carbon dioxide to separate muscle and fat from organs, and the gallbladder is sucked out through the navel. Instead of safety pins holding up her pants, Pearlie jokes, now she'll have staples in her belly button.

But the problem is with the anesthesia: At her age, it could cause a heart attack, a stroke, or even death. She can't help thinking about Yetta, her friend from Silvercrest, who went in for a simple operation on her leg and died. Or her brother Marty, who had gallbladder surgery and died a year later. What's the point of risking her life for this operation? Does it make sense to prolong a life, at 93? Hasn't she lived long enough?

The questions crowd her mind, as she sits in the waiting room of another specialist. Suddenly, her mood perks up as she eyes a wildly unattractive woman walking by. She's reminded of how Moe would nickname someone like that Good Looking. "He had a habit," she says of my grandfather, "if he wanted to go somewhere early and he needed help from, like, a waitress who could be as homely as sin, he'd say, 'Okay, Good Looking.' He'd call them Good Looking."

She goes weak with laughter. "And he used to say another thing. If people would fart, he'd say, 'If you were there, wouldn't you want to come out?' "

Thankfully, my mother arrives. She kisses Grandma and me, leaving lipstick marks on our cheeks. Then, she takes a seat between us, removing her black leather jacket. Since my mother's energy has been consumed by taking my father to and from chemotherapy treatments—dealing with his loss of appetite, his terrible bouts of nausea, his depression—my sister Shari and I have inherited the job of taking Pearlie to the doctor. But on this morning, Mom has shored herself to offer Pearlie support, too. Seeing my mother is the best medication in the world for Grandma.

"The thing is, what am I fighting for, Shirley?" Pearlie asks my mother.

"What do you mean?" Mom asks Grandma. "Living and enjoying!"

"But there's a time to stop," Pearl replies, looking defeated. "Let 'em go *cockin'*, already."

"That's not Pearl talking," my mother says.

Grandma takes Mom's hand and kisses it, threading their fingers together. "Maybe this way, I can *kvetch* for another year," she says. I laugh. Pearlie looks across the room at another patient.

"My granddaughter and my daughter!" she boasts to the stranger, who nods approvingly. "The best!" Chatting up strangers in the doctor's office is Pearlie's forte. Like a heat-seeking missile, she knows how to zoom in on love—show it, find it, create it.

Almost forty years ago, it was just such a display in her ophthalmologist's office that landed her a husband for Deedee. Always on the lookout for a nice Jewish doctor for her daughter, Pearlie also needed new glasses. So she went to see Dr. Schwartz, the eye doctor her mother Annie adored so much she'd travel an hour each way just to see him. The ophthalmologist's son, Elliott, was working as a receptionist that summer day, trying to make chitchat with the patients, since his father was notoriously late. Pearlie liked him right away and was eager to find out more about this friendly, tall man with a goatee. Besides, she had just put the kibosh on Deedee's relationship with her then-boyfriend, worried her child "was being used."

"When I got home and I told her about him, she didn't want to meet him for no money in the world," Pearlie remembers of Elliott. She mistakenly thought he was studying medicine, but when she discovered he was an up-and-coming composer, Pearlie billed him as the next Leonard Bernstein. "And DeeDee said, 'No! And don't fix me up with anybody! I'll get my own guy!' Anyway, the thing is, he did call, and I was standing there, and I said, 'Now you make an appointment with him. You make an appointment.' And so she did. But she didn't do it the first time. She said, 'Call me up again.' So, the next time he called, she went out with him. And she says, 'That's it, Mama. Don't make any appointments for me. Don't pick out my fellas for me. I don't want him. Nothing. Forget about it.' But he called again, and he took her out. And after a few times she got to like him." They've been married for thirty-five years.

Making a *shiddach* (match). It's thought to be a *mitzvah,* or good deed. Is it an inherited trait, this ability to hook up two people for life? Thinking back on my own matchmaking successes—four couples, creating eight children, including two nephews—I wonder if my own impulses aren't really Pearlie's, two generations removed. But then my mother's voice shakes me out of the reverie.

"Did you see the TV movie last night with Olympia Dukakis?" she asks Pearl. "She's a widow who hears Frank Sinatra telling her to do it *her* way."

"No, I saw the one with the woman who married the Jewish doctor." She means Mary Tyler Moore. *Ordinary People.*

"So the thing is, what am I fighting for—another year, maybe?" Pearlie asks again. "And nobody can tell you what to do. And another thing: That surgeon, did you see how bad her lower teeth are?"

Sometimes, it strikes me that Grandma feels so close to my mother that she acts like they're different parts of the same person. Even their anxiety seems contagious. "What I'm happy about is my mind is good, Shoiley," Grandma says after taking a treadmill test to verify that her heart can withstand surgery. "I didn't lose it."

I, on the other hand, worry I'm losing mine. The fear in my

mother's eyes sears through me like wildfire. "I feel like I'm on a carousel going faster and faster," Mom says, smiling.

❦

What kind of funeral do you want?

TESSIE: A lot of people. Yeah. Why not? I went to a lot of funerals, so I deserve [pronounced "desoyve"] it.

PEARLIE: I think about it often. I don't want the children to have too much trouble with me, so I took out this funeral insurance about seven years ago. Other than that, just a simple funeral is fine. You know, like a regular funeral. Like they bury you and put you in the ground. And I have a reservation there next to my husband, Morris Feldman.

❦

TUESDAY, MARCH 21, 1995. "*Shmendrick!*" PEARLIE BELLOWS OVER the phone at me. "How do we know he's not a *shmendrick!*" This word can mean anything from a pipsqueak to a little penis. Who's a *shmendrick?* I ask.

The more I try to answer Pearlie's questions, the more she sucks me into the vortex of her anxiety. It is three nights before she will enter the hospital for gallbladder surgery, and I switch on my phone machine. She leaves a series of messages:

6:00 P.M.: "Hello, Joyala, I haven't talked to you for some time."

6:15 P.M.: "Yeah, it's Grandma Pearlie for Joy. What time do I have to go to the hospital?"

6:30 P.M.: "Forget about getting a second opinion from a non-surgical doctor."

6:45 P.M.: "What time do I have to go to the hospital, Joyala?"

6:55 P.M.: "Yes, Joy, what about the pre-op tests?"

7:00 P.M.: "Joyala, tell me. What do we know about that *shmendrick?* The anesthesiologist?"

Though I've answered each question countless times, she can't hear me. In part, I think, her worry is wrapped up in her past.

The last time she was hospitalized, back in 1971, she had cataract surgery, which went well. At the time, though, my grandfather was succumbing to Alzheimer's disease, though no one called it that then. We thought it was a series of little strokes that made him act so strange—like thinking our refrigerator was a urinal on one of their visits west. He would have moments of weird clarity and then lapse into a fog.

When Pearlie thinks of going into the hospital, her mind turns to a tableau of grief. A series of five or six images pop up in her head, over and over. A car mechanic advising her that he wouldn't trust her husband with a baby carriage, despite Moe's insistence that he take the Cadillac for a spin. In the flickering television light, Moe thinking the people in the TV set were out to get him. Pearlie riding with Moe on the train all day, to nowhere—just to tire him out. The phone call from Jerry, saying he was going to go home because he wasn't feeling well. And then, the phone call from Jerry's son, Dickie: Jerry had had a heart attack on the subway that morning and died. Moe, laughing and kibitzing at Jerry's funeral, and then asking Pearl when Jerry was coming over. Moe, with his head propped up on pillows, looking Buddha-like, and the doctors disconnecting the tubes and catheters helping to sustain his breath when he was dying.

Now, facing her own mortality is like diving into a pool of grief. It washes over her, no matter how long ago the loss. Swimming back to the surface—regaining her breath—is the hard part, her love having been so deep.

After dinner one night, I go out to my office and flip through some of her letters, which she wrote after Jerry's death. What becomes clear to me now, reading them again, is how in taking care of her husband, who couldn't abide her tears, she had no time to mourn. "You couldn't say good-bye to Grandpa," she's told me. "He wouldn't accept it. He'd make a joke of it."

April 13, 1975
Rockaway Park, NY

Dear DeeDee,

Today it felt like it was 80 hours to the day. Thursday night I kept thinking about Jerry and couldn't sleep. So I got very tired and finally fell into a deep sleep. I dreamt about Jerry the first time and DeeDee he seemed so real to me. He was talking to me so seriously, like he would talk to me how to handle Daddy. He seemed so real that in my dream I really thought he was alive. He said to me something about Helen whether I should tell her something or what I woke up. I was shaking like a leaf and kept calling him and my heart was beating so fast I could just feel it knocking. He seemed so alive I couldn't face I guess getting up and knowing my wonderful Jerry wasn't here any more. Losing a child is like some part of your body is missing.

You know the Saturday before I left I heard you talking to Elliott about the professor from England how he should handle him and DeeDee you are so smart and so wise. You have all Jerry's goodness. Secretly I enjoyed the way Elliott listened to you and respected you for your suggestions.

Daddy is calling me so I must say adios.

Love lots of xxxxx
Mom

June 1975

Dear DeeDee,

Somehow I was always so happy with life that my children and grandchildren were well and happy why can't I feel this way now? If it wasn't that I felt the responsibility of taking care of Daddy I feel what's the use of life? It just seems so futile without Jerry. It's like I have no heart left.

DeeDee forgive me if I am so morbid it is just one of those days that we miss Jerry so much. Like Daddy told me the other day, he asked me about Jerry and I said, "Moe, you know he is gone," and he said, "To me, he will never be gone. He always will be alive to me." For a person that is confused at times he says such wise things.

xxxxx

Sept 1975

Our Dearest Son,

To say "Happy New Year" how can it be a Happy New Year without you.

I once received a beautiful gift on my birthday—our son. Who could be happier? But my gift was taken from us.

I look at the ocean, moon and the stars, but just can't find an answer. We all miss you so, your wonderful smile, good will to all and goodness itself.

The hurt is so deep and painful, the lonesomeness of not seeing or hearing you say, "How are you Mom? How is Pop?"

I don't want to hurt Dad, it is so painful for him to see me cry and tells me it wouldn't do me any good, but I have no control of my feelings.

Jan. 4, 1976

Jerry Dear,

To-day it just a year since you are gone.

Dad has gotten much weaker in health and I don't know what the next day will bring. But even in his weakened mind there isn't a day that goes by that he doesn't talk about his Jerala.

We all went to schule today for your memorial and Dad, Helen and the children felt your nearness the love we all feel for you.

Sue and Dicky took such care of Dad, it brought back cherished memories of how good you were to us and the sweet words we never will forget "How are you Mominue? How is Totishku?"

Our love will always be with you till we die and can once again join you.

Mom and Dad

Feb. 8, 1976

Dear Jerry,

Today is our birthday but I know I can never share it with you in life. I can only live with the memories. You would have been 54 years old today and here I am 74 years old. How willingly I would have exchanged your place if you could have lived. Daddy keeps asking for you continually and when we talk about you his eyes light up full of love and sadness. As time goes by the wound only deepens. Nothing in this world can compensate our loss of you with the words ringing in my ears Happy Birthday Mom.

July 17, 1976

Jerry Dear,

Life is so hard to bear. Each day is an eternity. It hurts me so much to see Daddy drifting more and more into a confused mind. I just can't stand by to see him suffer. I love him so and want to take care of him with all the dignity and respect he deserves. My husband and my children were my whole world.

I just can't accept my loss. The Bible says honor thy father and mother. What son could have bestowed more honor and blessing than you, Jerry? Yes, I don't understand.

Mom and Dad

November 13, 1976

Dear Jerry,

Jerry darling it hurts so much I feel sometimes I just can't continue to live but Daddy needs care and this is what keeps me. Good night, our angel Jerry.

Mother and Dad

March 3, 1977

Dear Jerry,

You always said we were the best parents in the world but I must disagree with you. I know you said you were fine when I asked you the last time you were here how you felt but I should not have accepted that answer. Sometimes I wonder if we are really living or just floating along like the clouds in the sky.

Mom and Dad

Oct. 9, 1977

Jerry Dear,

Daddy has been in the hospital ten days now and to me each day has been an eternity. He is so sick. Last week he was so sick that I thought he wouldn't be able to see Monday morning. Now he is in the incessant [sic] care. Doctor says Dad has congestive heart failure. I felt your presence twice today with Sue and Dicky, who came to the hospital. Please give me the strength to continue. Please Jerry ease his pain. I need him so to continue my life. I am waiting for Dicky to take me to the hospital. I am almost afraid to go. It is almost morning and I can hardly wait to see Dad.

Mom

Dec. 7, 1977

Dear Jerry,

Daddy has gone to rest. Daddy passed away Nov 23, 1977 and the funeral was Nov. 25, 1977. Why? Why? It seems God couldn't see him suffer so much. He was in the hospital for

*seven weeks. They couldn't find any more skin for his injec-
tions and he fought so hard to remain here with me. Twice he
came out of a coma but the third time it was just too much for
his heart and like you, never complained about anything
hurting him. I miss him so Jerry.*

*I have no one to call me the endearing name that only
Daddy could call me Pearlala where are you. I have no one to
cover me at night if I am cold or to see that I eat and only with
Daddy. I miss him so his sweet smile and how his eyes would light
up with a twinkle when I would wear something he liked.*

Jerry darling, what am I living for? Who needs me now?

June 25, 1978

Dear Jerela,

*We had the unveiling of the stone for Daddy. Susala was
right there to take me around and hold me closer when my feelings got the best of me and I found that I was not alone.
Helen came and Dickala came too and I felt part of you was
there too. When we paid you a visit, Jerela, I wanted to talk to
you so, but how can I talk to a stone? But as I stood there I saw
your beautiful face with those beautiful eyes of yours telling me,
it's okay Mom, just carry on, which I am trying to do.*

Goodnight my son.

Mom

When I call Pearlie back, after helping the kids with homework
and getting Lucy to bed, she's a puddle of apologies, "a nervous
meshuggeneh."

"So you'll come over tomorrow and we'll discuss this, darling?"
she asks me. "So you take notes on whatever information you get."
Somehow, I've seduced her into believing that my note taking—
everything has become material for the book—means that I
understand all that I write down. Nothing could be further from
the truth, however. My note taking is simply a defense. It allows
me to distance myself and thus serves as a kind of armor. A shield.
If I'm an observer, then I'm not actually participating. Only report-
ing what I see.

"You see how I'm fighting to live, darling?" she asks. "I didn't
think I wanted to live so much. I'm finding out things. Life is so
precious." I write it all down.

IN THE HOURS AFTER HER SURGERY, WHEN I RETURN TO VISIT
Pearlie at Santa Monica Hospital up on the sixth floor, she seems
to be in a state of manic exhaustion. Her "happy juice" has yet to
wear off, and everything strikes her as hilariously funny. She tells
me when she woke up, she thought she was in jail! The *shmendrick* Dr. Einstein is so wonderful! Such dimples! He jammed the
breathing tube so hard down her throat he knocked her loose
tooth into place! And he didn't charge her a dental fee! (Hysterical
laughter.) Maybe he pushed that pipe all the way down to her
shmitchek, because that problem she was having with water
buildup is gone!

She's screaming, laughing, tears streaking her face. Suddenly,
her raspy voice drops to a conspiratorial whisper. "BD," she says,
speaking in code and looking out her private room for snoops.

"BD?" I ask, confused.

"The *bubbe* doll," she says, whispering because she's worried
someone might steal her idea. She's refined her vision: The doll
will have accessories—a cane, orthopedic hose, a pocketbook,
removable teeth. Unlike Barbie, she must have sagging breasts! So
girls can see what dames are really about! Get a realistic picture of
old broads! And she wants my father to confer psychological blessings, a sort of fumphiologist seal of approval.

Grandma, in her fuchsia robe, has made friends with all the
nurses. When they check her blood pressure and take her temperature, she makes sure to show them her volunteer ID badge to get
the best possible service. Aunt DeeDee, who is sleeping overnight
at the hospital with Grandma, recounts how, when lined up in
a row of gurneys beside other people awaiting surgery, Pearlie
made small talk with the young woman beside her. The woman
said she was onto her third attempt at in vitro fertilization—trying
to make a baby. Pearlie assured her that 3 was a magic number. It
would work this time.

"That sounds like Pearlie," I said, "making other people feel
good when she's most nervous."

"Let me tell ya," Pearlie agrees. "We were all shittin' in our
pants there." She turns to me, lucid for a moment. "Go home to
the children. They come foist. Go, Tootsala."

❦

I CALL TESSIE TO SEE HOW SHE'S FEELING. "I'M FINE," SHE LIES. "Getting younger every day."

I ask her to tell me the truth. "*Ach*, I've got no *koyach*," she says to me. "You know what's *koyach*? Strength. I've got no strength. I felt this week terrible. The weather is so miserable. Now, I feel according to the weather.

"But I guess you gotta suffer already more. It's not so easy to die, either." She asks after my kids. I tell her about them in descending order: Trevor is in Arizona for a basketball All-Star game and he's James in the school play of *James and the Giant Peach*; Gussie got $3 from the tooth fairy and just gained admission to the Money Magicians' Club at school; Lucy, at 20 months, announced that she wanted an "Ee-ay ee-ay-oh burger," meaning a hamburger from McDonald's: She combined the lyrics from "Old MacDonald" with her favorite fast food.

"Oh, my God!" Grandma says, delighted. "*Oy. Oy.* God bless her! She's so smart. You can't imagine. I saw this little baby last summer and now she talks!"

The sun was shining when I first called, she tells me. But now it's suddenly gone gray. "Maybe it's the end of the world," she tells me. "I personally wouldn't care. I'm selfish."

Her insomnia is back. "I don't sleep so well at night," she says. This is code for worry. Maybe telling her about Dad was not wise. Both Cynthia and Bobbie recently came to California to visit my father, but neither of them told Tessie what they saw, presumably because they didn't want to cause her further pain. "They don't tell me, I don't ask," she says. "I don't know." Playing dumb is an integral part of her belief system.

She tells me she also believes in fate. "I do," she says. "When they call you, you go. That's all."

Who's "they"? "You know—the Upstairs People." We've gone from the Man Upstairs to the Upstairs People. Maybe she's grown less sexist.

I tell her I'll be seeing her in a few weeks. "Bring your earplugs," she advises me. "And say hello to my lovah boy."

❦

Heading west on the Belt Parkway to visit Ellis Island, Grandma Tessie and I pass a sign for Sheepshead Bay. It sparks a memory of a family gathering there decades ago, the first time she's thought of it in ages. "It's so many years," she says, her gray eyes glistening. "To see a name. It gives me, like, a thrill."

We're sitting in the back seat of a limousine. I've promised Grandma comfort, having rented a town car but lucking out with a stretch limo, instead. With her cane at her side, she extends her black Rockport shoes onto the thick oriental rug adorning the car's flooring. She's a picture of purple, from the silken scarf draped around her neck to her parka and slacks. Her fingernails, as usual, are bright red.

Still, every trip out of the apartment is exhausting. Just this morning, she needed to take several Tylenols and curl back up in bed, because her head felt like it might split open. Any dip in barometric pressure—there would be a rain shower the next day—her body feels hours in advance. But the dogwoods and cherry blossoms are blooming outside. She makes a good show of it, for my sake.

I toy with the television set in the limo, changing channels. And I offer her a drink. But she asks about our picnic provisions, lox and cream cheese sandwiches on rye bread. She's even packed one for the Israeli limo driver, Dov, who might well have been sent over by central casting. He lives in Williamsburg, her old neighborhood, near Lee Avenue. The place causes her mind to settle on an old beau.

No matter how old you get, you never stop thinking about old boyfriends. "From Europe I know him yet," Tessie says. "We came from the same town. He wanted to marry me. He was a very nice guy, but I didn't want to marry him. 'Cause I didn't want to pluck chickens. There were six brothers. All six brothers were butchers. This guy came to America same time as I did. He was a *landsman*. A woman asked him if a chicken was tough. She meant hard. There, if you say tough, it means good. So, sure, sure. Oh, we used to have fun with him. That was only about, what, seventy years ago?" She laughs softly.

Her mind offers a series of jump cuts in time, fast-forwarding and rewinding images from the 1970s. She best remembers New Year's Day, 1971, in Pasadena. My brother Steve had convinced Grandma she would be his good-luck charm in the Rose Bowl. Watching him set a record (since broken) for kicking a 48-yard field goal for Stanford against Ohio State, the longest in Rose Bowl history, Tessie had no idea what was happening on the field. "In front of me sat a woman and a girl from Ohio," Tessie says. "When they were applauding, I knew I should keep quiet. Stanford won the game. Don't ask . . ."

The limousine darkens, passing through the Brooklyn Battery Tunnel. Grandma grows quiet. Any time she drives through a tunnel, she's reminded of riding in the hearse to Izzy's funeral in New Jersey. It's as if no time has passed at all. Dots of yellow light lining the sides of the tunnel whoosh by, like electrons in a particle smasher.

Her traveling days are behind her now. After Sam died in 1965, she and her sisters became more inseparable than ever. Tessie was there to bring soup to her sister Rosie at Creedmore, to nurse her sister-in-law Ida who was stricken with cancer, to take Gussie to the doctor for her goiter problems, to cook up dinners for Leah when her asthma was especially bad. For enjoyment, she spent summers "in the country," playing cards with Leah and Gussie all day at Skopps, a rundown collection of bungalows offering *kochalayn* (cooking facilities) in the Catskills, not far from Grossinger's in South Fallsburg. And winters, she'd soak up the California sunshine, staying with my family in Beverly Hills. This is when she and I first bunked together, because neither of my sisters could

Tessie with (from left) Shirley, Steve, Shari, Peggy, Mike, and me in 1968.

tolerate her snoring. I, on the other hand, found it oddly comforting: It reminded me of Curly from the Three Stooges.

She turns toward me. "One time, I'll never forget," she says. "You and your daddy played a violin duet for me. You were barefoot. It was Sunday morning. And you said, 'Daddy, you made a mistake.' And he said, 'Oh yeah?' With your bare foot, stomping the floor. I just can see it now. That, to me, was the best because you criticized Daddy, not Daddy you." I had almost forgotten that my father and I played violin duets together.

She leans forward, to speak to Dov, the driver. "I want to go back to Israel," she tells him. "I hope in my lifetime." The last time she was in Israel, on a tour in 1975, she dreamed of returning forever. But then she came to believe that your children can move away from you, but you can't move away from your children. In 1976, she moved from Jamaica to her current apartment, which used to be right next door to her daughter Cynthia's.

Having arrived at Battery Park, I wheel her past a young black man, playing the theme to *Exodus* on a violin. I'm deeply moved by the haunting melody. "Oy," she says.

Nearby, another musician plays the theme to *The Godfather* on steel drums. "Big deal," she says, meaning precisely the opposite.

As we line up at the dock for the ferryboat, we watch a gymnast leaping in circles, midair. I applaud. Tessie looks puzzled. "Why does he do it, even?" she wants to know.

To save her strength, Grandma allows me to push her around in a wheelchair. She calls it "the worst curse," being seen in public this way. She wonders aloud whether this indignity might not be a form of divine retribution.

"When we were small and we saw a cripple walking, we would laugh," she says. "Mama used to tell us, 'You mustn't laugh at someone that is sick, because God is gonna punish you: If you laugh at a cripple, you'll be a cripple.' She said, 'You can only laugh at an old person so you can get old.' " She pauses for a moment. "So maybe I did." For Tessie, old age isn't a blessing so much as a punishment.

But she brightens upon discovering one of the perks of riding in a wheelchair: first come, first served. We bypass all the tourists queued up for the ferry as a young uniformed boat employee suddenly spins Tessie around, doing wheelies with her onto the boat.

"That's one thing, sveethot," she tells me, as I maneuver the wheelchair over to a window seat to get a better view of the Statue of Liberty. There is a lineup of tourists, snapping pictures and buying ice cream and covering their heads with those dreadful Styrofoam Miss Liberty crowns. "I can't die young. That's all."

✄ ☞

IT SEEMED LIKE A GOOD IDEA: TAKE GRANDMA TESSIE BACK TO Ellis Island, seventy-five years after she arrived in America. It would be her first trip back. It would be a chance for grandmother and granddaughter to soak up the contours of their mutual history. It would be a sentimental journey of remembrance and connection. In fact, it would be a whopping disappointment: too much emotion, too much memory, too much unresolved pain.

"What is that, the Pacific?" she asks, looking blankly at the ocean.

Uh-oh. "C'mon, Grandma, you know it's the Atlantic," I say, wondering if I've waited too long for this outing.

She laughs. "I forgot for a second where I was. For just a moment, I saw you, and I thought I was in California, too."

We look at the Statue of Liberty together. "Oh, was I seasick coming to this country," she recalls. "You see, Mama was only afraid for my father. He was a very delicate man, and my sister Sylvia was a very skinny little girl. She was afraid for them, they were going to get seasick. And I was the strong one. And Mama was the strong one. So we both got sick. And they weren't even sick." She laughs at the irony of it all.

More than the magnificent bronze statue in the distance, she zones in on an elderly woman in a pink jacket nearby. "She's got trouble," Tessie whis-

Grandma Tessie returns to Ellis Island with me, spring 1995.

pers to me, as if she's known this stranger forever. "I can see it. In her eyes. Her thoughts are so low. Maybe she's alone. Maybe she doesn't want to talk to her daughter or daughter-in-law. Something's wrong. I can judge." I love these pronouncements of hers, whether they're based on fantasy or projection, because when I look at the woman in pink, all I see is another tourist. My grandmother's lay analytical skills are in evidence much of the time.

But most of Tessie's musings on this day are ones of sadness. Even before I wheel her into the majestic brick building with turrets on the rooftop, she says, "Let's go home." Though she claims to be concerned about my *shlepping* her around, the truth is, she's worried she'll have a coughing jag. Or she'll need to use the bathroom. Or worse still, she'll see nothing that looks familiar.

"Take a picture and let's go," she says. "Then we can show everyone we got here."

She finally agrees to at least let me take her inside. "I don't see anything I recognize yet," she says, looking further agitated. She expected iron cots and got a museum with displays, instead. At one of them, we see a collection of towering colored discs, stacked up heavenward, that illustrates the projected growth of Central American immigration in the United States. It makes the huge wave of Eastern European immigration that Tessie came in on look microscopic by comparison.

"Let's go," she says again. "There is nothing for me to learn here."

The exhibits on immigration patterns disturb her further. There is one, showing how the U.S. government refused an exemption to immigration law that would have admitted twenty thousand German children in 1939. "Those children went to Auschwitz," she says, flatly. Another display, showing how federal law was designed to exclude Eastern Europeans in the decade after she arrived, reminds her of begging Izzy to send for his sisters in Europe. They, too, were denied refuge in the United States and emigrated to South America, instead. She never met them.

Even the straw suitcases on exhibition are irritating. They remind her of her first job in New York, sewing linings into straw bags with her brother Max. During World War I, Max, who was two years older than her, left Galicia and moved to Vienna in order to escape the draft. Toby grew accustomed to pretending that she was the oldest child in the family, depending only on herself, since her older sisters had all moved to America. It fell to Toby to help support her parents, journeying out in the middle of the night to buy sugar for the makeshift teahouse they set up during the war. "See, I felt a responsibility," she says.

By the time she arrived at Ellis Island, she was at once naive and wizened. She truly believed the streets were paved with gold. Mostly, she felt grateful to her sisters, who had pawned their jewelry to buy tickets for her to come to America. She'd do anything for them. In the old country, too, she used to prove her love by lying for them. If Leah wanted face powder, forbidden for young girls at the time, it was Toby who would make up a story to buy it for her from the village apothecary. If Frank wanted cigarettes, Toby would figure out a way to smuggle them to him.

"I did what they told me, and I was their confidential," she says. "In Europe, you don't dare to smoke. My aunt would say, 'Tobeleh, for whom do you buy the tobacco?' I said it was Mikola, one of my father's workers."

She stops, thinking of what she's revealed. "No, no, I'm going too deep in," she says. But her eyes flash with excitement. "I would even lie for them. Because they were older. I felt I owed them everything that they brought us to America. I never really paid them back." By 1979, even her baby sister, Sylvia, would die before her.

She stares icily at the glass-enclosed display, which a curator has entitled All Their Worldly Possessions. "I was only nineteen years old," she says, softly. "And I was thinking, What should I expect in America? Will I be happy or sad? But I was happy. I had my parents. I had my family here." She had her whole life ahead of her.

"Now, towards the end of it, okay," she says, meaning the opposite. "That's all right. I'm not disappointed. I'm not very thrilled, but I had a good seventy-five years. Let's say I had forty percent good and sixty percent medium." She thinks for a moment and revises her assessment downward. "No, say fifty medium, forty good, and ten nothing."

Ten nothing? "Disappointment," she says. "Let's go."

Not exactly a rave review of one's life.

⋙ ⋘

As it happens, what was really bothering Grandma at Ellis Island was the knowledge that her name is not engraved on the immigrant wall of honor. That's because no one in our family bothered to send the required fee to get her name up there. So I call the Statue of Liberty–Ellis Island Foundation to inquire about including Tessie's name.

"Unfortunately, that's been closed," says Florence Kaplan, a foundation volunteer. "We sold all the spaces." She explains that there are currently four hundred thousand names on the American Immigrant Wall, each costing $100. At the moment, there is room for only another one hundred thousand names, and my grandmother has missed the March 1995 deadline. Would she care to be wait-listed?

That night, Brock calls from California to see how Tessie enjoyed returning to Ellis Island. "Beauty-ful," she tells him. "It was a beautiful day." She hands me the phone, offering damage control. "Tell them it was beautiful."

TESSIE READS HER TABLOID NEWSPAPER AS I PACK UP MY LUGGAGE to return home, stacking my carry-on bag, a backpack, and a paper bag brimming with goodies for my kids beside the front door. She shuffles into the kitchen and retrieves a large plastic bag.

"Sweetheart, here's another bag," she says, clearly offended by the precarious way I've packed.

"I don't need it," I tell her.

"Look," she continues, "it'll fall out."

"Really, Grandma, I'm okay," I say, growing annoyed. I just want her to leave me alone.

"Look," she says, now shaking my things out of the paper bag to make her point.

"Grandma, you want the next headline to be 'Granddaughter Kills *Bubbe*'?"

"You'll do me a favor," she says. "If you want to do it, go ahead."

"You're driving me nuts," I tell her.

She puts my paper bag inside the large plastic one and knots the handles.

"Now," she says, "I feel better. I feel safe. You don't need even the double bag."

I put on my coat and discover a few wadded-up dollar bills in the pocket, which always makes me feel lucky. But Tessie disapproves, because I've stuffed the money into my wallet. "You must respect money," she advises, straightening each bill and neatly stacking them, from highest to lowest. She didn't work as a grocery checker for nothing.

Of course, the thing that infuriates me about both of these encounters—beyond the fact that she acts like a know-it-all and treats me like a child—is that she's right.

⊰⊱

BACK HOME, I CALL TESSIE TO LET HER KNOW I'VE ARRIVED safely. Silence, long distance, can be deafening.

"Okay, baby," she says, eager to hang up, "we're using up your money." She sounds so far away. Why?

"My son, he wanted to be so smart," she says, sarcastically. "He wants to be cremated. That hurt me very, very much." She's referring to a conversation she had with my father several years ago in which he expressed his desire to be cremated when he dies. Cremation is expressly forbidden to observant Jews, because it is considered disrespectful to the human body, God's creation.

"Between you and me, he doesn't have a designated place," she says, her tone ominously disapproving. One of the first things my grandmother's family did when she arrived in America was to buy a burial plot. Now, the fact that my parents have avoided dealing with such matters is cause for worry. Of more concern to me is whether she's managed to tell my father how much she loves him.

"For a mother to tell her son she loves him?" she asks, incredulous. Her tone suggests the idea is nothing short of revolutionary. "Absolutely—there are no need for words."

I disagree completely. "Thank you for mentioning it," she says, sounding genuinely grateful. "It makes sense, what you say."

Easy Veggie Soup

You take a package of—it doesn't matter—Manischewitz or Steits. I don't want to give anybody a break. I buy the split peas and yellow peas or barley and mushroom.

I take a piece of wax paper in the kitchen, not over the pot, and I dice in about two pieces of celery and two carrots. Throw it in.

Then when it cooks an hour, let's say, then I take the little package inside and put that in, too. I beat up an egg in a little dish. A drop of salt. Two tablespoons of matzo meal. Mix it up. Then, as the soup is boiling, I take one big spoon and a little teaspoon. I just take off little drops and throw it in the soup. I used to make, like, little marbles. But it's a waste of time. All in all, it cooks slowly for two hours.

CHAPTER II

Vitz: A Wisecrack

*Pearlie and Tessie outside my parents'
house in Beverly Hills, 1989.*

"DON'T START WITH ME! YOU START WITH ME, I'M LEAVING."

Eva is yelling at Tessie, who couldn't be happier. To be bossed around by someone you love. It reminds her of her sisters or her mother. They're all gone now. But Eva is here, having just arrived on a bright Monday morning in early spring. She shoots Tessie a look. "Only a mother could love such a face on payday," Tessie teases.

Pretending not to hear, Eva turns to me. "If I don't hit her, nobody will."

Eva Lovi is Grandma Tessie's best friend. She also happens to be her 85-year-old niece by marriage. Eva's father was the brother of Sam, Tessie's second husband. When they were both girls in Kozowa, it was Eva's greatest thrill to accompany Tessie to the oil factory, where she mixed up huge batches of cottonseed oil. "Vee vent in the vintertime," Eva tells me. For the past twenty years, the two women have celebrated Passover together at Eva's home in Lakewood, New Jersey. And, without fail, they talk on the phone every Monday night.

Now, having been dropped off by her son-in-law, Eva demands that Tessie sit down, but Tessie insists that Eva not wait on her. Both want to serve the other.

"I'm on a diet," she says, handing Tessie a coffee canister filled with her homemade chocolate chip cookies and a freshly baked potatonik, a crusty potato pie the size of Tessie's TV screen. Wearing a brown suit, rubber-soled shoes, and a gold Star of David necklace with tiny rubies, she parts her straight gray hair to one side, conferring a certain elegance with her warm, inviting eyes. I've never met her before this moment, though Tessie speaks of her often.

"She's a real, real *baleboosteh*," Tessie says, paying a high compliment with her use of the Yiddish word for either homemaker or bossy woman. Eva is the only person Tessie allows to work in her kitchen, other than her daughters. "She knows how to cook. She knows how to serve. She knows how to talk to you, you should eat. She really tortures me."

Tessie smiles and sits down at the dining room table beside her girlfriend. She looks at me, then at Eva. "Company, for me, is the best medicine," she says. Ever since the 1980s, when her building went co-op, repairs on her apartment have been slow in coming. The ceilings are cracked and the walls need paint, but she hasn't attended to it and feels self-conscious about inviting people over.

Eva studies Tessie's face, quilted with lines. "Something about her face is very remarkable," she says to me of Grandma. "Somehow it's the same, like always."

"You mean I was that ugly when I was a young girl?" Tessie asks. Slowly, she rises. "All right," she says, standing to pour a cup of coffee for her guest.

Eva, protesting, gets up from the table, too. "Stop it."

"No way," Tessie says, shoving Eva aside in the kitchen.

"Will you please?" Eva moans.

"Shut up."

"Grandma!" I say, protesting.

"I'm older than her. I can say it." But it's all a little ruse, a *baleboosteh* shuffle of mutual admiration and respect. The layers of feeling run deep. Tessie was there to soothe Eva's sorrow when her son George, a world-renowned astronomer, died of cancer a few years back. These days, it is Eva to whom Tessie confides her worry over my father's illness.

Before arriving, Eva felt compelled to stop at the cemetery nearby. "I didn't make them alive anymore," she says, now teary over her visit to the grave sites of her two sons, her husband, and other family members. "At least I saw the stones. I admired the beautiful flowers there. The buds completely out. My father's was full with evergreen all over. Everything just beautiful. What can I tell? A lot of times I'm ashamed of myself that I'm alive and they are dead."

By the time they sit down together for a feast of bagels, lox, cream cheese, fruit, potatonik, and coffee, they eat in silence. It gives Tessie the opportunity to relate a good *vitz* (joke) she just picked up.

"Somebody invited a *landsman* for dinner," Tessie begins. "So, he came in. He was sitting. He was eating. He enjoyed it. He was a poor man, an *oyrech* [guest]. He said, 'Where do you come from?' He says, 'I come from, let's say, Kozowa.' 'Oh, you come from Kozowa? I'm from Kozowa, too. Tell me, how's Moishe?' *Gershtorben* [dead]. 'How is Yankel?' *Gershtorben*. 'Oh, did you know the family so and so?' *Gershtorben*. And he says to him, 'I don't understand. You mean the whole town died out?' He said, 'When I eat, everybody's dead.' "

Tessie and Eva chuckle together. In the kitchen, Lucy is just finishing up. She walks to the front hall closet and reaches for her jacket. "Okay, see you tomorrow morning," Tessie says.

"Okay," says Lucy.

"I got help now," Tessie says of Eva. "I don't need your help."

"Oh, you see?" Lucy says, feigning hurt over her dispensability.

"That's it," says Tessie.

"But she's nice," Lucy says of Tessie, assuring Eva and me that they're just teasing each other. "Very, very nice. She gives me good advice. When I need."

"She asks me questions and I answer," Tessie shrugs.

"Good advice," says Lucy. "She got experience, you know. She is good."

"Yeah," Tessie mutters. "Good for what? Good for nothing."

"Good for nothing!" Lucy roars with laughter.

"So where you going now?" Tessies asks her.

"My second guy. But I'm going to buy something first."

Tessie wags a finger. "Don't spend all the money."

"No. No."

"So you can have carfare to come tomorrow."

TESSIE LIFTS HER WHITE COFFEE MUG TO HER LIPS. THE TOPIC is potatoes. "I paid one dollar and fifty-nine cents for five pounds," she says.

"I paid two dollars and forty-eight cents," says Eva. "They make it less and give you a bargain. I don't like it, they're not Idahos. You peel 'em and they're gone."

Grandma stands. "*Oy,* what's going to become of me?" she asks. "I know. A corpse." She sits back down.

Two *baleboostehs,* two memory banks. Mostly, they speak Yiddish to each other. I understand nothing. When they revert to English, it's for my benefit, retrieving memories of an earlier life in America.

"Every Monday was washday," Eva says, "and every woman, standing at the sink washing the clothes. We dried clothes over the stove. We'd cook on the stove, too. I hated it."

Tessie agrees. "It's unbelievable that we did it," she says. "It's so strange. A rat bit Sylvia's ear." This reminds her of her sisters. "Ya know, they're all gone. Like they were never here."

Eva remembers the first advertisement in the *New York Times* for a television. "We just couldn't believe it," she says, perfectly peeling a McIntosh apple. Tessie free-associates to images of her old railroad flat, one room after the other. Summertime, people climbing out on roofs to cool off. Women sleeping on fire escapes. "Even rich ones couldn't have air-conditioning," she says.

Their conversation veers from their opposition to communities

for older people, which they think are "like a living cemetery," to the need for children in one's life, to the joy of seeing everything go green again in the spring. Both agree that given the chance, they'd never return to Kozowa.

"Who would want to go there?" Eva asks. "You know what they did? They took all the stones from the Jewish cemetery."

Tessie interrupts. "They made a ballpark. Of the Jewish cemetery."

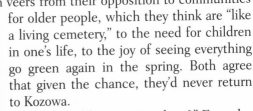

Tessie and Eva, baleboostehs *and best friends.*

"And the stones were made to sidewalks," Eva says.

"We were in America then," Tessie adds. "It was the Nazi regime." Silence. She shakes her head. "They made a ballpark."

Eva sees a vacant look cross Tessie's face. "Go lie down," she instructs her.

"Never!" Tessie replies.

"I can see in your eyes, you need it."

"Like my son," says Grandma, "he naps for eight minutes."

"Go on. If you don't, I'm leaving."

Grandma gets up and gropes her way to the bedroom. She shrugs. "The more you live, the more you learn, the more you forget. *Farshtayst?*"

A Bubbe Takes on Plastic Surgery

What do you think of the current plastic surgery craze?

PEARLIE: Do you love a person less if they're not as good-looking as before? Or if they have less of a beautiful face? I've seen people that have been done over—skin done over—and their faces look so much more drawn than even with the wrinkles.

Of course, it's not pleasant to meet old age. I know even for myself. You don't like to see your wrinkles coming in and your face drawn back and your eyes change and you get little things on your skin. You may not see them on me now, but they're coming. They're coming, darling. It's part of nature. If you sometimes see a tree and then, say thirty or forty years you come around that neighborhood, the tree is bent. It's not as straight as it used to be. You know, nature is nature, and a person's nature is a natural thing. But you don't like to see it happen to yourself.

So you put a little paint on, you put a little powder on. Everything is there. I think the heart of the person is the most important thing in the whole world. You can love a person even if they're not nice-looking, but you can never love a mean person, a person that's hateful. Those persons aren't to love.

I've seen so many of them, they get these face-lifts,

and afterwards it falls down again, and they have to go
through that over and over again. And it must be a terrible thing. You don't have to think of yourself as mean
and ugly and not nice-looking. It's much better than a
face. A soulful person.

TESSIE: I wouldn't. What for? Who are you fooling? Yourself?
You go through all the pain? For what? So what, you're
going to look for a new husband?

If you get older, you start to wrinkle, crinkle, whatever
it is. So who cares? I don't care what people on the face
look. I look what's inside. My own wrinkles—that's a different story. I don't like them. I wish I wouldn't have
them. It's getting so that it's even hard to put on a little
powder or rouge or so, because it's such deep wrinkles I
have. And if you would say to me today, I'll pay the
expense and you wouldn't have no pain or nothing, just
do it! I might. But now, it's only one way for me: just
cope. Whatever way you go, go. I do care how I look. I
have to wash my face.

"THE QUESTION IS: THIS OR THIS?" PEARLIE ASKS ME, HOLDING
up a purple cape in one hand and a fuchsia cape in the other. On
a day when she's feeling weak, or *shvach,* her question underscores an important lesson in the female psyche: Never underestimate the transformative powers of a new outfit.

I choose the purple crocheted cape to go with her ensemble—a
long lavender dress, purple tam, pink bobby socks trimmed with
white ruffles, and sneakers. It is just a week after her surgery, and
Pearlie looks for strength wherever she can find it. She never fails,
for example, to revel in her body—hitching up her jumper to show
off her new scars at the first opportunity. She's not one for modesty.

"No, no, no," she says, sliding the cape around her shoulders.
"The body is beautiful, whether it's a baby or adult. It's just wonderful to have all parts of your body." Especially when they work, I
point out. "Yeah," she agrees, putting on the finishing touches of her
Clinique Rose Apricot lipstick plus her big, dangly hoop earrings.

This is Grandma's first foray out since her return from the hospital. On her way to her surgeon's office for a post-op visit, she

takes her cane and turns off the light. I notice that the crocheted sweater she had offered me and I rejected days before has a new life, as a pillow on her couch.

Downstairs, stepping out of the elevator into the Silvercrest foyer, Pearlie is practically gasping for air. But smiling. Always smiling.

"You're so elegant!" says her friend Mary, appreciating the purple outfit.

"We missed you at the bash Friday night," says Joe. Pearlie hasn't left her apartment in days, feeling too weak to go out. DeeDee, on another one of her trips from Maine, has been cooking her meals.

"The thing is, it takes a while to get your strength back," Pearlie tells her friends, going out the door. "You don't know if you're a cookie." As in, ready to crumble.

"You look great!" says Nancy, the receptionist.

"Is that Pearl?" asks Colleen, from her administration office. She comes out to see for herself, then wraps her arms around Pearl. "Welcome back!"

Pearlie, leaning on her cane, shakes her hips, like Elvis.

"Rock and roll!" says Robert, another friend.

"Rock and roll!" says Pearl, waving her fist heavenward. "To rest is to rust."

🖚 🖛

IN MY CAR, SHE SHEDS HER PUBLIC PERSONA. HER VOICE TREM-bles. "Why am I afraid to go out?" she asks.

What are you afraid of? I ask. "I'm afraid I'm losing my vitality," she tells me. "You get so angry with yourself. You think you're losing your mentality." I park the car in an underground parking lot, near the surgeon's office. Pearlie inches out of her seat, checking that she has her cane, her pocketbook, her glasses slung around her neck. Waiting at the elevator, she loops her arm into mine and kisses my elbow, an expression of appreciation.

In the hallway, up on the tenth floor of the Santa Monica Medical Building, she walks by a mother in jogging shorts, wheeling her infant in a stroller. "Hi, baby," Pearlie says, grinning. "What a beautiful child."

Starting over. It is a theme that underscores much of Pearlie's life. How to begin anew. But now, at 93, she's not so sure how to do it. Out of the hospital—and what? Back to what? Her mind drifts back to how she felt, taking care of my grandfather toward the end of his life.

"To know I was living with someone who wasn't in his right mind, now I wonder how I lived through it," she says. When she finally agreed to move him to a nursing home, visiting him every day, he became furious with her, asking only when she'd be taking him back home. "I must be strong inside. You wring it and wring it and wring it until it wrings dry. I wrang dry."

But she pushed herself to do volunteer work at the Peninsula Hospital, where Moe had died. "I saw people there that couldn't take care of themselves," she tells me. "I realized I could take care of myself. I could overcome my loss. So I respected myself. And I figured, if God gave me so much strength to overcome this, I must give back some of this to people that need it.

"At first, I went to people that had strokes. I showed them they could still use their hands. They could write. They could crochet. It gave me a real appreciation of what it means to use what you've got."

Pearlie has always covered up her pain with a smile. As far as cover-ups go, it strikes me that this is not a bad way to go. This is one reason she loved her husband so much. "All the time he was in the nursing home, he knew everything that was going on. Ya know, he didn't want to let on that he was sick. Always with the smile, always with the jokes. He was very funny, in his way. But ya know, coming from that family, no matter how depressed they were inside, they wouldn't show it on the outside. Never. Never."

For Pearlie, it took eight long years after Moe's death until she was ready for change. Day by day, she'd "push the days away" by volunteering time at the hospital. She knew she'd ultimately move closer to DeeDee or Shirley. Since the weather in Maine was too cold for her "rheumatics," she would pack everything up for California. My mother remembers feeling quite "terrified" at the thought, not having lived near Pearlie for nearly forty years. Pearlie, on the other hand, would adjust quickly by focusing on a lifelong obsession, her weight.

Santa Monica, California
December 24, 1985

Dear DeeDee,
   Today I had my checkup with my doctor. He took a urine test and found it okay but in the blood test he found that I had

tryglicerides. I don't know how you spell it, but it is fat in the body or veins and he said the only way to cure it or help lower it is to lose weight.

I put on about 10 pounds and weigh 135 pounds and my doctor said for my height of five feet, I shouldn't weigh no more than 105 pounds. I think I will eliminate all the wonderful cakes and pies they bake here and try and eat smaller portions. But boy, it's hard to stay on a diet, especially now with Christmas right around the corner.

Last week, we had a party where Ramsdale's wife had 12 candles lit on her head with a sponge artificial pie under it. They lit them all up and sang Praise the Lord and I said Praise to my God that they shouldn't start a fire.

Please take care how you drive Christmas week, especially with the drunken drivers.

Kiss the children and xxx to all.

Mom

Now, sitting in the doctor's waiting room with its red plaid carpeting, she's not sure how to proceed. She fills out the medical forms on the clipboard, asking for family history. She thinks of her siblings—Maxie, Marty, and Stella. All of them gone now. How much she misses them. "It's funny, when they're alive, you don't think you're close," she says. "When you lose them, that's when you realize how close you really are. There's such an empty feeling." The nurse calls her into the examining room.

"She's one strong lady," Dr. Marjorie Fine says of Pearlie. As if I didn't know. "Made of the right stuff." Dr. Fine bears a minor resemblance to Mary Poppins, with her hair tied back in a bow. She wears a prim white lace blouse and a skirt. She gently removes the surgical tape over Pearlie's incisions and inspects her work, replacing the worn-out tape with fresh, clear patches.

"The *lupichka,* Doctor," Pearlie says, pinpointing pain in her bony back.

"You know what you need there?" the doctor replies. "More fat. You need padding."

Music to Pearlie's ears. "Oh, you're so wonderful. I love ya! What should I eat?"

"It doesn't matter," says Dr. Fine. "Now that your gallbladder is out, eat what appeals to you. The gallbladder doesn't have a real function. It just stores the bile your liver makes. So, there are no

Pearlie and six of her great-grandchildren in Happy Face vests she crocheted.

restrictions. Nowadays, they figure that old people like you have beaten the odds, already."

"Ice cream, Doctor?" Pearlie asks of a favorite indulgence she's avoided in recent months.

"Yeah, it's good for you. You gotta get some meat on your bones."

Pearlie wonders about her hiatal hernia.

"That we didn't fix," says Dr. Fine.

"Why didn't ya?" Pearlie counters.

"Why couldn't we turn back the clock?" Dr. Fine asks, smiling.

Pearlie needs practical advice. "The Axid, dahling, how should I take it?" The surgeon recommends she take her hernia medication before going to bed. And she says something else, something my mother and aunt keep telling Grandma: "You don't have to prove anything to anyone. Just get well."

"All right, doll," Pearl says to her doctor. "Have yourself a good vacation."

❧

IT IS 1914 OR 1915. KAISER WILHELM HAS COME TO INVESTIGATE the soldiers invading Austria. And he passes by a little house right near the highway. A teenage girl, peering out her window, watches him come and go.

"Not many cars," Tessie remembers. "I can see it now."

Actually, what she also sees at this moment, killing time before company comes over on a Sunday afternoon, is her nose. For the first time, she tells me the story behind her snoring. "I always had trouble with my nose, my breathing," Tessie remembers. "It's from when I was ten years old. Yom Kippur. The law said you had to sell tobacco or cigarettes. You had to stay open. I was in my aunt's house, to keep *traffica*. It means you can sell tobacco. In her kitchen, she had a closet. And a few packages of tobacco.

"Outside the house, there was a pump for water, so you didn't have to go to the well. A girl I hated, she lived far away from our neighborhood. She was worse than a boy, more than a tomboy. Her older sister wanted to go into the field with a jug of water. I wanted to get even with her sister. She was really mean to everybody. They really hated Jews—a big family, known for treating the Jews horrible. Don't mention no names, because I don't want to have any trouble.

"As she went to the pump for water, I took the jug away. The pump hit me in the nose. My nose started bleeding. I was afraid to tell my father. Years later, when I got my tonsils taken out, I was twenty. And I was hemorrhaging. This is how I suffered all my life. And I never told anybody. It was, like, beyond my dignity that I had faults."

Why did she have it in for this girl? "Because she was stronger than I."

The phone rings. It's Cynthia, checking to see what else she can bring Grandma, besides pastrami and cucumber salad and deli food for dinner. When she hangs up, Tessie washes a few dishes. Then she sits back down. She says she washes the dishes "on installment." It helps to preserve her energy.

I ask her to tell me the story again of her sisters in America, mourning their father's death, while he was still alive. It is one of my favorites, depicting the vagaries of chance and circumstance.

"During the First World War, you couldn't write from Europe to America," she says, standing to wash another dish. "Switzerland was neutral. One of my cousins lived in Vienna, and Vienna you could write to Switzerland. My cousin wrote to Switzerland. Her name was Gitel Karpin. Her mother was my mother's cousin and her father was my father's cousin. That's why we were so close.

"Her father had a cousin in a different city also had children in America. But Gitel made a mistake. She wrote she got a letter from Europe.

"To make it short and sweet—somebody wrote to her that their father died in Europe. At the same time, she was writing to her mother's cousins and her father's cousins. But instead of putting in the letter to her father's cousins, she put in the letter to her mother's cousins—my sisters in America. In the letter, she wrote to tell them their father had died.

"So, my sisters sat *shivah* for him. The letter said, 'I don't know when he died, but you have to say Kaddish for him.' And my sister Rose named her son Chaim, after him. So this was around 1918. When there was peace, you could write to America. The censor didn't allow you to write Jewish to America. So I wrote in Polish. And my father signed the letter. Then, they knew he was alive."

Chaim loved teasing his daughters about his death: How did you cry for me? he'd ask them. "And my sister talked to a rabbi who told her to change her son's name to Arthur, or Alter in Yiddish. That means old. But imagine how my father felt. He was supposed to be dead. And he was alive.

"All the children, they came to see us in Ellis Island. They took the little boat, you know. And they saw that my father was there. Leah, she nearly fainted to see her father is really there. I climbed up on the window to see downstairs. On Ellis Island we were on the first or second floor. And through a window I saw a woman walking around. Everybody was looking for their own. I was standing there. It was a Saturday morning. No, Friday morning. We came there Friday, and I hear a woman says, 'Do you know a family—in Yiddish—named Teitel?' I said, 'What did you say?' 'Chaim Teitel?' she asks. Leah was pregnant with Anna that time.

"Sylvia was standing near me. I said, 'Sylvia, hurry up. Go down and bring up Papa to that window.' Leah nearly fainted there that she sees her father. And they were crying about, oh—"

Suddenly, she stops midsentence. "Now it's no use," she says.

"What's no use?" I ask.

"Even to think about anything. Nothing. It's nothing. Worth nothing."

What do you dream about these days?

PEARLIE: You know, I dream very little. Isn't that strange? In fact, I can't remember the last time I dreamed. Maybe it's because I listen to the TV till I'm very tired. When I hit the hay, that's it. I sleep only three hours a time. Get up at five. Seldom do I dream. The next time I dream, I'll let you know. It'll be about a handsome guy, that I can tell you.

TESSIE: I don't sleep too much. I sleep an hour on, an hour off. Lately? No. I really mean it. And another thing, I don't remember my dreams. When I was in the country, Mrs. B, she used to tell me what she dreamt about. I'd love to remember. But I never can remember my dreams. It's very seldom I can remember. Most of the time, I see dead ones: my mother, father, sisters. We talk together like we used to do, fifty years ago. It must be very serious, very scary or so, that I should wake up. My mother used to say you're not allowed to believe in dreams, because sometimes you dream very bad things and it doesn't happen. She says, in Jewish, a dream is silly and God is the boss of us. We shouldn't believe in dreams to begin with. Maybe that's why I don't remember them. She used to tell me exactly what she dreamt, and I thought she'd made it up.

✌✌

TESSIE AND CYNTHIA ARE ARGUING IN THE KITCHEN. "You purposely spoke low," Tessie snaps.

"I did not."

"You did, Cynthia. You did!"

"I did not. Why would I purposely speak low? You're really deaf. Why would I speak low?"

Tessie considers the question as she cleans up one of the Empire kosher chickens Cynthia has just brought over on a sparkling Sunday afternoon. Their argument, like so many others, is about past slights—both real and imagined. In this case, it concerns a recent doctor's visit, when both were nervous about tests to determine if Tessie's esophagus might have a growth on it. The tests turned out negative. But mother and daughter are positively fuming with each other: Tessie feels the doctor and Cynthia were conspiring to exclude her from the truth about her test results, speaking in hushed tones. Cynthia thinks her mother is becoming paranoid. Or deaf. Or maybe both.

"I don't know why," she answers. "It's not nice to talk loud. And the doctor spoke also very low. I even interrupted a few times. I said, 'What's going on?' " Grandma turns to me. "They would explain to me and talk low again. I feel a little, like, I'm still somebody! And they talk low. It's probably I don't have to hear."

I want to crawl under the table. But I ask a question instead. "You really think Grandma's paranoid?" I ask Cynthia.

"Why would I talk low with the doctor?" she asks. In our family, there is a long-standing history of hiding medical truths. Cancer, especially, is a big bugaboo. When Tessie nursed her mother before her death from colon cancer, her children had no idea their grandmother had cancer. When my father had colon cancer when I was 18, I didn't learn the truth about his illness—he later said he wanted to protect his patients and his good professional standing—until several years later. Sometimes, denial is a good thing, Sometimes, it backfires.

Grandma wants to be fair to her daughter. They're talking to each other through me now. "She is very, very concerned and she is—she tried for me more than anybody would. Even more than I would do for her. And yet, if I say one word, she threatens me. That's all. And then I don't have the nerve to say anything. So, instead of answering, I keep quiet. 'Cause I'm afraid I'll lose her."

"She's afraid she's going to lose her legs," Cynthia snipes, referring to herself. It is primarily she who buys food and clothing for Tessie now. "You know what I mean?"

"Lose what?" Tessie asks.

"Her legs," Cynthia says, explaining that she has become Tessie's legs.

"Her what?" Grandma asks me again. "Her egg?"

"Legs, legs, for God's sake." I find myself yelling at her now, too.

"The doctor is up to her, anyways," Cynthia continues, sounding exasperated. "He gives her medication. Then she doesn't do what he says. What's the difference?"

"There is nothing to like in a medication," Tessie counters. "Did you ever like a medicine? There's no such thing that you like it. You take it because you have to take it. Maybe I didn't finish it. It's possible."

Cynthia softens. "Excuse me," she says, eyeing a package of chicken and wanting to be of help to her mother. "You have chicken on the counter. Could I put it in the freezer?"

"You couldn't put it in," Tessie says, surveying how much extra food she has. "Ya know, you can get smothered by love, too," she adds.

"I don't buy anything she doesn't ask for," Cynthia snaps.

I can only wonder if I'm going to be like this with my mother. When she needs my help to shop, will she snub my efforts to be of assistance? At once angry with herself for being in this position but also grateful to have a daughter who helps? Or will we circle each other warily, the mother-daughter compass shifting in ways that defy logic as dependency and love grow inverted over time?

IN MINING MY GRANDMOTHERS' LIFE STORIES, SOMETIMES THE tables get turned. For example, I discover a letter of Pearlie's, dated June 12, 1986, about me during a low point of my life.

> *Thursday*
> *June 12, 1986*
> *Santa Monica*
>
> *Dear DeeDee,*
>
> *I think Joy will be able to get a hold of herself. I spoke to her yesterday and she seems much better. Her article about the new picture that Robert Redford is in will be published in the* New York Times *magazine, and her name underneath is Joy Horowitz. She gets good money for her articles. Did I tell you that they buried the baby in a non-sectarian cemetery and there is a field for only babies and lots of them are born brain dead? Shirley says they are still working on what the cause of death was for Joy's child, but so far it had choked in the uterus and also they think it had someting to do with the baby didn't grow completely. They are not sure and still don't know the results of the test. Norman came to the funeral from work. Mike, Shirley, Shari, Peggy, Steve, Debby, Brock's father, mother, sister. There were flowers from Brock's studio, and so many flowers in the house and on the grave. It was very sad. And Brock and Joy wrote a beautiful eulogy. And then Mike and a few of them put the yamakies on their head and he said the Jewish prayer. I think it is a good thing they did what they did because that finished it. Joy called the baby therapist at*

the hospital and asked how to explain the baby to Trevor, and she told him the baby's name was Jake and he died. Trevor seemed very relieved. Did I tell you after the funeral we all went back to Joy's house and I brought over cake and cookies and we had coffee and her garden is so beautiful.

Love you all,
xxxxxMom

P.S. Because I entertained in a few places with the dancing dolls I was given an invitation to go to Disneyland with the group in a bus and they are going to give me a box lunch. That is this Wednesday.

Reading that letter left me reeling. It's not just that I was the subject of her reportage, and the details of my loss became fodder for Pearlie's pen. More, I saw my own story from Pearlie's perspective and realized how she buried the lead. One of the most incomprehensible moments of my life took second billing to a magazine assignment about a Robert Redford movie. Or how much I got paid to write about it.

Would my attempts at mining Pearlie's life prove to be equally *farblondjet* (mixed up)?

☞

FRIDAY, APRIL 14, 1995. AT OUR PASSOVER SEDER AT MY PARENTS' house in Beverly Hills, my father holds forth mightily, even if slightly stoned on Marinol, the marijuana derivative for cancer patients.

Pearlie, too, is in top form, having crocheted a yarmulke for each person at the table, including Lucy. It is the first time I've felt comfortable enough to wear the Jewish skullcap, traditionally worn by men during religious rituals. That's because Pearlie has put her creative stamp on each one, making us all look very bohemian and very egalitarian, the purple and blue and silver yarn interwoven like crowns of love.

During the Seder, which Dad typically runs through at a dizzying pace—trying to avert a matzo meltdown by one of the children but also focusing his attention on them—my sister Peggy, on a visit from Austin, Texas, breaks rank to stand and offer a Hebrew prayer of thanks, the *shechyanu*. Unspoken but clear is her gratitude that Dad is still here with us, though his ashen countenance has me wondering if he is Elijah in human form, or maybe Casper, the friendly cartoon ghost. Pearlie nods approvingly at Peggy, whose daily practice of meditation Grandma now refers to as "that swanee thing." She means "swami," as in guru.

When we drive Pearlie home, she sits in the front seat, beside Brock. I'm perched in the "way back," behind Lucy, Trev, and Gus. We listen to Lucy and Pearlie, singing along with Raffi, the bearded children's balladeer. The blend of their voices makes me wish I had pilfered some of Dad's Marinol for the ride.

"I want to tell ya," Pearlie announces to her captive audience, my sons, "there's nothing in the whole world like having your mama and daddy love ya. It's so good to see you good to each other. And God gave you a little sister.

"I'm telling ya, this is it. Ya got your family, you got everything." There follows a moment of silence, as sweet and contemplative as any that I can recall. My kids seem to understand what she means. It is a *bubbe* benediction.

"Release me!" Pearl instructs Brock, as the car pulls up in front of her building. He unfastens her seat belt. "Joyala, you better watch out," she says, meaning she might steal Brock from me. "I could get used to this. Such soy-vuss."

Gus leans out the window. "Good-bye, Graham Cracker," he yells, waving.

❧ ❧

O~N THE DAY OF THE~ O~KLAHOMA~ C~ITY BOMBING,~ P~EARLIE IS~ profoundly upset. "How could people want to do things like that—set off bombs?" she asks, her voice shaky. "We're here to live, not to die. It's just so hard to believe there's so much hatred."

She sighs deeply. "God puts us here for a reason: to be getting along together and for feeling for each other."

I've come to visit her on this day with a video camera in hand, because she wants to show me her latest creation—the *bubbe* doll, Pearlie's answer to Barbie—and I want this on film for posterity. At a craft shop nearby, she bought a ready-made doll with gray hair and then crocheted an outfit for it: purple knit dress, purple cape, matching purse, and headband. It is beautiful, in a childlike way.

"It'll remind kids that they have a grandma," she says of her doll. She checks the plastic legs, which don't move. She laughs. "She's kinda stiff. She can't bend too easy—but isn't that a replica of people as they get older?" She's also crocheted a cane and glasses that hang on a thread around the doll's neck.

Pearlie dabs the sides of her mouth with a handkerchief. Suddenly, she jabs the doll into the air, as if it's dancing, like a Japanese Kabuki puppet. "So, *bubbe* doll," she says in a singsongy way, "just sing and be happy. Be happy while we can. Yes. Yes. Yes. Everybody should be well and get along together in this world. And be happy.

"Don't you think so, Joy?"

A Bubbe Bake-Off

GRANDMA PEARLIE'S

Stuffed Cabbage

You know that station I watch with Regis Philbin? Her mother made it one time on TV. Kathie Lee's mother. It was similar to what I make. It's a wonderful thing, 'cause you can prepare it. It freezes. It's the most wonderful thing for freezing. You can make it exotic, with raisins—white or red. There's so many ways to make it tasty.

The big thing on stuffed cabbage is getting the cabbage soft and rolling it. You gotta boil it up. With a steamer, if you can. It mustn't be split 'cause the meat comes out. I make it sweet and sour and I put in ginger snaps. This is Jonathan and Elliott's best dish.

You boil the water and put the cabbage in and cover it. I put the whole cabbage in. As it softens, I peel it off. It's hard to take out. You need prongs to take it out. Use cold water to get the cabbage leaves off.

Use two eight-ounce cans of tomato sauce. And a third cup of water. You can use salt and you don't have to. Two tablespoons of sugar. One onion diced up. Half a cup of raisins is optional. If they like 'em, all right. If not, it's just as good without it. And two or three ginger snaps, crumbled. And a little lemon juice, too.

You take the rice, raw. You take about a cup of rice. A little salt. And an egg. And you mix the onion, rice, egg, salt, and meat. About a pound and a half of meat, as lean as possible mix in. Then you roll out your cabbage rolls. On the bottom where the bone is, you have to cut that out because it's easier to roll the cabbage. Then you put a tablespoon of the meat mixture in each cabbage roll. Make it like a package, you fold each side over into the center and roll it up, like a package. Put it in the tomato sauce diluted with water. The extra cabbage you cut up and throw on top. You bring it to a boil. Then you cover it. Let it cook for about an hour. You gotta watch it, it shouldn't burn. You have to lower the flame. Don't be afraid to add water. After an hour, you can put in the ginger snaps. And add some sugar. Not too much. It's not hard, but it's a job. It can stay in the Frigidaire, frozen, for six months. It's always ready for ya.

Stuffed Cabbage

(With Eva's Hungarian Recipe Thrown in for Good Luck)

This is really a chore, to make cholipshes—in Polish, it's galumkis—not only to make it, but you take a day off just to prepare yourself to make the cabbage. First, you try to buy the leanest meat you can get. When you buy the cabbage, you see it shouldn't be hard, the leaves. I don't like the tight ones. I like the loose ones. So, you boil up the cabbage in a pot of water. And you cut the heart, the top, the middle. You cut away the hard part, it shouldn't crack.

And you got to prepare the meat before you start. This I forgot to say. So you take the rice, and a pound of ground beef, and put it in a bowl to mix it together. How much rice? I don't know. A half pound is too much. Two handfuls, two fistfuls of rice is good. Of course if you want you can wash it. Then, you chop up an onion or two, whatever you like. Salt, too, you need. For the meat. I don't know your meat, but our meat is already koshered, so it's got salt. But it needs a little bit more. Then, you make it into round things. You roll them up. Put a tablespoon of meat in each one. It just depends how big the leaf is. You can cover it, you can close it from both sides. Like an envelope. And then you cook it about two hours. Then, you taste it.

The tomato sauce? Oh, yeah. That's right. We'll make it tomorrow. We'll look at Eva's recipe for sure. Today, I can't think no more so good. Turn off that tape recorder already.

SAUCE

12 ounces tomato paste
1 can jellied cranberry sauce
1 cup McIntosh apples, chopped
1 16-ounce can saurekraut
honey, to taste

Chop remaining cabbage leaves—mix together with the saurekraut and chopped apple. Layer the mixture in the pot, alternating with the stuffed cabbage. Combine the sauce ingredients. Mix together with enough water to cover the cabbage. Pour the sauce mixture over the stuffed cabbage in the pot. On a slow fire, it simmers about two and half to three hours. You got to make sure it cooks. You can't be a shlump about it.

CHAPTER 12

Hok a Tchynik: Blab Enough

My son Gussie and Tessie share a laugh.

BREAD AND RABBITS. THIS IS HOW MY GRANDMOTHERS REMEM-
ber their grandmothers. Pearlie's paternal grandmother, whose
name escapes her, came to America three times and three times
moved back to Israel. It was her black bread, sliced and smothered in butter, that Pearlie remembers best of all from trips to
Harlem, where her brothers received their Hebrew instruction.
Tessie's maternal grandma, Ceil, slept with a cage of twelve white
rabbits beneath her straw bed to cure her rheumatism.

Now, I remember my grandmothers as believers in redemption.
No one, they think, is beyond hope, even if they see it from different perspectives.

"You have no idea how good people are, Joyala," Pearlie tells me.

"I believe in retribution," Tessie says. "Everything is an echo in
the world. We echo ourselves." And yet, the very core of their
selves is wrapped up in the same idea: In the end, all that matters
is the love we've shared while alive.

Take heaven, for instance. Neither Tessie nor Pearlie believes
in an afterlife. No pearly gates or angels on high. They are both of
the school that what you see is what you get. For my grandmoth-

ers, the finality of death is not some scary concept. It is the truth. *Finito*. Done.

Consequently, the idea of hanging on to life for all it's worth runs deep. If this is all there is, you do it. You survive. And if you're lucky, you can even find a slice of heaven on earth. In the people you love, the water you drink, the bread you eat.

"Bread is the main nourishment you need," Tessie says one morning over mouthfuls of a hardened bagel, practically prehistoric. On another day, she drinks coffee and munches on a piece of seedless rye for breakfast. It is a Saturday morning, and the burner on her stove stays lit all day, in keeping with the rules of the Sabbath. "This is the heel," she says, appreciating her favorite part of the loaf. "I love it here."

According to Tessie, it is a sin to throw away food, particularly bread. There is sacrament in using up scraps languishing in the fridge, rather than buying something fresh to replace it. The way she pushes on, day in and day out—her hands wobbly, her feet unsteady, her stubborn insistence on using up what she's got— makes me think of a modern-day Job. Her life may be slowly sputtering out, but her very essence, her spirit, is still her own.

"If you have to suffer, you live," she is fond of saying. At first blush, it seems a deeply pessimistic worldview. Does that mean if you don't suffer, you don't live? I ask. She answers by way of a parable. "Years ago, a woman in my building tried to commit suicide," Grandma begins. "Italian girl. And she jumped down from the second-floor window. But the lines, the wash lines, used to go to the rear of the building. You don't know how we used to dry our clothes. Anyway, one building was connected to the other in the backyards. And the wash lines kept her back, broke her fall. I mean, she did fall, and she got broken hips. I don't know what else. And she remained in the hospital and came back, and she says, 'I have to suffer, so I live.' So that's what I keep on saying."

Dying, in other words, is not so easy. Though Tessie believes suicide to be a sin, she is also not one to advocate prolonging life when it really is a matter of prolonging a death. Contradictions persist. Her phone book includes an entry for an organization, Concern for Dying, because she doesn't want extraordinary measures taken on her behalf, should the time come. But she also dubs Jack Kevorkian, the so-called suicide doctor, "Dr. CaCa."

When I imagine my grandmothers side by side, what occasionally comes to mind is a line from Rudyard Kipling: "If you can meet triumph and disaster, treat those two imposters just the same." Like a chimera of joy and pain, Pearlie and Tessie have unwittingly devolved into a total paradox: me.

⊲⊲ ⊳⊳

M<small>OTHER</small>'<small>S</small> D<small>AY</small>, M<small>AY</small> 14, 1995. 2 P.M. I<small>NSIDE MY KITCHEN, ALONE</small> with Pearl.

"Joyala, I want you to have it," Pearlie says to me.

"I couldn't," I tell her.

"It's yours, really."

"No, Grandma, I can't take it."

"I gave it to your mother and then she gave it back to me when I moved out here. Now, please, it's for you." Pearlie is bequeathing to me a family heirloom that would be thrown in a junk heap by anyone else. But to me, this is a most remarkable present: her mother's aluminum pot for stuffed cabbage. It is more than a century old.

I feel guilty the second I take it, worried about my place in the family. About going out of order, taking my turn too soon. Like taking "butts" (cutting in line) on the playground. Shouldn't my mother be next? Or my aunt? Or my older sister? It is a middle child's obsession. But, I think, Grandma has given this to me because I'm the one who's asked to learn how to make her stuffed cabbage. The pot is perfect. I thank her.

To celebrate Mother's Day, I've invited over Pearlie, Mom and Dad, Shari and her family. Our kids are charging in and out of the house. Dad is too sick to join us. Over cappuccinos and SnackWell chocolate fat-free cookies and fruit, the rest of us sit at the kitchen table and feel his absence. I watch Shirley watching Pearlie, holding hands and saying nothing, grateful to have each other as mother and daughter, as friends. We talk about other things.

"It's hard," Pearlie says of her postoperative life. "Ya gotta get used to the body. But it's not the same body. I'm not enjoying it, the way it is." I give her a gift—foot cream to rub into her soles— for her "numby" feet.

And yet, she continues, "it's strange. I don't think anyone really, really wants to kick off. Most of the time, we're forced to go. I figure if I kick off, it'll be hard, transportation-wise." It reminds her of a joke.

"A guy takes his wife to the doctor's office. She's not well. The doctor says, 'You stay here while I examine your wife.' The doctor examines her and then sends her to the waiting room and asks for the husband. The guy says, 'What's wrong with my wife?' The doctor says she has to have sex three times a week. The husband says, 'I'll drive her once but she has to take the bus the other two times.'"

Later, I call Grandma Tessie, while stitching name tags into Trevor's clothing for his first summer at Camp Takajo, a Maine sleepaway camp. She asks after my children but quickly grows annoyed with herself, because she's forgotten Trevor's name. I tell her he's taken to playing an electric Stratocaster guitar, like Jimi Hendrix, though the reference is lost on her. I tell her Gussie smacked a triple in Little League. And I tell her Lucy's latest linguistic accomplishments. Her favorite declarative sentence is, "I like the CooCoo man so much," a reference to her love for the ice cream man.

Tessie laughs. In anticipation of Dad's six-month chemotherapy regime ending, he and Mom will take a Caribbean cruise next month. Though I have my doubts about the wisdom of such a trip, especially on a day like today when he can barely lift his head, he and Mom are trudging onward. They want to swim in clear water together. On their way back, they plan on visiting Tessie in New York for one night.

When my father told Grandma about his plans, she replied, "You can afford it?" Translation: Why can't he stay longer?

He asked her how much she'd want him to stay, and she didn't hesitate to reply: "Forever."

❦

Saturday morning. June 10, 1995. Watching Gus play Little League baseball while soaking up the morning sun, Brock turns to me in the bleachers and says, "Here is my religion." He points to Lucy, sitting on his lap and dripping a Popsicle down her elbows onto his khaki pants. "Here is my altar." He softly kisses the back of her head.

At first, avoidance was our favored approach to religion. When we were married, we promised to one day visit Israel and Ireland, our ancestral homes. But we haven't gone to either country yet. Then, holidays became a smorgasbord delight of commercial indulgence, a feast of stuff but a spiritual famine. Over time, I wanted more.

It was after Trevor's birth that I tacked up a mezuzah on our doorpost. It was after Gussie's birth that I decided to give the kids a Jewish education. It was after Lucy's birth that I mysteriously found myself whipping up braided loaves of challah on Friday. When our babies Jacob and Isaac died, I wondered about their souls: Where did they go? Was I being punished by God, or was this a little cosmic joke? Where does faith come from, anyway?

My grandmothers haven't been much help, instructionally speaking. According to Orthodox Jewish theology, an infant does not have a soul until it's lived thirty days, which suggests that mourning a baby's death is pretty much a waste of time. No soul, no grief. Poof—gone. To her credit, Pearlie came to Jacob's funeral. That day is a horrible blur in my memory, but I do remember standing in the baby burial section of the cemetery—something about the size of that casket changed my view about life forever—and holding Pearlie's hand. Then, I listened as my father said Kaddish, the Jewish prayer for the dead, and Brock's father recited the Lord's Prayer. It was our do-it-yourself burial.

After Trevor's birth, we called Tessie to tell her our good news and to inform her of her new great-grandson's name. "That's not so good," she said, meaning it wasn't Jewish enough. The night before our baby Isaac died, she called me in the hospital. I asked her how she'd feel if I named the baby after Izzy. "Yeah, that would be nice," she said. We did. The name on his marker is Isaac Horowitz Walsh.

Pearlie offers mixed messages. On the one hand, she advises me not to make a big deal of religion with Brock. "Don't push it, Joyala. Religion is in the heart. You're married to such a wonderful guy. He's your better half." On the other hand, she crochets a yarmulke, not just for each of my children's bar or bas mitzvah down the road but also one for Brock. Just in case.

Maybe because of the Jewish law of matrilineal descent, I've taken much for granted. Though Trevor and Gus attend Hebrew school now, the whole matter of organized religion continues to elude our family. We've suggested alternatives to a bar mitzvah for Trevor, like a trip to Israel or an overnight camping trip in the mountains, where we could celebrate his thirteenth birthday. He said he preferred a ceremony in the synagogue.

Brock calls me a hypocrite, rarely attending temple myself but still advocating Sunday school for the kids. I want them to know about their culture, their history. It's part of my tradition, my heritage, and it's inescapable—like breathing. I never thought when we married I'd see it this way. Now I do.

Still, the most fundamental yearning for us all is to be a family. Connected. Whole. But as a Jew, my spiritual search will have to be one of my own making. One thing is certain: Spending time with my grandmothers feels as holy as anything I know. And I know this: I want my children to feel proud of who they are. To hide, never. To question, always. Brock asked Trevor recently what he expected of him for his bar mitzvah, and Trevor answered with a question of his own: "You'll come, won't you?"

❧☙

THE MORNING FOG IS THICK, ROLLING IN OFF THE OCEAN AND making the entire sky gray and overcast on this Friday in late spring. The front door to the Silvercrest is still locked, requiring entry through the telephone system perched beside the door. On the bulletin board inside, there is a picture from 1987 of Pearlie and other Silvercrest residents who volunteered their services in the community. Pearl is easy to spot in the photo, her hands holding those of the women lined up behind her. In the elevator, there is a sign tacked up that reads "Join Us! Silvercrest Bible Study," an activity Pearlie will skip.

At 7:45 A.M., Pearlie fixes herself a bowl of Cream of Wheat and a cup of tea. Dressed in her striped flannel nightgown, navy blue bathrobe, and slippers, she's already put on a dab of pink lipstick. Gary, the Arrowhead Water delivery man, will be here this morning, and she wants to make a good impression.

"I'll tell ya the truth," Pearlie says to me, between bites of her hot cereal, "I've gotten to the point where food don't mean anything to me." This, perhaps more than any of her physical maladies, makes my heart ache. Food was Pearlie's channel to high society. It was an expression of love for her family. It was an evil to be wary of. It was her everything.

Is losing your appetite another part of the aging process? "That's what I'd like to know," she says, her voice going high and reedy. "Food was something to enjoy. It meant so many things. It meant warmth. It meant getting together with people.

"When I hear people are going on diets, depriving themselves of so much pleasure . . ." Her voice trails off as she shakes her head. "We have food to look to as friendliness, home. Now, people feel it isn't doing them any good. Instead, people eat because they know they have to, not because they want to."

It's staggering, really, to think about how much has changed in Pearlie's life, just relative to food preparation. When she was a teenager, before the advent of refrigerators and freezers, half of all American women had at least five children and spent an average of five hours in the kitchen each day. But, I tell her, a recent article in the *New York Times* reported that women today have an average of two children and spend about fifteen minutes just preparing dinner.

"That's why the divorce rate is so high," Pearlie says, spooning hot cereal into her mouth. I roll my eyes. When she was involved in the sisterhood at Temple Beth El in Manhattan Beach, she remembers getting meat and other food for free from local merchants, charging $1.50 per plate for a lunch she'd make, and then distributing the proceeds to poor people.

"I really enjoyed doing that," she says. She rises to show me an invitation she's received for an upcoming volunteer appreciation luncheon she plans on attending in honor of her work at the Santa Monica Hospital.

On the chair by her TV, a book sits open. It is Dominick Dunne's *The Mansions of Limbo*. "It tells about the stars and where they have their parties," she explains. "Ooh, do they spend money. Wow."

She looks at what I'm wearing—a T-shirt under a cotton blouse and blue jeans. "You go out like this without a jacket and it's cool," she says. "You're not dressed warm enough." I said the exact same thing to Trevor when I dropped him off at school before arriving here.

She hands me her FHP card and a prescription to be filled at the pharmacy. She needs to get the generic form of Cardizem, her blood pressure medication, and of Paxil, a new antianxiety pill Dr. Lutsky has prescribed for her "noyves."

"They charged me the genetic price," she says.

"You mean generic," I say, correcting her.

"Yeah, right."

Her skin is glowing this morning, the first time in weeks that she's not had a sallow complexion. She attributes it to using petroleum jelly, a beauty technique she picked up from a woman in the building who has translucent skin. "Maybe it grows hair on the face," Pearlie quips. "Don't put that in the book."

The doorbell rings. "Oh, here's my Gary," she says, opening the door. A handsome blond man with blue eyes and thick biceps walks through the door. "Gary, come meet my granddaughter. She's the one writing the book."

Gary Anderson strides in, carrying a couple of plastic gallon jugs of water. Strangely, when I see him, I'm reminded of the photographs Grandma has shown me of Sam, her father, minus the Vandyke beard.

"It's a pleasure for me to see Pearl every two weeks," he says to me. He gives Pearl a wink. "This relationship is more than just a water man–customer thing."

"Yeah, right," Pearl says, guffawing. "Gary's married, ya know."

"She won't let anyone else bring her water," he says, teasingly, "which means I can't go on vacation." In his Arrowhead delivery uniform of a red striped shirt and blue shorts, Gary looks like a Good Humor man for the nineties. His sunglasses, slung around his neck on a black cord, rest on his chest. A giant tattoo peeks out from beneath his right sleeve. He says the tattoo makes people think he's a tough guy. But, in fact, he got it during his stint in the Marines, when he was stationed in Haifa, integrated with the Israeli special elite force, during the Beirut war. Pearlie thought he was in his twenties but he's really 32, with Scandinavian roots.

"I'm middle-aged," Gary crows. He crouches down, studying Pearlie's water supply beneath her kitchen table. "I know you're having company next week," he says. Obviously, Pearlie has filled him in on the family's affairs; DeeDee will be here next week from Maine for another visit. "It looks like you're down to eight bottles," he says. "I think you have enough. If not, just call me."

He scribbles down his phone number for Pearl. "So Pearlie, this is my number, okay?" he asks, handing her a card. "You can call just to say hello if you like." He walks over to her refrigerator and circles the date of his next visit in two weeks on her calendar.

Gary turns to me. "She makes my day," he says. Pearlie blushes. "I guess I make hers, too." They look at each other, fondly. Though I've teased her about this relationship being another one of her many flirtations, I see I was dead wrong. In fact, theirs is a real friendship, new and tentative and tender.

"Pearlie's told me to make the most of each day," he says. "You never know when your calling will be. I take that very seriously. People are really good. You hear so much bad stuff in the media. But there's so many wonderful people in the world. Right, Pearl?" She looks at him with pride, nodding, as a teacher to a student. That a 93-year-old woman and a 32-year-old man could strike up a relationship over water bottles—Pearlie calls them "bah-uls"—is a basic lesson in charity: to open one's heart to another so the small gestures, the day-to-day kindnesses, matter most.

Gary opens the door to leave. "Have a great day, love," he says to Pearlie.

Eyeing the phone number in her hand, she asks when the best time to call him would be. He answers, "Any time." Leaning out her blue door as he walks down the hallway, Pearlie, the ever-hopeful femme fatale, calls after him, "Your wife won't get jealous?"

<hr />

IT IS LITTLE WONDER THAT A BRICK-MAKER'S DAUGHTER WOULD end up in this part of Queens. As far as the eye can see, there is red brick in Tessie's neighborhood. Apartment houses, stores, single-family homes, restaurants—all made of brick. It must truly feel like home for Tessie. It must remind her of her father. But just about everything does.

On the kitchen counter by Tessie's wall phone, she keeps an address book she picked up years ago on one of her California visits. It is covered in brown vinyl and is from one of those cheapo stores where everything costs 99 cents. But what started out as a simple address book, so Grandma could keep up her tradition of sending cards on birthdays and anniversaries, has evolved into something else.

Now, it is a book of the living and the dead. In the back, she has a listing of deceased relatives and friends—their birth dates and their death dates, including by the Jewish calendar. The sheer volume of these listings has begun to outnumber the living ones. There is her sister, Gussie Scheffler, 1-3-72. Her sister, Leah Becker, 1-14-73. Her brother-in-law, Lou Benedon, 9-20-83. Her sister, Sylvia Benedon, 8-30-79. Her brother, Max Title, 6-24-83. Her sister-in-law, Ida Title, 2-21-67. Her father, Chaim Teitel, 8-8-34. Her mother, Charna Teitel, 3-8-46. Her husband, Isadore Horowitz, 10-23-51. Her husband, Sam Weinreb, 1-20-65. There is even a listing she has left blank for herself, Tessie Horowitz Weinreb.

Next to her name, she has written the name she wants on her tombstone: Toby Bat Chaim Teitel, meaning Toby, the daughter of Chaim. Not her mother, too? I ask.

"No," she says. "This is the way I like it."

The father-daughter connection, for Tessie and for Pearlie, seems a key component of their inner strength. In some ways, I've come to believe that their long-term reserves are derived almost entirely from that devotion, as middle daughters tied to their father's affection. It's a bond I know well.

If nothing else, Tessie and Pearlie stand for the proposition that behind every strong woman there is a father. He could be a *shlub*. He could be a crackpot. He could be a saint. He could even be God. But the primacy of this connection in forging a woman's tenacity is indisputable.

Not to besmirch motherhood. Mothers we need for roots: the tit, the food, the succor. But fathers are our wings, our emancipators, our key to survival. Without Chaim and Sam, Tessie and Pearlie would be lost girls, their womanhood impossible.

It is often presumed that the mother-son relationship is the cornerstore of the patriarchy of Judaism: While women are the rulers of the domestic front, men have traditionally been the spiritual leaders and scholars, beginning their day with a simple prayer that thanks God for not making them women. But what's missing from that equation is the father-daughter attachment, a sort of blacksheep bond that is rarely acknowledged. And here, I think, is where a deeper truth lies.

The only mention ever made in the Old Testament of a woman in terms of the father-daughter relationship is of Dina, and that is because she has been raped. The story implies that it takes her being defiled for a father to care about a daughter's worth. Also implicit is that the men who created the tale were projecting their own fantasies about their daughters onto Dina. For his part, Freud focused on latency issues, which for Tessie and Pearlie come under the heading Oedipus Shmoedipus.

My grandmothers' self-esteem grew steady and true because they identified with their fathers at a time when women's roles were hopelessly limited. It is precisely because of their fathers' love that they carried on.

For Tessie, there was Chaim—the autocrat, patriarch, pious believer, and man of a thousand *zetz* (blows), not one to shy away from slapping an errant child now and again. In wartime Europe, she struggled to protect him. In America, she turned over her first-born child—my father—to his care. My great-grandfather looked like either Moses or God, with his long white beard. In America, he never earned a dime, though he did work as a *melamed,* teaching young children Hebrew.

"You wouldn't dare to open your mouth to Mama," Tessie says, "but Papa was different." It was, in fact, considered an honor to argue with Chaim. And he liked to spar with Toby. Growing up, she rarely saw him, except at the dinner table Friday nights when the children were barred from making any noise. "If he went like this," she says, tapping her foot beneath the table, "it was, 'Who did it?' Got to be quiet. Oh, the respect at the table was beautiful."

But he was willing to learn from his daughter, too. For example, she came home from school one day and announced that the earth was round. At first, he railed that this was impossible. His Jewish studies had spoken of the four corners of the earth. But Toby prevailed, showing him her textbook with an illustration to prove her point. "My father always said, 'If you want to argue, argue with a smarter one than you. Don't argue with an illiterate person: Keep away.' " Her father made her believe she was smart.

For Pearlie, there was Sam—the Austrian farmer and son of a rabbi who wrapped the *tefillin* around his arms each morning in prayer. When he came to America, he went to night school and learned how to read and speak English. Anna, his wife, spoke English but never learned how to read or write. "That bothered us children very much," Pearlie says of her mother's illiteracy.

"My father would come home at night and get the Jewish paper and read my mother everything that was happening. See, my mother was a little fighter, ya know. She demanded things and she got them. She was a very good soul. But it was my father who showed his affection more. My mother was glad to get my father and the kids out of the house, 'cause every minute it was dinner, supper, things like that. So, Papa would get us dressed and take us, like, for the fireworks July Fourth." He made her feel loved. Safe.

I think of my own father now. The psychologist who came to the dinner table, making up stories about his flatulent patients—

no names, ever—to deflect his worry about their anger and sadness with jokes, instead, for our amusement. Or run to the phone (the upstairs extension for privacy) to speak to another soul in crisis. Once strong and strapping—the Daddy I was thrilled to accompany to Vinny's Hardware Store or the car wash on Saturdays. Who would lift me atop the refrigerator when he'd come home and make me feel like I was literally on top of the world. Now, frail, diminished, struggling to hold on to his dignity in the chemotherapy crush that has wasted his anemic body to the point of wicked exhaustion.

Without my father's support, without his love, I'd be nothing, unable to dream. I think of him because I worry I'm about to lose him. So do my grandmothers.

"Every night, I pray to God that he should take me instead of my children," says Pearl.

"Just because I don't say anything doesn't mean I'm not thinking of him every minute, every second," says Tessie.

And yet, in piecing together the story of my grandmothers' lives, I'm struck by certain mythical aspects of their fathers, the unspoken part. Neither was able to hold on to a job in America. Neither tolerated dissent. Chaim, depending on whose version of the story you believe, might have even killed a man. Sam was forced to work for Moe, a son-in-law he didn't respect. Maybe it is precisely because they wanted more than they got that their daughters loved them so much. Maybe it is her father's weakness that a daughter best understands. My own father's vulnerability—his tears—says more now than his strength ever could.

Or maybe the truth is simpler. "My father was affectionate," Pearlie says of Sam. "He thought about big things and came out short," Tessie says of Chaim.

❦

THE PHONE RINGS. IT'S TESSIE, AND SHE SOUNDS EDGY.

It is ten-thirty at night, New York time, way past her usual bedtime, and she's worried. She can't get to sleep. My mother and father have just flown home from New York, and Grandma hasn't yet heard whether their flight got in safely.

"I need him to call," she says of my father, who is 72 years old. Will this be me, worrying about my sons when they're old?

I try to reassure her that he'll call when he returns home. And I ask her how her visit with Dad went.

"I cannot express what I feel," she says, simply. "At first, I felt my heart was bleeding. Then I got used to it." She means she got used to the sight of her son, stooped and withered. "When I saw him, I make believe it's nothing."

This is hard to believe. "What's there to talk about?" she asks, her voice betraying her. "My heart cries. I can do nothing. I hope for the best. That's all. His hair grows back. All right. Better than nothing." It's true, Dad's hair is sprouting back in.

But five days later, my father is greeted by shocking news from his oncologist: His cancer, considered fatal and incurable, is now in remission. A CAT scan shows that there is only scar tissue where the tumor once grew. The chemotherapy, at least for now, has worked.

Dad tells me his doctor friends, whom he plays poker with, are suggesting he's not out of the woods yet: No one they've heard about has yet to escape the destruction of mesothelioma. But when he returns to a meeting of his psychoanalytic institute, he greets his colleagues with these words: "I have a very short speech: I'm back." Like his grandfather Chaim, my father has managed to outlive his own death.

Shari, Steve, Peggy, and I chip in to buy him a fruit and vegetable juicer for Father's Day, and we spend a perfect afternoon together at the ballpark, watching Trevor play in a Little League championship game. When I ask him, Dad tells me that he attributes his recovery to the love of his family, proper medical treatment, and a certain degree of masochism, which he thinks he inherited from his mother. Mom tells me she thinks Tessie has a direct line, as in a direct line to God.

I call Grandma to share our elation. "I hope it's true," she tells me. "I hope I'm not sleepin'." What is possible in the world, she seems to be teaching me, can be found only among the shards of the impossible. Together, we can imagine anything and make it so. My father's cancer, and its current state of remission, is a metaphor of that. She hopes only when there is reason for it.

Does she think it's a miracle, my father's recovery? "Well, I believe in God," she says.

"You think God answered your prayers?"

"I don't want to say," she replies. "We don't know the outcome yet." But who ever knows the outcome, except when it's a memory, looking back?

In the beginning of September, a state court jury in San Francisco will award my father $2 million against Lorillard Inc., the manufacturer of Kent cigarettes, saying his cancer was caused by asbestos in the filters. My father's case will prove to be the tobacco industry's biggest defeat in the history of tobacco litigation, though the media barely pick up on the story. His triumph in court, though, will be a Pyrrhic victory: Lorillard vows to appeal the verdict. And in the week following the trial, my father will resume chemotherapy. For now, his prognosis remains grim even as he's made legal history.

"If there's one thing my mother taught me," he tells me, "it's that you've got to keep fighting. What else is there?" Beyond love and family, which inevitably must die, I now understand that there is only one thing that lasts: duty. It is a duty to go on, to observe our humanness in the face of suffering. And in this ordinary pursuit, extraordinary things can happen.

⤜❧⤝

ON A WARM SUMMER FRIDAY, EARLY IN THE EVENING, THE streets appear deserted, the pedestrians home now; and there she is, all by herself, tidying up the living room, puffing up a seat cushion, then resting on an armrest, a solitary silhouette bending and stooping and finally staring off through her venetian blinds into the thickening New York dusk.

"This," she says of my visit with my son Gus, "is to me like a blessing. Do you know that the last two days, I did not have even a Tylenol? I don't want to even talk about it." Though she says she's not superstitious, to talk about good things is to risk the evil eye.

Did she not take Tylenol because she was feeling good or because she had to prove to herself she didn't need it? It is Friday night, the longest day of the year, and Tessie is waiting for the appropriate moment to light the *Shabbes* candles.

"I'm on strike," she says, of taking medication. "The last two days—absolutely no medication at all. Yet when do I walk around so much in a day as I did today? If I walk a tenth what I did today, that would be a lot. I sit and either I read the paper, or I play solitaire, or I lay down. That's all. I don't look forward to anything. I don't expect anything.

"Here, I got a guest. I got my granddaughter. I got my great-grandson. No jokes. Thank God, I cook today and I'm going to eat today, too.

"Before you came home, I start feeling my old way. And I say, 'Dear God, please don't do it to me now, because I have to do it. I must do it. Give me strength.' "

What is the "old way"? "I have certain days that I don't feel good. It's like I'm disappearing. Takes only a few seconds. I take a minute or two, I don't think I could last that long. I have to hold on. I don't know where the hell—"

I interrupt. "Is is overwhelming exhaustion?"

"Not tired. I start feeling, like, hot. And then I don't know anything. I feel I'm going to fall, so I grab whatever. Here, I sit here, and I hold on tight to the table. It takes only a few seconds."

To feel like you're disappearing. Expiring. And then to will it away. To me, this seems like a form of magic, making your invisibility vanish.

"Some days, I don't even recognize myself. I'm not me. I haven't got the strength even to argue. I'm like an old washcloth."

Other days, though, she takes much pride in her abilities, however limited. On this evening in June, she's made Gus and me a dinner of spaghetti and meatballs, Gussie's favorite. It has taken her all day to prepare. Remembering her days in the store, she serves it up to Gus as "shmagetti." He laughs, slurping noodles into his mouth.

Her eyes brighten. "I really accomplished something," she says of making dinner for her granddaughter and great-grandson. "All right. It's nothing to brag about."

Maybe it's good to push yourself? She nods. "What did I do? Chopped onions for stewing them. Made the meatballs. Noodles. I'd sit down if I was tired."

She looks happy. "I'm tired," she tells me. "But it's healthy tired, not sick tired."

In honor of her ninety-fourth birthday, I've bought her a white pocketbook. "*Oy vaysmere,*" she says, "how did you know?" (Cynthia told me.) She opens it. "Where's the check for $1 million?" she asks.

She can give, but she can't take. I ask her to show Gus how she fashions a squirrel out of a hanky, like her father used to do. At first, she denies that she can remember how to do it. Then, she immediately tucks in a corner, then another, and makes it hop out of her hand, amid Gus's squeals of delight. She calls her creation "Ms. Squirrel." Very up-to-date. Pish-posh.

But when I try to extract knowledge from her, say, about religion, I'm left in a spiritual vacuum. To question Tessie about her faith is a lesson in futility. Ask her what happens if you blow out the *Shabbes* candles, considered a sin by observant Jews, and she replies, "What happens? It gets dark." Ask her if it bothers her that a woman in Orthodox Judaism cannot be part of a minyan to say Kaddish, and she replies, "If you want to do it, you do. That's all."

But when Gus questions her on matters of biblical scholarship, she chooses her words carefully. "Is it true," Gussie asked Grandma one night, "that Moses spoke to God at the burning bush?"

Grandma smiled. "Yes, it's true," she said. "Yes, definitely. I was there."

⊰⊢⊱

IN THE DARKNESS, LYING BETWEEN MY SON AND MY GRAND-mother, I listen to the soul of a city. The crickets. An occasional boombox blasting by in a car. Another airplane, leaving Kennedy International Airport. A car alarm.

Grandma takes one pillow and folds it in half, under her right shoulder. Then, she snores. Gus, sleeping on the floor beside me, snores, too. Soft, buzzy breathing in unison. The golden glow of the Sabbath candles lights the anterior room. I am between my past and my future. Together, even just for this moment, I am happy falling asleep.

Grandma stirs. She coughs deeply but tries to suppress it with a sour candy she stores in the night-table drawer beside her bed. I thank her for everything, for service better than the Waldorf. "We're a couple a lucky kids," she says, softly, turning over. "Thank you. Someone to talk to."

But as Gus and I are about to leave the next morning, she barks out orders, like a drill sergeant. A litany of criticism erupts.

"Your pants are up in back."

"Fix your collar."

"Can't you dry your hair?"

"Don't you dare go out by yourself!" (To Gus.)

"Again, with the security blanket?" (To Gus.) She looks at me, and I feel only disapproval. She is cranky, unsparing, and not ready to settle for any answers that do not ask the most of us.

Then, I realize this is the only way she knows to express her love. Another parting. Another day by herself to look forward to. She doesn't want me to go. I can't seem to say good-bye, either, fearful this could be the last time. The cab honks for us outside.

"Give me a hug good-bye," I tell Grandma.

She does. Then she buttons the top button of my blouse, worried about the cold.

"Health," she says to me, her eyes watery from a tear duct on the fritz. "What else can I say?"

But the cab driver neglects to fetch my luggage. "He shoulda come in and taken your bags," she says, offering parting instructions. "Don't you dare give him more than a dollar tip, tops."

HERE'S THE THING ABOUT MY GRANDMOTHERS: THEY'RE THE smartest women I know. It's not that they're book-smart or intellectually brilliant. But in the ways of life—in the stuff that matters—they're geniuses. This, of course, may be the greatest irony they teach me: that the poorest girl can wind up the richest woman. "They say even a fool has a prophecy," Tessie explains.

No matter how I cut it, growing old is an impossibly hideous concept. But my grandmothers have given me a new perspective. Like, for instance, middle age may be a time of a widening ass, but if I get very old, I can look forward to my backside shrinking. That's vaguely comforting. "It's a time you think more of yourself than ever before," Pearlie says of old age. "You can't make no contract with God."

Tessie, too, is a realist. "Let's not fool ourselves," she says of her current situation, feeling lousy from a barometric change in air pressure. "I'm lookin' at reality: Better I can't expect. To feel better? Why? All right, this is it. It's fine. It's good. I'm here. And if not, you know what to do."

Yes, I know what to put on her tombstone. I know she wants a lot of people at her funeral. "Yeah," she says, "and if they don't come, I'll be calling them at night." We both laugh.

In a time of instant celebrity and the media's creation of false idols, our real heroes live anonymous lives—unknown, remote, lost to history. My grandmothers, and those of their generation, are among these true, if invisible, pioneers. To me, each of their memories is like a gift of hope. Their stories and reminiscences transmit values that have grown anachronistic: Loyalty. Continuity. Faith. A belief in what is simple and true—the love of family. Theirs is not the politics of "family values." It is, instead, a trust in what can be.

Though I've come to see my own adaptation of these values as variations on a theme, I connect with each one, time and again. Tessie calls me her profit, but she is my prophet. Pearlie says I am her future, but she is my bridge there. They allow me to piece together the story of a life: a collection of fears, memories, hope—of selves over time, shifting, changing, evolving, and even staying put.

So now, for example, I light the Sabbath candles in my own peculiar way. In our house, it is not just the mother's place to say thanks for the blessings of being together at the end of a workweek. My sons say the blessing with me. My daughter, when she can remember, will, too. And my husband makes a peace offering of kisses and hugs and good wishes. It's all part of the same package, I think. Being together and respecting our differences. Offering up prayers and wishes about light in the face of darkness.

My *mishling* (Yiddish for "hybrid") children understand this best. At bedtime each night, Lucy requests three songs: "Tura Lura," an Irish lullaby; "*Dayenu*," a Passover song; and "In My Life," by John Lennon. Last Christmas, it was their Jewish Great-Grandma Pearl who left silver dollars in their stockings. At Chanukah, it was their Protestant Nana who sent eight little presents for each night they lit a candle on the menorah. It is a contradiction. It is schizophrenic. It is my life, at once evolving and staying the same.

To have my grandmothers in my life, to see them enjoy my children—their great-grandchildren—is to uphold a wonder of nature. Like standing at the ocean's edge or observing the vast expanse of a mountain range, it is impossible for me to spend time with Pearlie and Tessie and not believe in something bigger than ourselves. It's not just that I feel a deep sentiment in their presence—which I do. It's more that there is a oneness I feel, among them and me and God. A clarity of connection that transcends age and time. Irrational and eternal.

"So, you want some more shmagetti?" Tessie asks Gus on our recent visit.

"I got that new beret for the baby all ready for ya," Pearlie tells me. "When you comin' over?"

My *bubbes*. How will I live without them?

☜ ☞

WHEN THE FEDERAL EXPRESS PACKAGE ARRIVES, I KNOW IMMEdiately what's inside: Grandma Tessie's passport to America. For months, she's promised to look for it, and now, she's passed it on to Cynthia, who has sent it overnight delivery.

Wrapped inside a white plastic bag is another plastic freezer bag, and inside that are two pieces of cardboard held together with two rubber bands. Four passports fall out, one for each family member who traveled to America. Her father. Her mother. Her sister. And Grandma herself, whose name on the Polish passport was Toni, because, she'd later explain, she wanted to be fancy-shmancy.

The passports smell like the perfumed drawer liners from Tessie's bedroom. As I leaf through each three-by-five page, now yellowed but remarkably well preserved and embossed with golden links around the letters *RP*, for Republic of Poland, I feel a clutch of tenderness. The way she signs her name now is fundamentally the same, with her curlicue *T*'s.

In my mind, I can trace my grandmother's journey, as she leaves Poland at age 18 and travels by train to Rotterdam for passage to her new country. Hers is Passport No. 4553. There is the purple stamp of the American consulate in Warsaw, dated July 2, 1920, which cost $9, or 1,440 marks. And the lavender stamp the following day from the French consulate. Another official stamp from Germany, five days later. And another from the Netherlands. In large block letters on the back of the passport, it reads: VACCINATED. And listed under destination, my grandmother has written *Ameryki (Nowego Yorku) Broklyn. do famili*. She's going to America. New York. Brooklyn. To be with family.

Thumbing through each page, I suddenly begin to weep. It is her grit that echoes across these pages. That she has chosen to so meticulously preserve these passports—the last vestige of another time, another place, another life—speaks of a connection that transcends age. It speaks of love.

But I'm puzzled by two things. Why is it that the picture of my great-grandfather—he bears a certain resemblance to Aleksandr Solzhenitsyn, with his long beard, high cheekbones, clunky overcoat, and almond-shaped eyes—remains in his passport book while the women's photographs have been removed? And what does this Polish word, *"prywatna,"* mean?

I call Tessie for answers. She tells me she and her mother and sister tore their pictures up the minute they arrived in New York because they thought they looked so awful. It makes me wonder how women's vanity has altered the work of historians over the years: If Tessie and my female ancestors deleted themselves from their own photographic annals because of unflattering snapshots, then maybe historical accountability has less to do with shoddy research than pride or a bad hair day.

As for *"prywatna,"* which she wrote in the space for her profession, she translates it as "private." "It means I don't work for nobody," she says simply. Fiercely independent even then, she would determine her own fate. And she has, no matter how treacherous.

"I think," she says, "that you make your life."

❧

A PIGEON LANDS ON PEARLIE'S BALCONY RAILING.

"They make babies," she says of the little bird. "They make you crazy. They leave their *krebbes,* their droppings. Shit droppings. Oh, it's terrible. So listen, Joyala, you said you wanted to ask me something?"

I say: I wondered if you've come to accept being 93, and you told me you fight it. Right?

"You feel, Why can't you do the things that you always want to do? And the insecurity you feel, you don't want to feel that. You try to overcome it and it's hard, because you're like in a different character. You're like a different person, Joyala. Not you.

"Yesterday, it's a strange thing. I went downstairs. I said, 'No, I'm not going to make it.' Then I says to myself, I'm going to fight it. And I went around the block. I see I'm doing fine. I came back, and I really did feel better.

"And I planned so many things ahead I was going to do. I'll start crocheting again and doing things. And then, blup, all of a sudden."

"Blup?"

"Blup. Just like that. It's not me, ya know. I get so tired so easily. I don't know what it is. I feel so weak. Then again, it could be old age. Just coming on."

Just coming on? "Yeah." We cackle together.

"I think you can't expect better. For me, it's a new experience."

"It took you long enough," I say.

"Yeah!" She giggles. Her laugh is infectious.

"Listen, ya gotta take everything in stride. You gotta accept certain things. Like, it was hard for me to slow down. Everything is a chore now—being able to go downstairs. Enjoying the walk. Not getting dizzy. Not getting tired. You have limitations where you didn't before. If you go over the limit, you get pains and get tired and cranky."

She wipes the sides of her mouth with her thumb and index finger. "Everybody wants to reach old age," she says, "but it isn't easy. You pay for living long."

She rises. "All right," she says, "I've been *hokking* you *a tchynik* [yakking enough]."

As I leave, she asks after Gus, who has bronchitis. Pearlie is a world-class worrywart. By imagining the worst, she tries to prevent it from happening. Magical thinking, to be sure, but sometimes her magic works. It is an expression of love, her worry. I tell her she must be one of the world's greatest worriers.

"Yeah," she says, "if ya got any worries, just send them over to me."

I kiss her good-bye, and she turns the silver chrome doorknob. Then, as I walk down the carpeted corridor, she throws the double lock on her heavy blue door.

❧❦

I LEAVE FIFTH STREET AT THE SOUTHERN END OF SANTA MONica. The one-way road slices through the old commercial section of town—the now defunct bus terminal, a cluster of office buildings, a pawn shop, a corner bar, the Art Deco post office painted peach, the Chevron station—and turns to homes and apartments just north of Wilshire Boulevard. Giant palm trees with long, comical necks, reminiscent of Dr. Seuss characters, border the shoulders, forming a green-gray tunnel that echoes with the rippling of the ocean air. Already, the morning fog cover has lifted. The sun shines through the fanned leaves as if through stained glass, and they chatter softly in a rising breeze.

Turning east on Montana Avenue, I see the familiar haunts. The Starbucks crowd, lounging like lizards in the sun, the morning joggers, the crossing guard at the elementary school, which has a sign slung on the chain-link fence: Determination. The shopping district dips into a copse of trendy boutiques and then rises again, emerging along a concrete slope dotted with antiques stores and fashionable eateries. To the northeast, a view opens across the Santa Monica mountains. My home lies ahead, a California Craftsman of brown shingles surrounded by birds-of-paradise.

For an instant, I hear Pearlie's words in my head: "Enjoy your family." I hear Tessie's: "If I had a fantasy, it would be to be fifty years younger." My age. My mind veers to an image of my mother, smiling in her purple socks at a breast cancer support group I dragged her to, with me blubbering and Mom looking steadfast and stoical. Then, my father on the phone, ecstatic to be untethered from his doctor's office again. Having beaten the medical odds, he's on to Las Vegas to do some real damage. "Honey," he reminds me, "I'm a man of duty." It's the duty to carry on.

I climb the brick walkway, ringed with the scent of jasmine, to the mahogany front door. A mezuzah, given to me by Tessie for good luck ten years ago, is nailed at an angle on the doorpost. The words "Mommy's home!" spill out of the front door even before I turn the key. The walls are covered with morning prisms of light as I enter the front hallway. Lucy's books are scattered on the Navajo rug, Trevor's electric guitar leans against the bookcase, and Gus's backpack lies in a heap of sports equipment beneath the hat rack. There is a sweet tang of maple syrup and Eggo waffles.

Past the frayed couch with Pearlie's afghan covering dirt stains, I turn and look back outside. It is a panoply of light and color. Beyond the wisteria, the garden is studded with brilliant green pine and lighter stands of melaleuca and lemon and orange blossoms. Through the lavender jacaranda tree and pink roses, a green-jacketed hummingbird moves into my field of view, teetering on an updraft. Then my children, playing basketball on the driveway with Brock, each one sweaty and filled with promise.

They fight, of course. There are tears. A scuffed knee. A broken heart. The chaos of being human.

I wonder: How long can I embrace this sense of awe? The gratitude my grandmothers granted me? To appreciate what we take for granted every day? For now, there is no doubt: I am home—in paradise.

ACKNOWLEDGMENTS

First, I am deeply indebted to my "subjects," my grandmothers, without whom I wouldn't be here. To them, their patience with me, their openness, their generosity, their trust, and their love, I owe infinite thanks and more. I suspect there will be parts of this book that they will disapprove of, but I take full responsibility for all of it.

To say that this book has been a family affair is a huge understatement. My parents, Mike and Shirley Horowitz, have kept me honest and on a steady course during a most difficult time. They have been generous and courageous beyond my expectation. And the support, as well, of their sisters: DeeDee Schwartz, for her openness and ready access to Pearl's correspondence; Cynthia Reynolds, for her encouragement; Bobbie Winograd, for helping to extract a recipe from Tessie's memory bank. Bea Schofield was especially generous in contributing to the Rosenwasser family history. Arnie Title helped set me straight on the Teitels' story. Ned Schwartz deserves credit for his photographic skills. And to Bernie Leffenfeld and Thelma Benjamin for their family trees, I am grateful.

I owe thanks to many friends and colleagues as well, especially to Barry Siegel and Carol Lysaght, whose great insight in reading early versions of the manuscript proved invaluable. My sister, Shari Epstein, offered counsel, as did Liv Ballard, Liberty Godshall, Edward Zwick, Amy Spies, and Denise Worrell. Ellen Baskin's research assistance was essential. I got help and comfort and support from the following: Lindy Lowy, Jeff Perry, Stuart and Carol Oken, Nancy Rapp, Robert Goldstein, Karen Bell, Laura Plotkin, Kathy Broyles, Sue Clamage, Freddie Odlum, Elliott Schwartz, Sue Elwell, Ruth Sohn, April Smith, Doug Brayfield,

Fred Scheffler, Ethel Wasserman, Eva Lovi, and Virginia and Maurice Walsh. My brother, Steve Horowitz, and my sister, Peggy Horowitz, offered gentle guidance along the way.

Earlier versions of "Shmegegge" and "Shmitchek" were published in the *Los Angeles Times Magazine*, thanks to Susan Brenneman, Brett Israel, and John Lindsay. I am greatly indebted to my gracious editors at Scribner, Susan Moldow and Nan Graham, who lent their personal support early on, and especially to Jane Rosenman, whose sharp editorial mind and loving hand is evident on every page. To my agent Sandy Dijkstra, whose enthusiasm never flagged, I am grateful. Finally, my special thanks to someone who has known the subjects in this book, and who has helped to give this book impetus and shape, my editor, adviser, friend, and husband, Brock Walsh, without whose love and humor and cappuccinos this project could not have happened. He is my inspiration, always.

Family Tree

FELDMAN FAMILY
(Austria and Russia)

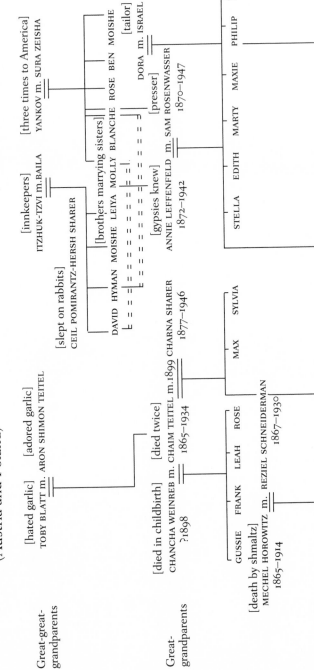

[innkeepers]
ITZHUK-TZVI m. BAILA

[three times to America]
YANKOV m. SURA ZEISHA

[slept on rabbits]
CEIL POMIRANTZ-HERSH SHARER

[brothers marrying sisters]
DAVID HYMAN MOISHE LEIYA MOLLY BLANCHE ROSE BEN MOISHE

[tailor]
DORA m. ISRAEL

[gypsies knew]
ANNIE LEFFENFELD m. SAM ROSENWASSER [presser]
1872–1942   1870–1947

STELLA EDITH MARTY MAXIE PHILIP ?

HOROWITZ FAMILY
(Austria and Poland)

Great-great-grandparents

Great-grandparents

[hated garlic]   [adored garlic]
TOBY BLATT m. ARON SHIMON TEITEL

[died twice]

[died in childbirth]
CHANCHA WEINREB m. CHAIM TEITEL m.1899 CHARNA SHARER
?1898   1865–1934   1877–1946

MAX   SYLVIA

[death by shmaltz]
MECHEL HOROWITZ m. REZIEL SCHNEIDERMAN
1865–1914   1867–1930

GUSSIE FRANK LEAH ROSE

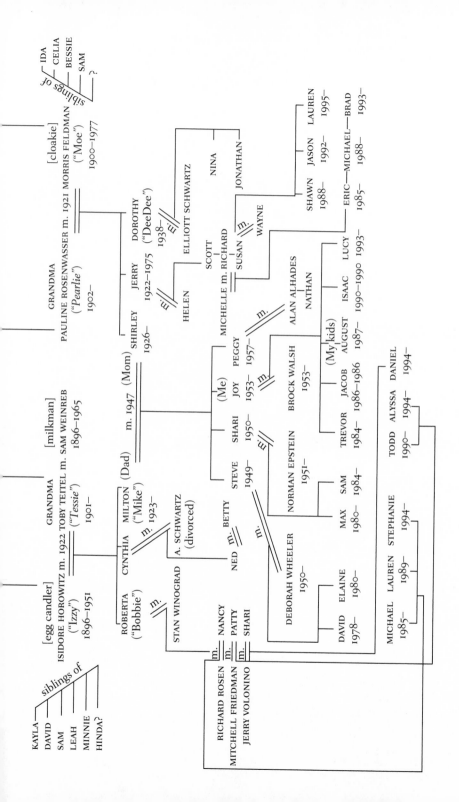